HEROISM IN THE NEW BLACK POETRY

HEROISM IN THE NEW BLACK POETRY

Introductions & Interviews

D. H. Melhem

THE UNIVERSITY PRESS OF KENTUCKY

Published by The University Press of Kentucky

Scholarly publisher for the Commonwealth,
serving Bellarmine College, Berea College, Centre
College of Kentucky, Eastern Kentucky University,
The Filson Club, Georgetown College, Kentucky
Historical Society, Kentucky State University,
Morehead State University, Murray State University,
Northern Kentucky University, Transylvania University,
University of Kentucky, University of Louisville,
and Western Kentucky University.

Editorial and Sales Offices: Lexington, Kentucky 40506-0336

Library of Congress Cataloging-in-Publication Data
Melhem, D. H.
    Heroism in the new Black poetry : introductions and interviews /
D. H. Melhem.
        p.   cm.
    Includes bibliographical references.
    ISBN 0-8131-1709-7 :
    1. American poetry—Afro-American authors—History and criticism.
2. American poetry—20th century—History and criticism.   3. Poets,
American—20th century—Interviews.   4. Afro-American poets—
Interviews.   5. Afro-Americans in literature.   6. Heroes in
literature.   I. Title.
PS153.N5M4   1989   89-22756
811'.5409896073—dc20

CONTENTS

To Gwendolyn Brooks, Dudley Randall, Sonia Sanchez,
Haki R. Madhubuti, Jayne Cortez, and Amiri Baraka

To all the Black poets mentioned in this study

To those who are not

ACKNOWLEDGMENTS

My first debt is to the National Endowment for the Humanities, whose fellowship (1980-81) aided in launching this project. The work has been endowed by the friendly cooperation and encouragement of the poets studied, who have kindly given me permission to quote from their work and from the interviews. I also thank their families, who have contributed in various ways. Thanks are due particularly to Henry Blakely II and daughter Nora Blakely, with regard to Gwendolyn Brooks and their own creative interests. The assistance of Beryl Zitch, director of the Contemporary Forum, has also been generously extended in a familial as well as a professional sense regarding Brooks and other Black artists.

Research on the book was conducted primarily at the Schomburg Center for Research in Black Culture, the New York Public Library, where I have been readily accommodated over the years, earlier by Ernest Kaiser and his now-eponymous Kaiser Index, and continuously by the skill and knowledge that librarian Betty Gubert has put freely at my disposal. The General Research Division of the main library on Forty-second Street and the Music Division at Lincoln Center have been helpful. Valuable information has been provided by the Newark Public Library.

Harold M. Proshansky, president of the Graduate School and University Center of the City University of New York, has supported my studies in Black poetry with practical assistance at critical times.

Excerpts of varying lengths from earlier versions of the chapters have appeared in the following literary journals: *Black American Literature Forum* ("Revolution: The Constancy of Change: An Interview with Amiri Baraka," Vol. 16, Fall 1982; "Dudley Randall: A Humanist View," vol. 17, Winter 1983); *The Greenfield Review* ("Jayne Cortez: Supersurrealism," vol. 11, Summer/Fall 1983); *MELUS* ("Sonia Sanchez: Will and Spirit," vol. 12, Fall 1985); *Steppingstones* tribute, *Amiri Baraka: The Kaleidoscopic Torch* ("Amiri Baraka: This Constant Mutability," 1985); *Time Capsule* ("Gwendolyn Brooks: The Social Act of Poetry," vol. 7, Summer/Fall 1983); and *Western Journal of Black Studies* ("Black Nationalism and the Poet Activist: An Interview with Haki R. Madhubuti," vol. 9, Summer 1985). A paper based on the Brooks chapter, given in March 1989 at Colorado State University, appears in *Colorado Review* ("Gwendolyn Brooks," vol. 16, Spring/Summer 1989). To each of the foregoing publications, grateful acknowledgment is made.

The benign presence of my family, whether near or far, has graced the austere regions of this labor.

INTRODUCTION

Listen to the Winds, O God the Reader,
that wail across the whip-cords stretched
taut on broken human hearts; listen to the
Bones, the bare bleached bones of slaves,
that line the lanes of Seven Seas and beat
eternal tom-toms in the forests of the
laboring deep; listen to the Blood, the cold
thick blood that spills its filth across the
fields and flowers of the Free; listen to the
Souls that wing and thrill and weep and
scream and sob and sing above it all. What
shall these things mean, O God the Reader?
You know. You know.
                                        —W. E. B. Du Bois

A new poetry, strong and true, has been developing in this country. Energized by the constant quest in the Black community for emancipation and leadership, this poetry shares idealistic strains with the dominant culture and expresses the democratic intentions of American civilization. In response to decadence and isolation, it offers vigor and commonality, a cohesiveness both spiritual and heroic. The poets themselves, often describing the literature as "revolutionary," view it as a politicized spiritual force.

I use the word *heroism* as extending the concept of leadership, by the stylistic appeal and content of the work and/or by the actions and examples of the poets themselves, a concept defined ultimately by both personality and art. The impulse to leadership in the lives and works of these poets suggests the development of what may be called a heroic genre.[1] It recalls the once elevated expectations of poets held by Percy Bysshe Shelley, Ralph Waldo Emerson, Thomas Carlyle, Ezra Pound, and others, who saw them as forerunners, expressing the needs and aspirations of the group and "Advancing the Race."[2] The six introduced and interviewed here represent a range of Black poets who are assuming comparable functions of leadership, antithetical to the poets who diffuse into history (the given, traditional "culture") and who seek "to bring us to a condition of serenity, stillness, and reconciliation."[3] These leaders connect with the past in order to understand the present and, where necessary, to change it. They offer not reconciliation with but reconstruction of history, literature, and society. They serve Black life and, in so doing, affect its context.[4] They figure prominently, moreover, in the abundance that may, indeed, be accounted a second Black literary renaissance.[5]

The three men and three women included in this volume are presented in dramatic and associative order. Brooks was the first to be recognized and to wield significant influence. Randall's Broadside Press brought not only his own and much of Brook's work but also that of many Black poets to public notice. Madhubuti's position as Chicago poet and publisher offers contrasts and comparisons with Randall; most pertinently, however, there are many cross-references between Brooks and Randall and Madhubuti, a circumstance in which geography as well as affinity plays a part. Moreover, the ties of both Sanchez and Madhubuti to Brooks and Randall have been close since the 1960s. Cortez and Baraka—the former teaching for years in New Jersey and living in New York, the latter reversing the pattern—seem compatible in the political directions of their poetry.

Brooks and Baraka, the most prominent woman and the most prominent man of the group, occupy the emphatic first and last positions of narrative order. And since they require less introduction to general audiences, and since works by and about them are more readily available, they have been given less introductory space here, Baraka the least of all. The other four, particularly Randall, have not received the general critical attention they merit and are less available to readers. Consequently, their poetry has been accorded relatively more representation and discussion. As for the interviews, those with Randall, Sanchez, and Madhubuti appear here fully for the first time. Both the Cortez and the Baraka have new additions; no part of the Brooks interview has been published previously. Editing has been minimal to convey style along with substance. Unattributed quotations from the poets are taken from the interviews.

I first met both Sonia Sanchez and Jayne Cortez in 1970, when they were separately featured in a poetry reading series arranged by the late Paul Blackburn at Doctor Generosity's Cafe in New York

City.[6] Their art and its presentation encouraged audiences to react; they conveyed something urgent, musical, distinct. Ignoring the prevailing modes of nonengagement, they seemed to read under banners proclaiming, "Speak the truth to the people!"[7] And they were doing so in experimental ways. The aesthetic process was involved intricately in a dialogue of leadership that utilized rapping, the resonance of call-and-response, and the poetry embedded in and embellishing vernacular language. These were strong virtuoso performances of voice, movement, music, and oratory that dramatized the living theatre of Black lives.

The following year, at the City College of New York, I audited the workshop of Gwendolyn Brooks, a poet I had long admired. Deepened study of her poetry made possible that aesthetic leap which enables a reader to experience a given work from the inside, as it were, and so to gain awareness at the vital heart of composition.[8] That center was, as Brooks put it in "The Second Sermon on the Warpland," "tom-tom hearted," African and African American, infused with the jazz and blues of Black music and with the sermonic power that varyingly touches all the poets in this study. Brooks would be the key to unlock the secrets of energy and excitement generated by their work. This became clear when Dudley Randall and Haki R. Madhubuti came to read to her class and, in 1977 when I audited Amiri Baraka's class on "Art and Marxism" at the New School for Social Research. Art, he demonstrated socratically, even when disguised as apolitical, is propaganda.

While Brooks's poetry draws on a confluence of Black and white elements, conventional forms are more important for Randall who, like Claude McKay, usually sets them to the measure of contemporary issues. Sanchez favors the Japanese haiku, which she also uses as a pedagogical tool in her workshops. Baraka's early work, influenced by the Beats, Objectivists, and Projectivists, initiates his appeal to rhetoric. Madhubuti shares his caustic wit, his punning, and his later rhetorical motives. Cortez is closely allied to Surrealism and to painting, yet her imagery, tempered in the furnace of a committed imagination, fuses with concrete reality.

Common to all are the strong incursions of Black music and the Black sermon, its poetry of the pulpit.[9] Most of these poets have written prophetic works. At times they meld poetry and prose: the verse journalism, preachments, prose poems, and poetic prose of

Brooks; the letter poems of Sanchez; the speech poems of Baraka, Sanchez, Cortez, and Madhubuti. Since the content shaping the form is political, the art of persuasion becomes part of the technique. And music, itself potentially the quick route to the heart and to action, not unexpectedly participates in the process. The result is something new, embedded in social utility.[10]

The story of avant-garde literature has been a tale of revolution, its topography strewn with anthropophagous offspring suggesting Harold Bloom's anxious literary parricides, who simultaneously destroy and renew through reinterpretation or "misreading" of a text.[11] Significant novelty in any art form is rarely welcomed with rejoicing, hospitality, or even civility, but rather with skepticism: "Why are you being difficult? Different? Deficient!" Even so, the modern and postmodern canons have absorbed Surrealism, Imagism, Vorticism, Objectism, Objectivism, Projectivism, Concrete poetry, prose poetry, minimalism, and language poetry. But the maverick that has never been given any sort of respectable contemporary poetic quarter—except as an example of what is *bad* poetry (in the standard negative sense)—is rhetoric. A sure way to damn a work to Tartarus has ever been to call it "rhetorical." Or else it may lack a mysterious quota of "hard, dry" images.[12] Even when accompanied by that second-class citizen the lyric, rhetoric is no less unwelcome. We have been carefully taught to "go in fear of abstractions."[13] and to beware "the lyrical interference of the individual as ego"[14] and that there are "no ideas but in things."[15]

We may courteously or condescendingly admit that certain speeches and sermons are "poetic." Perhaps Martin Luther King's "I Have a Dream" speech is very like a poem. The epigraph to this introduction, Du Bois's "Postscript" to *The Gift of Black Folk* (1924), may indeed be a prose poem. And some musical incursions (blues and jazz) may be admissible, in certain instances, to a kind of racy exotic privilege, but the degree and purpose must be questioned. The most incisive comment, however, remains Charles Olson's: "Who knows what a poem ought to sound like? until it's thar?"[16]

Like new stars and constellations, beautiful art forms are constantly coming into being. The poem as cosmos emerges from a complex of sensibility and occasion (the "cry of its occasion," Wallace Stevens noted).[17] It inscribes a dual conception and need: the self and the self-in-society, reflecting culture and historic urgency. It is attuned to a spiritual music that we must be taught again to hear, music that emanates from Whitman, Emerson, and Dickinson, from Malcolm, Martin, and Du Bois; from Harriet Tubman, Sojourner Truth, Bessie Smith, and Billie Holiday.[18] It comes to us by way of such dormant, deprecated, or ignored sources as the Transcendentalists and the Romantic poets. It comes to us by way of Africa and African American slave routes and roots, the spirituals, chants, hollers, and work songs, and it is born alive into literature by way of Du Bois; it is the light in the sermon, the poem, the blues, and the jazz.

Society conditions our expectation of labels, so that names confirm, even bestow materiality. The word is rightly potent, but its absence can wrongly imply nonexistence. And so we label this heroic Black poetry avant-garde. ExperiMENTAL. With or without labels, the poets will continue to "make it new" in their own sense as well as Pound's,[19] inventing, reinventing, discovering, and creating their own dazzling identities. Dwight Bolinger, writing of the fall from favor of successive linguistic theories because of their refusal to accommodate change, states: "It seems that the seeds of revolution are apt to lie in that part of the field to which the attitudes in vogue deny importance. The neglected evidence is shut out on one excuse or another . . . but it keeps accumulating, and all of a sudden its freshness and brightness outshines the turned and polished but too-familiar face of the ruling idea."[20]

Perhaps critics are surprised because, as Paul Carter Harrison observed to a mutual friend, regarding a drama critic's unknowledgeable review of his *Anchorman*, "White people don't expect Black writers to be avant-garde." Whatever the circumstances, the new poetry demands new, informed attitudes and a new criticism—a *renewed* criticism, to distinguish it from the New Criticism, which was designed to support its own kind of poetry. This renewed criticism has the task of recognizing novelty, of defining its attributes whenever they appear, without fossilizing its organic life into rigid canons that will invite their own demise. The terror of abstraction, of emotion, and of the lyrical ego are the aesthetic progeny of the post-Victorian and post-World War I moral debacle that involved a loss of faith in slogans and, to a crucial extent, in language itself. It seemed necessary to affirm that "a rose is a rose," to return to nouns, verbs, and images purged of modifiers that could corrupt objective reality with spurious feelings. The process, however, pushed to extremes, has turned Modernist and post-Modernist insight into blind poetic dogma with no redeeming Homeric grace.

The immediate question for the renewed criticism is not "Is it poetry?" but "What kind of poetry is it?" What are its objectives? Do the poets achieve them imaginatively? Do the poems "refresh life," as Stevens expects them to?[21] The poetic dimensions, once revealed, will determine the criteria of judgment. The renewed criticism, open to the sound of novelty as well as to its sense, will responsibly enrich our multiculture. It will perceive Black poets of the new heroic genre as a fluid yet fully grown indigenous avant-garde movement. It will read their works "with eyes open. And hearts, too," as Brooks would say.[22] It will rejoice in these writers who—using differing means to translate hope, pride, cohesion, morality, and effort—bring messages of regeneration to an entire society.

Notes

1. For aspects of the heroic other than the focus here, including the slave, the "trickster," and the outlaw, see Lawrence W. Levine, *Black Culture and Black Consciousness: Afro-American Folk Thought from Slavery to Freedom* (Oxford: Oxford Univ. Press, 1977), chap. 6, "A Pantheon of Heroes." See also the "toasts," epical poetic narratives (pp. 378-80) that often concerned the Signifying Monkey, whose stories were first gathered in the folklore studies of Roger D. Abrahams, such as *Deep Down in the Jungle: Negro Narrative from the Streets of Phildelphia* (Chicago: Aldine, 1964). A compelling dramatic presentation of the trickster hero is Paul Carter Harrison's play *Anchorman*, with music by Julius Hemphill, which opened at Theatre Four in New York City on Feb. 11, 1988.

2. "Advancing the Race" is one of five "axes of life" that describe the essential Black Life of "Bronzeville" in the important study by St. Clair Drake and Horace R. Cayton, *Black Metropolis: A Study of Negro Life in a Northern City*, rev. ed. (1945; rpt. New York: Harper & Row, 1962), vol. 2, esp. chap. 14, "Bronzeville."

3. T.S. Eliot, *On Poetry and Poets* (New York: Farrar Straus, 1957), 94.

4. I originally planned, too ambitiously, to include other poets in this study: Audre Lorde, June Jordan, Nikki Giovanni, and Etheridge Knight, for example. (Lorde and Knight are discussed in my paper "Cultural Challenge, Heroic Response: Gwendolyn Brooks and the New Black Poetry," presented at

the Popular Culture Association Convention in Baltimore, 1977, and forth-coming in a PCA collection of papers, *Perspectives in Black Popular Culture*.) I had also hoped to include Robert Hayden, whom Dudley Randall once paired with Gwendolyn Brooks as "the two best living black poets in the country" (*The Black Poets* [New York: Bantam Books, 1971] xxiii) and whose major works are seared with a heroic Black consciousness.

5. See John A. Williams, "The Harlem Renaissance: Its Artists, Its Impact, Its Meaning," *Black World* 20 (Nov. 1970): 17-18. See also C. W. E. Bigsby, *Second Black Renaissance: Essays in Black Literature* (Westport, Conn.: Greenwood Press, 1980), a perceptive inquiry that locates the begin-ning of the second renaissance in the works of Richard Wright. For an indispensable guide to the new Black poetry and its astonishing dimensions, see Eugene B. Redmond, *Drumvoices: The Mission of Afro-American Poetry: A Critical History* (Garden City, N.Y.: Doubleday/Anchor, 1976).

6. Paul Blackburn was a prominent poet and translator of troubadour poetry. An associate of Charles Olson and the Projectivists, he died in 1971 at the age of forty-four.

7. This is the title of a poem by Mari Evans, which appears in *I Am a Black Woman* (1970), reprinted in *Confirmation: An Anthology of African American Women*, ed. Amiri and Amina Baraka (New York: Quill/Morrow, 1983), 105-6.

8. Referred to as "sympathetic identification" in my essay "On the Poetics of Charles Olson," *For Now*, no. 15 (n.d.): 40-56.

9. See the pioneering work in James Weldon Johnson's *God's Trom-bones: Some Negro Sermons in Verse* (London: Allen & Unwin, 1929); in Bruce A. Rosenberg, *The Art of the American Folk Preacher* (New York: Oxford Univ. Press, 1970); and in Stephen Henderson, *Understanding the New Black Poetry: Black Speech and Black Music as Poetic References* (New York: Morrow, 1973).

10. I have also imagined a "jazz heroic" as rubric for the pervasive register of jazz as a vital juncture of pride, music, and language, with appreciation of its liberating elements, such as improvisation. Many fine poets have rendered homage—directly or indirectly—to the music, among them Lucille Clifton, Mari Evans, Michael Harper, Calvin C. Hernton, Ted Joans, Percy E. Johnston, Raymond R. Patterson, Quincy Troupe, Magaret Walker, Sherley Anne Williams, and the late Larry Neal. The jazz heroic, moreover, may be considered by future scholars in the light cast by William J. Harris and his conception of a "jazz aesthetic" (see Chapter 6, n.3, below).

11. See Harold Bloom, *The Anxiety of Influence* (New York: Oxford Univ. Press, 1973) and *A Map of Misreading* (New York: Oxford Univ. Press, 1975).

12. T. E. Hulme, who impressed Ezra Pound, writes: "The thing has got so bad now that a poem which is all dry and hard, a properly classical poem, would not be considered poetry at all." In *Speculations: Essays on Humanism*

and the Philosophy of Art, ed. Herbert Read (1924; rpt. New York: Harcourt, 1967), 126.

13. Ezra Pound, "A Retrospect," in *Literary Essays,* ed. and introd. T. S. Eliot (New York: New Directions, 1968), 5.

14. "Objectism is the getting rid of the lyrical interference of the individual as ego, of the 'subject' and his soul, that peculiar presumption by which western man has interposed himself between what he is as a creature of nature (with certain instructions to carry out) and those other creations of nature which we may, with no derogation, call objects." "Projective Verse," in Charles Olson, *Selected Writings,* ed. Robert Creeley (New York: New Directions, 1966), 24.

15. "—Say it, no ideas but in things," in William Carlos Williams, *Paterson,* Book I:1 (New York: New Directions), 14.

16. Charles Olson, *Human Universe* (1965; rpt. New York: Grove Press, 1967), 79.

17. "The poem is the cry of its occasion, / Part of the res itself and not about it." From "An Ordinary Evening in New Haven," in *The Collected Poems of Wallace Stevens* (New York: Knopf, 1971), 473.

18. See Michele Russell's "Slave Codes and Liner Notes," an essay that acknowledges Black women singers as "the bearers of the self-determination tradition in Black women's blues. Unsentimental. Historical. Materialist," in *All the Women Are White, All the Blacks Are Men, But Some of Us Are Brave,* ed. Gloria T. Hull, Patricia Bell Scott, and Barbara Smith (New York: Feminist Press, 1982), 129-40. See also Gerda Lerner, ed., *Black Women in White America: A Documentary* (New York: Random House/Vintage, 1972), for an important early survey.

19. See Ezra Pound, *Make It New* (1934; New Haven, Conn.: Yale Univ. Press, 1935).

20. Dwight Bolinger, *Aspects of Language* (New York: Harcourt, 1968), 209.

21. "The poem refreshes life so that we share, / For a moment, the first idea . . . ," in "Notes Toward a Supreme Fiction," *Collected Poems,* 382.

22. Brooks advises young writers to become educated, read widely, and write, and she adds, "A writer needs to live richly with eyes open, and heart, too." *Report from Part One* (Detroit: Broadside Press, 1972), 146.

Bill Tague

1. GWENDOLYN BROOKS
Humanism and Heroism

In September 1971 Gwendolyn Brooks, appointed Distinguished Professor in the Arts by the City College of New York, commuted weekly from her home in Chicago to teach two poetry workshops. I recall her entering the classroom: alert, elegant, slim, her lustrous skin a deep brown, expressive eyes and hands like those in a painting by El Greco, a woman charged with enormous vitality. One was struck by the tonal range of her voice, by the intelligence, candid and ironic, that confronted the trite or insincere. When her first book, *A Street in Bronzeville,* was published in 1945, she had been shy in public. Now, she seemed warm and self-assured. Time, success, and the new Black pride of the 1960s—her "surprised queenhood in the new black sun" (*Report from Part One,* 86)— had all played their parts. Even more critically, her conception of the poet's social role had registered in her personality and in the very nature of her poetry.

Brooks encouraged her students to work with and modify conventional forms, to develop their own, and to publish a magazine, which they called *Twelve and a Half.* She introduced figures from her literary world—Dudley Randall, Haki R. Madhubuti (Don. L. Lee), Diane Wakoski, agent Roslyn Targ—and invited some to speak to the master's class. But it was hearing her read to a large, enthusiastic audience at the college that explained the interaction between her personality, her work, and even its form. This was no ordinary reading. It was an urgent reaching out, especially to Black members of the audience. With humor and conviction Brooks commented on the poems, commanding rapt and responsive attention. She was friend, teacher, social prophet, expressing everyday concerns and speaking of lives seemingly humble yet potentially heroic. Her voice was the voice of leadership calling to this energy.

What sort of history, personal as well as sociopolitical, had produced this poet? Brooks's autobiography, *Report from Part One,* credits the support of her parents: Keziah Wims Brooks, a former fifth grade teacher in Topeka, Kansas, who played the piano and harbored a wish to write; David Anderson Brooks, son of a runaway slave, a janitor with "rich Artistic Abilities" who had spent a year at Fisk University in Nashville. It was a close family into which the poet was born on June 7, 1917, in Topeka, Kansas. Having returned there for the birth, Mrs. Brooks took her infant daughter back to Chicago a month or so later. Brooks showed early characteristics of the literary prodigy. Yet, despite literary and academic achievements, upon graduation from Wilson Junior College (now Kennedy-King), she was obliged to work as a domestic.

While school and job discrimination disclosed the true nature of the intra- and interracial scene, her home environment (the family included a younger brother, Raymond) supported her confidence. Raised in a Black neighborhood in Chicago, "semi-poor" (Brooks's description), churchgoing, she began writing at the age of seven. "*You* are going to be the *lady* Paul Laurence Dunbar," her mother soon predicted (*RPO,* 56). First published at eleven with four poems in the *Hyde Parker* (a Chicago newspaper) and then at thirteen in *American Childhood,* by sixteen she was a weekly contributor to the *Chicago Defender* column "Lights and Shadows"; seventy-five of her poems were printed there within two years. The pervasive Black heritage of music was fostered by both parents, with church as a creative center. Church was where Brooks's mother took her to meet James Weldon Johnson and Langston Hughes. Hughes in particular became an inspiration and later a friend.

Early publishing, marriage to Henry Blakely II, motherhood (a son, Henry, Jr., was born in 1940 and a daughter, Nora, in 1951), the warm critical reception of *A Street in Bronzeville,* and careful supervision of her publishing career by editor Elizabeth Lawrence at Harper & Row all helped to develop Brooks's poise and to nurture her growth as a public figure. The 1950 Pulitzer Prize for poetry (for *Annie Allen,* 1949) fixed national attention upon her, the first Black to be thus honored. Subsequent awards included two

Guggenheim fellowships, an American Academy of Arts and Letters grant in literature, the first Kuumba Liberation Award, and the Shelley Memorial Award of the Poetry Society of America. She was the first Black woman to be appointed Consultant in Poetry to the Library of Congress and elected to the National Institute of Arts and Letters.

Brooks's honors continue to mount. Her honorary doctorates now exceed fifty. In 1988, she received the *Essence* Literary Award. On November 15, the same year, she was inducted (along with astronaut Sally Ride) into the National Women's Hall of Fame in Rochester, New York. The following year, on April 28, she became the first Black woman recipient of the Poetry Society of America's Frost Medal, its most prestigious award. Shortly before her birthday, she was notified of a Senior Fellowship in Literature grant from the National Endowment for the Arts in recognition, as an official put it, of "the spirit of the work and the life of the author."

Brooks's generosity is equally legendary. Succeeding Carl Sandburg as Poet Laureate of Illinois upon his death in 1968, she established annual Poet Laureate Awards the next year and has endowed many other prizes throughout the United States. By encouraging writing in schools, in prisons, in her own neighborhood, and wherever she travels, she has probably done more to promote the writing of poetry than any other individual in this country.

An overview of Brooks's art reveals two of its essential features: a humane vision and a heroic voice. The former is caritas, a caring; maternal and clear-eyed, Brooks offers guidance and understanding to the young. Poems like "We Real Cool" and "The Life of Lincoln West," and books like *Bronzeville Boys and Girls* (1956) and *Young Poet's Primer* (1980) illustrate her abiding concern. In her very first book, "the mother" examines abortion from one woman's anguished perspective. Brooks supports family values, though not uncritically, in her novel *Maud Martha* (1953), and she depicts Blackness in family terms in *Family Pictures* (1970).

The poet champions civil rights in "Riders to the Blood-red Wrath" and *The Bean Eaters* (1960) and tells what it is like to grow up Black in an inhospitable white—and sometimes even Black—world. She decries war and segregation in "Gay Chaps at the Bar," poverty and discrimination in "the children of the poor," using the strict sonnet form in both sequences. Brooks punctures fallacies of romanticism, whether they be personal or local or national, the latter two expressed in racism and war. She can hurl a righteous anger and still maintain that "we are each other's / harvest: / we are each other's / business: / we are each other's / magnitude and bond."[1] Her wry humor extends from irony in earlier works to satire and allegory in later ones. Drawing her subjects mainly from common life, she is, in the words of Hortense Spillers, "probably the most democratic poet of our time."[2]

Brooks's poetry indicates an indomitable ego strength and a commitment whose roots are fed, as George E. Kent points out, by a "religious consciousness, from which dogma has been ground away."[3] Brooks herself says, "My religion is . . . PEOPLE. LIVING," and she has often remarked, "My religion is kindness."[4]

This attitude of caritas, nurtured by a sense of African identity, translates the poet's humane vision into the second basic aspect of her work, a heroic voice that responds to the needs of the Black community for pride, liberty, and leadership. I use the term "heroic" here in a dual context: the personal and sociopolitical aspect connotes action, example, and leadership; the artistic aspect denotes Brooks's distinctive style and voice.[5] While addressing herself primarily to Blacks, she also points out, "I know that the black emphasis must be, not *against white*, but *FOR black*" (*RPO*, 45). Although she has spoken of wishing to "blacken" her language, its diction is primarily standard; she has, however, turned from the sometimes elliptical mode of earlier work to one that she terms "clarifying, not simple" (*GB*, 103). Alluding to Amiri Baraka's poem "SOS," she aims to "call" Black people to unity and pride, and raises the communicative power of poetry to the rhetoric of music. The poetic structures combine the energy of African drums, the rhythms of Black blues and jazz, and the power of the Black sermon, particularly in its chanted genre, the Anglo-Saxon alliterative poetic, the ballad, and the sonnet; the presences of Walt Whitman and Emily Dickinson; the range of modern poetry from Langston Hughes and such lesser-known Black women as Anne Spencer to Robert Frost, Edna St. Vincent Millay, and T. S. Eliot. The Black poet, she says, "has the American experience and he also has the black experience; so he's very rich" (*RPO*, 166).

Brooks's audiences respond with enthusiasm to her warmth, to her vital presence, to the sound and sense of her poems, and to her unique musical inflections. The works that have aroused this devotion and esteem begin with *A Street in Bronzeville* (1945), in which a series of vignettes of Black life introduces the book's major theme of entrapment. The next section offers detailed and contrasting portraits that reinforce both humane and heroic concerns through their vivid personae and focus on "black-and-tan" conflicts as well as black-and-white.[6] "Gay Chaps at the Bar," a sequence of twelve antiwar sonnets inspired by letters from soldiers, concludes the book with impassioned perceptions of the Black experience of segregation in World War II. Her first book demonstrates Brooks's comprehensive sensibility, technical skill, and social commitment.

Annie Allen (1949), an antiromantic poem sequence about a young Black woman's prewar illusions and postwar realities, again identifies the pressures of daily life. Its mock heroic centerpiece is "The Anniad," written in a trotting, heavily alliterated tetrameter. "Sweet and chocolate" young Annie dreams of a mythic "paladin / Which no woman ever had." Her reality is a male chauvinist "man of tan" who goes to war, develops tuberculosis, and returns disillusioned, puzzled by postwar life. He fathers Annie's children, then escapes into debauchery and finally into death. The closing "Womanhood" poems, beginning with the superb five-sonnet sequence "the children of the poor," portray a brave yet circumspect Annie, impelled by motherhood, looking out from her own problems toward a world she would like to reform. Her psychic growth and sturdy triumph have inspired Nikki Giovanni to recognize Annie as "my mother."[7]

Following the triumph of *Annie Allen* with a book whose history affirms the poet's perseverance, Brooks presented her unique "autobiographical novel" *Maud Martha*.[8] An impressionistic *Bildungsroman* that is currently being given warm attention, particularly by Black feminist critics, it lattices personal narrative with social themes: black-and-tan, black-and-white, economic hardship, female dependence and muted defiance. Although distinct from later fiery survivors, like the noble proletarian "sheroes" of Sarah E. Wright's brilliant *This Child's Gonna Live* (1969) and those of the searing novels of Toni Morrison and Alice Walker, Maud's frayed but tenacious idealism—and anger—nurture the seeds of potential political action.

Returning to poetry, Brooks responded directly to current events in *The Bean Eaters*: lynching in Mississippi, school integration in Little Rock, housing integration. This book reflects the dual acceleration of the Civil Rights Movement and confrontation politics. In its mixed reception Brooks encountered what might be called the "Stay as Sweet as You Are" genre of criticism, which negatively prejudges both technical novelty and political substance. Accused of "forsaking lyricism for polemics" (*RPO*, 165), she observed, "To be Black is political" and added later, in a manuscript comment to me, "Of course, to be *any*thing in this world as it is 'socially' constructed, is 'political.' "[9]

The tempo of militancy inspires a shifting of emphasis in this volume. In her first book, for example, "Ballad of Pearl May Lee" allocates guilt both to Sammy's taste for "pink and white honey" and to the lynchers themselves; in *The Bean Eaters*, "A Bronzeville Mother" unequivocally blames the lynchers and their sympathizers. The black-and-tan motif reduces to one poem, "Jessie Mitchell's Mother," in which the new Black pride overcomes the old valuing of whiteness and the dominant culture. Class-consciousness pervades "The Lovers of the Poor" and "A Man of the Middle Class."

Women and children receive Brooks's continuing attention. "A Sunset of the City" portrays an older woman abandoned by family; valiant "Old Mary" proclaims, "My last defense / is the present tense." One of the most interesting poems technically is Brooks's most widely anthologized piece, "We Real Cool," a maternal poem presented in the collective voice of the pool-playing gang. Gently scolding yet deeply sorrowing, it identifies the hopelessness of the boys, who retaliate against defeat, despair, social cruelty, and indifference by "coolness" to their environment. Alienation turns their hostility against themselves in a wasteful aggression and futile bravado that the poet mourns.

Selected Poems (1963), which Brooks originally called "Contemporary Fact" after Whitman's dictum "Vivify the contemporary fact," culls mainly from previous volumes but contains some important new work as well. The heroic matrix of "Riders to the Blood-red Wrath," her tribute to the Freedom Riders (and, as she notes in a stanza-by-stanza commentary, to "their fellows the sit-ins, the wade-ins, pray-ins, vote-ins, and all related strugglers for what is reliably right"; *RPO*, 187–89), and her approach to a larger framework with "A Catch of Shy Fish" sound the deepest markings of her progress. The latter, a remarkable sequence of eight vignettes, depicts Blacks who are powerless in the socioracial structure, though they are, as she puts it, "hard to 'net down'—hard to 'net *up*'" (*GB*, 143). But the allegorical, typical, and individual identities apply to all "shy fish" who populate the seas of existence. "Big Bessie throws her son into the street" ends the sequence and the book with an expression of modest yet persistent valor and returns to Brooks's theme of crippling illusion.

In 1967, at the Second Fisk University Writers' Conference in Nashville, Brooks met the artistic manifestation of the Black Rebellion: the Black Arts Movement and its founder, Amiri Baraka (LeRoi Jones). At Fisk, Brooks's humane vision converged with her sense of the heroic. *In the Mecca* appeared a year later, at the height of political turbulence: assassinations, antiwar protests, urban riots.

The book, first conceived in 1954 as a teenage novel, had undergone a long metamorphosis. With encouragement from Elizabeth Lawrence, Brooks transformed the conception into poetry. What Haki Madhubuti calls her "epic of Black humanity" (*RPO*, preface, 22) is up-to-the-minute, infused with current events and figures. A creative prime meridian for the poet, it sounds the oracular voice, prescriptive and prophetic. On the book jacket she comments: "I was to be a Watchful Eye; a Tuned Ear; a Super-Reporter." The concept of the Super-Reporter suggests a role of quasi-divine reportage, the prophetic role foreshadowed by the "Teller" in *Annie Allen* and confirmed in such later works as "In Montgomery" (1971), the major piece that introduces her "verse journalism."[10]

The 807-line title poem "In the Mecca," Brooks's longest single work, recounts the tragic quest of a mother for her child. Mrs. Sallie's frantic pilgrimage through the once elegant Mecca apartment building reveals the detritus of a failed socioeconomic system, a failed art, a failed religion, and their spawn of isolation and rage. A general want of caritas, Brooks's major theme here, defensively mirrors deficiencies of the white environment and reflects the Black Mecca as a microcosm. "How many care, Pepita?" Mrs. Sallie repeatedly cries. Technically, the multiple embedding of free verse and conventional forms and the cinematographic orchestration of styles open the dramatic narrative freely to content, achieving a political resonance of liberation. The poet calls for a "new art and anthem" that will redeem grief with "an essential sanity, black and electric" (ll. 501, 783).

The epilogic poems that follow offer tributes, hope, and direction. "The Wall" commemorates the dedication in August 1967 of the "Wall of Respect," part of a Chicago slum building that had been decorated by Black artists with a mural of outstanding Black personages, including Brooks herself. As eulogist, she enters the scene. When she mounts the rattling wood to address the crowd, she becomes part of her poem and a heroine of it, redeeming Mrs. Sallie who climbs "the sick and influential stair." Alliteration, epithet, compounding, metaphor, metonymy, and capitalization project a heroic voice, spiritually conceived. But it is the two "Sermon[s] on the Warpland" that confirm this "grand heroic" style, reinforcing its somewhat elevated mode with formal biblical inflections (as distinguished from the "plain heroic" colloquial or conversational diction of some later works).

The Sermons are the first of several poems that Brooks calls "preachments," which adapt the chanted sermon as an art form.[11] They clearly indicate the heroic and prophetic motives of her work in their use of imperatives, parallel constructions, and figurative language evoking the Bible. It is here that Brooks turns away from the sonnet, symbol of conventional form and the past, to a "tom-tom hearted" present. The First Sermon counsels, " 'My people, black and black, revile the River. / Say that the River turns, and turn the River.' " The Second Sermon commands, "This is the urgency: Live! . . . Conduct your blooming in the noise and whip of the whirlwind."

After *In the Mecca,* Brooks turned to the Black press. In 1969, Dudley Randall's Broadside Press published *Riot,* written in response to the disturbances following the assassination of Martin Luther King, Jr., on April 4, 1968. For Brooks, a riot must be compassionately understood in order to be truly reported. The epigraph to the title poem quotes Dr. King: "A riot is the language of the unheard." The book's three poems form a triptych that takes the heroic, prophetic, and journalistic impulses of *In the Mecca* into the immediacies of social chaos.

Family Pictures (1970) engages Brooks's major subject of the Black family, both individual and Nationalist. The main themes of its eight poems are self-esteem and self-acceptance, solidarity, and respect for difference. "The Life of Lincoln West," which Brooks calls "an identity poem," was originally a prose piece.[12] A favorite with the poet and her audiences, the narrative concerns a Black child who seems to offend everyone merely by his appearance. In this touching parable of the ugly duckling, Lincoln West, while not physically transformed, "ultimately becomes 'a swan' in his *own* opinion" [GB].[13] Overhearing a white man's insulting remarks about him—"Black, ugly, and odd. You / can see the savagery. The blunt / blankness. That is the real / thing"—little Lincoln, with brave selective attention, takes comfort and pride in being "the real thing." From this generating core emerge the "Young Heroes" of the three portraits that follow—Keorapetse (Willie) Kgositsile, a South African poet, Don L. Lee, and Walter Bradford, a youth worker—and a redefined concept of the beautiful within reordered ethical values. This is the larger significance of "Lincoln West" and its placement at the head of the volume. It moves to interpret the slogan "Black Is Beautiful" as attitude and action, as confidence, work, love. Other heroes are the "Young Africans," "Who take Today and jerk it out of joint"; the poem strides vigorously into the prophetic and grand heroic. Among the remaining pieces, "Paul Robeson" honors the great bass-baritone (who died in 1976). It is richly musical, expressing "The major Voice. . ·. . forgoing Rolling River, / forgoing tearful tale of bale and barge / and other symptoms of an old despond."[14]

Riot and *Family Pictures* crest the progressive mood of the Civil Rights Movement. They propel the hopeful announcements of *In the Mecca* and prophesy a salvageable future. "In Montgomery," however—her second-longest poem—describes something new. In 1971 Brooks was commissioned by *Ebony* magazine to report on contemporary Black life in Montgomery, Alabama, scene of the historic bus boycott of 1955-56, begun by Rosa Parks and successfully organized by Martin Luther King, Jr.—though Brooks observes that a self-imposed segregation was, in 1971, still in effect. Enhanced by the sensitive photographs of Moneta Sleet, Jr., "In Montgomery" documents Brooks's reaction to a city's complacency following the seismic sixties and reveals her dismaying prescience of the new decade. The seventies would reveal the governmental corruption of Watergate and bring the end of the tragic involvement in Vietnam. The nation's weariness with politics, coupled with satisfactions over modest gains in civil rights, would result in a concentration upon such daily exigencies as jobs and in a retrospective and escapist mentality. The national mood was changing and would register in Black life.

Brooks succeeds in becoming a "Watchful Eye, a Tuned Ear, a

Super-Reporter." Her prophetic voice, grand and heroic, frequently sermonic, combines interviews, sense impressions and observations, reportage, and photograph captions within her poetic vision. "Montgomery is a game leg. / After such walking!" she cries in the wilderness. She sees, at the top of "a mountain of sand," a Black youth "astride the Future"; more bitingly, after referring to Blacks, babies, and "establishment leashes," she poses the stanza, "A sleek long brown dog / is dead in the middle of the street." The poem represents a valuable contribution to the genre that Brooks calls "verse journalism" and ranks with "In the Mecca" among her most serious and sustained efforts.

In 1974 Brooks's brother Raymond died; the following year she published *Beckonings*, dedicated to him. It continues the prophetic remonstrance, at times muted by a somewhat elegiac tone. Of the twelve pieces, four are songs, one is a ballad, and another a lyric. Both the prevailing musical base and the vernacularizing reach out on directly emotive levels. Although Brooks is dissatisfied with some of her selections in *Beckonings*, it does contain several important pieces: for example, the ballad "The Boy Died in My Alley," the pastoral lyric "Horses Graze," and "Boys. Black," a preachment to the young (in the 1981 anthology *To Disembark* she incorporated sections of "Boys. Black" into a new poem, "Another Preachment to Blacks").

Though she helped edit her mother's *The Voice and Other Short Stories* (1975), Brooks did not publish another volume of her own work until 1980. After nursing Keziah through her final illness in 1978, she grieved deeply. Further, she was concerned over Black disunity and the suspension of Broadside Press and of *Black World* magazine. Eventually, she decided to assume total responsibility for her own publications, beginning with *Primer For Blacks* (1980); except for *To Disembark*, she has continued to do so, under the imprint of The David Company. *Primer For Blacks* defines Brooks's parameters of leadership. The title poem is a call to love and esteem the whole spectrum of Blackness. "To Those of My Sisters Who Kept Their Naturals" specifically addresses Black women who "have not bought Blondine," whose "hair is Celebration in the world!" "Requiem Before Revival," a prose poem essay, answers the need for "the essential Black statement of defense and definition." The poet is satisfied with this collection: "I like what the poems say," she affirms.

Brooks produced two books for young writers, *Young Poet's Primer* (1980) and *Very Young Poets* (1983), whose friendly, clear approach makes them useful to writers of any age. The second appeared in the year that Harold Washington became the first Black mayor of Chicago. Brooks had joined with Artists for Washington during the campaign, and she read at his two inaugurations. In "Mayor Harold Washington" the poet addressed him as "Mayor, Worldman, Historyman," and went on, "Beyond steps that occur and close, / your steps are echo-makers." The poem appears with two other Chicago-oriented poems in *Mayor Harold Washington and Chicago, the I Will City* (1983). Following his untimely death in 1987, her poem in memoriam, "Last Inauguration of Mayor Harold Washington," appeared in a special edition of the *Chicago Tribune* on December 8.

Brooks was named Consultant in Poetry to the Library of Congress for 1985-86; her lively response to the question "*What does the Consultant in Poetry do?*" reveals her typically vigorous, creative, and socially conscious approach.[15] In addition to office responsibilities and correspondence, she extended her duties to include visits to schools (often two and three in a day), universities, prisons, and drug rehabilitation centers; she organized poetry-writing competitions, inaugurated the Lunchtime Reading Series, and conducted regular monthly readings.

While Brooks's local and national concerns were making stringent demands on her time and energy, events abroad stirred her consciousness, as well. Moved by the turbulence in South Africa, in 1986 she published *The Near-Johannesburg Boy and Other Poems* and dedicated it to the students of Gwendolyn Brooks Junior High School in Harvey, Illinois. The book was the first to bear her new imprint, The David Company, named in honor of her late father. A strong collection, it sustains Brooks's collocation and melding of the humanist strain with the heroic. The title poem is, first of all, about a child; children remain an essential, recurrent subject. The poem also represents her African identity, its reality made vivid on her trips to East Africa in 1971 and to Ghana in 1974. The epigraph informs the reader that Black children are often "detained" in South Africa and that this boy's family is not permitted (implicitly because of apartheid) to live within the city of Johannesburg: hence the poem's title. In the dramatic monologue, a form that has served the poet well, empathy enables her to assume the boy's persona:

"My way is from woe to wonder. / A Black boy near Johannesburg, hot / in the Hot Time." She builds from simple narration, from a stately yet conversational meter, and from a child's simple declaratives:

> Those people
> do not like Black among the colors.
> They do not like our
> calling our country ours.
> They say our country is not ours.

"They" are the whites. To the boy, "Their bleach is puckered and cruel." He speaks with difficulty of his father' death: "It is work to speak of my Father. My Father. / His body was whole till they Stopped it" in an uprising. [GB: "'The Fist-and-the-Fury' refers to the father's brave FIRST response to his dilemma (life as a Blackman in contemporary South Afrika)."] The son will not accept the finality of absence. His stalwart mother survives: "this loud laugher . . . Oh a strong eye is my Mother." [GB: "But *she* 'slumps' when nobody is *looking*."]

The child turns from the past; he moves [GB: "I am *not* still"] "like a clean spear of fire," ready for the "inevitable" (Brooks's written insertion here) future conflict. The spear image invokes his tribal heritage. "I shall flail / in the Hot Time" [GB: "flail—uncertain, disorganized, thrashing"]. The verb is impeccably chosen. Consider its association with agriculture and threshing, with primitive weaponry and scourging, with erratic progress, abnormal mobility, and lack of response to controls, due to bodily damage, and then listen to and see its proximity *and* resistance to the word "fail."

The equipment of Brooks's grand heroic style resonates throughout. Alliteration, parallel syntax, hyphenated compounds (such as "the Fist-and-the-Fury") with elegant simplicity carve an intaglio. Here is the last stanza:

> Tonight I walk with
> a hundred of playmates to where
> the hurt Black of our skin is forbidden.
> There, in the dark that is our dark, there,
> a-pulse across earth that is our earth, there,
> there exulting, there Exactly, there redeeming, there Roaring Up

(oh my Father)
we shall forge with the Fist-and-the-Fury:
we shall flail in the Hot Time:
we shall
we shall

"We shall," iterated four times, acquires an increasingly imperative edge. And the lack of final punctuation indicates a continuing conflict ["and determination, and uncertainty"—GB]. The augmenting and transforming of "I shall flail" in the previous stanza into "we shall flail" indicates a Black solidarity; movement proceeds from the personal to the social, from the one to the many. The word "playmates" gives a wrenching emphasis to the youth of the protesters. It also summons the students killed in the Soweto demonstrations of 1976 and those "detained" and injured during the commemorative observances in 1986.

"Early Death" extends Brooks's concern with youth. A diptych comprising "To the Young Who Want to Die," it confronts the matter of despair and suicide among youth "of any race or 'persuasion.' " The poem's maternal cast reverts to "We Real Cool" and "Boys. Black," yet it differs from these and other poems on youth. It is an unmediated closeup that makes direct reference to suicide—a rare topic in the Brooks canon—and to drug addiction. Assessing the grief and loss, it eschews inspirational force and social focus for the proximity of a gentle parent or friend. Urging the young to stay, Brooks engages their curiosity about tomorrow and reminds them, "Graves grow no green that you can use." She directs a potent appeal to adolescents in their fragility of transition.

"Shorthand Possible" and "Infirm" further endorse Brooks's humanism. The first refers to Brooks's long marriage which "makes shorthand possible" and it reasserts her support of family life. The second, divinely compassionate, recognizes the infirmity and the beauty of all human beings. The immensely popular and deceptively simple piece mounts a complex voice. The poet enters the poem and, by the fourth line ("Oh. Mend me. Mend me. Lord"), she has become one of the disabled—she prefers the term "inconvenienced"—who call to God for help.

Today I
say to them
say to them

say to them, Lord:
look! I am beautiful, beautiful with
my wing that is wounded
my eye that is bonded
or my ear not funded
or my walk all a-wobble.
I'm enough to be beautiful.

You are
beautiful too.

The speaker becomes a composite of infirmities and presents them
to the Lord. The prayer is not for healing, however, or even for mere
acceptance, but for appreciation of difference so that difference no
longer equates with deficiency. With the ambiguity of the third "say
to them," the prayer speaks both to and for the afflicted, addressing
both them and the Lord. In the triumphant closing three lines, the
poet affirms that life per se is the beauty, sufficient to encompass
every frailty, every human being.

Brooks characteristically brings a human dimension to art.
Witness "Telephone Conversations," which records her memory of
a long "happy conversation" about William Faulkner with her
biographer, the late George Kent. In the poem, Brooks employs a
metaphor of the telephone dialogues as "little lives," each one a
baby that "prospers or declines." Or note her poem about Chi-
cago, "Buildings," which describes "a brave building / straining
high, and higher." The edifice reminds her of "the hands that put
that strength together." Despite the poet's affection for the city, she
observes that most of her Chicago poems were commissions, and
she states candidly, "I have a lot of semi-lousy poems about Chi-
cago."

Brooks expands her concern with art in "The Chicago Picasso,
1986." Revisiting the sculpture whose unveiling she had attended
and celebrated nearly twenty years before, she appreciatively com-
pares Art with "the tall cold of a Flower," then assumes first person
for the Picasso. Like Keats's Grecian Urn, it represents beauty
accepted for its own sake. Familiarity has not conferred an indige-
nous or local "Chicago Beauty": I tell you that although royal / I am
a mongrel opera strange in the street. / I am radical, rhymeless —
but warranted! / / Surely I shall remain." It is art set in the hetero-
geneous urban landscape yet not of it, of unknown or mixed and

unconventional parentage ("mongrel," "rhymeless"), needed. Thus Brooks eschews doctrinaire aesthetics. She retains a place for art qua art, the raucous radicalism of a Picasso, novelty that utters a cry for freedom as emphatically as a jazz improvisation.

The poet returns to the subject of aesthetics with "To a Proper Black Man": "It is not necessary, / Black Man, / that I bleat 'Black Man! Black Man! Black Man!' " she writes, precluding any attempt to influence her subject matter or stance. The Black man knows both himself and what she is writing about; proof of her commitment, she declares, is superfluous. [GB: "Still, she knows it is 'a honey' he appreciates hearing."]

Two poems reaffirm Brooks's attention to the pantheon of Black heroes. "Whitney Young" eulogizes the late civil rights leader and president of the Urban League, who drowned in 1971 at the age of fifty. "The Good Man" extols Haki Madhubuti, member of Brooks's poetry workshop in the late sixties and, in a sense, her spiritual son. Appreciating the unwavering quality of Madhubuti's commitment, which reflects her own, she calls for the poet to continue his guidance: "In the time of detachment, in the time of cold, in this time / tutor our difficult sunlight." Madhubuti's work as poet, publisher, and teacher offers hope in the "time of detachment," the self-centered present which invites sorrowful comparison with the enthusiasm and social activism of the sixties.

Brooks played a prominent role in Madhubuti's successful Twentieth Anniversary Conference on Literature and Society—celebrating two decades of his Third World Press—at Chicago State University in December 1987 (see Chapter 3). There she endowed the George Kent Awards, two annual grants of $500 each, and presented them to their first recipients: Mari Evans and Sonia Sanchez. Sharing with them a workshop, "The Writer and His/Her Social Responsibility," she listened as Evans urged Black writers "to deal with the issues of our times" and Sanchez called for teachers to "expel the myths" that dehumanize the image of Blacks in literature. Then Brooks addressed the necessity of a just portrayal of the Black family.

I believe that writers should be writing more about the Black family. The Black family is really being hounded and hounded these days, and I feel we "ordinary" Black people shouldn't leave all the assess-

ments of our essence to the likes of Bill Moyers, nor to Alvin Pouis-
saint. We have tongues. We have calculating eyes. [*Reading*]

THE BLACK FAMILY

I believe that many of you know some fine Black families. I believe that
many of you know some fine Black fathers. The BLACK FAMILY is,
the Black father is, the Black man is really being crucified these days.
Yet many of you and thousands outside these doors have self-sacrific-
ing, warm-hearted, survivor fathers or remember such fathers, a
father like mine who was home by six o'clock when he wasn't
working two jobs, for dinner with his BLACK FAMILY (almost
everywhere here that I have the phrase "BLACK FAMILY," it's in
capitals, so hear it that way), in a house rich with books, bought by
him for his BLACK FAMILY. And often after dinner, my mother
would play the piano, and my father, my mother, my brother, and I
would *sing*. Think of that. A BLACK FAMILY *singing*, singing in the
awful wilderness of Blackness. My father often would recite poetry to
us. We had all the works of Paul Laurence Dunbar, as well as the
Harvard Classics, for the delectation of our BLACK FAMILY. I grew
up, got married, my husband and I raised a son and daughter, both
doing just fine, thank you. They knew the same kind of wholesome
BLACK FAMILY life.

Yes, I know there are weaknesses, failings, fallings-off, but don't
you *ache* for balance in these contemporary reports? Don't you *ache*
for views, public views of amiable BLACK FAMILY, morally nour-
ished BLACK FAMILY, nice BLACK FAMILY, going on picnics,
having a BLACK FAMILY reunion, perhaps, with maybe 600 mem-
bers present—and that happens more than you might suppose—
laughing with each other, comparing memories, building schol-
arships for the young? There are such Black families, and they are not
few. It is not so much that we resent attention directed to the street-
corner hustler or heroin-handler or the unmarried teen-aged mother,
as it is that we resent the lack of comparable attention to the specific
stories of our lovely young women, our intelligent young women, and
our fine, strong, morally clean, serious young men and young wo-
men, to our Black young. We all expect you to be clean-willed,
decently adventurous, warm of heart, clear of spirit, reasonable, sane,
trying. We expect you to hold on, subscribe to the beauty and
nurturing potential of BLACK FAMILY. And here, at last, by BLACK
FAMILY I mean our entire range of categories: South Africa, South
State Street, the little babe just born in the South Bronx. Love *us*. Do
not try to wriggle out of our race. Approve new rules of discovery,
discovery founded on and referential to the nourishment of our past.

Salute all that is rich and right and civil within us. And go out of here knowing that you are beautiful; fine, beautiful.

Brooks was celebrating a special year in her life in 1987, engaged in the socially useful activity that fuels her energy. On June 7 she had spent her seventieth birthday conferring the eighteenth annual Poet Laureate Awards at the University of Chicago. Although the prizes were usually given to elementary and high school students, on this occasion Brooks additionally cited thirty-two outstanding adult poets of Illinois. Her total dispensation exceeded $7,000 of her own funds. Haki Madhubuti planned his own birthday surprise for her by editing a tribute anthology, *Say That the River Turns: The Impact of Gwendolyn Brooks* (Third World Press, 1987). It features poetry, prose, and reminiscences by an impressive gathering of writers, among them her husband and her daughter. In his introduction Madhubuti refers to the poet as "a Living National Treasure" and states, "It is her vision—her ability to see truths rather than trends, to seek meaning and not fads, to question ideas rather than gossip—that endears her to us. . . . She has the stature of a Queen Mother, but is always accessible and giving. Ms. Brooks is a woman who cannot live without her art, but who has never put her art above or before the people she writes about."

Among other significant events in Brooks's career that year, she became the first Black woman to be elected an Honorary Fellow of the Modern Language Association (Ralph Ellison and James Baldwin had preceded her), and the first special session on her work was held at the San Francisco MLA convention.[16] Her most ambitious and, she believes, her best publishing venture, the omnibus volume *Blacks,* made her earlier works obtainable once more. And for the seventy-fifth anniversary issue of *Poetry* magazine (October 1987), she submitted "Winnie" (Winnie Mandela), the first section of what would become a two-part work published both in *Gottschalk and the Grande Tarantelle* and as a separate volume in 1988.

"Winnie" affirms Brooks's ongoing concern with portraying exemplary yet accessible Black leadership figures and with sounding the heroic voice and the grand heroic mode. Technical accomplishment and subtle prosodic strategies join to exhort Black people to unity and pride, the clear messages of Brooks's oeuvre. We first see Winnie as "the non-fiction statement, the flight into

resolving fiction, / vivid over the landscape, a sumptuous sun,"
who nevertheless would sometimes "like to be a little girl again."
Brooks reaches easily into the personal core within the public
image, then pulls that image into the dimension of social action. In
the last line, we learn that the speaking persona is Nelson Man-
dela:

> Listen my Sisters, Brothers, all ye
> that dance on the brink of Blackness,
> never falling in:
> your vision your Code your Winnie is woman grown.

> I Nelson the Mandela tell you so.

[GB: "Mischievously, the poet wants you to understand that Nel-
son (like many *another* man) wants you to understand that HE
guarantees Winnie's Quality! (The very fact that he feels obliged to
make that statement indicates his understanding that Winnie's
strength, courage, and influence are independent! She is devoted to
and admiring of her husband, but she is capable of standing firmly
on her own feet.)"]

In the second section, "Song of Winnie," Brooks assumes the
subject's persona. Addressing "a melting pot of names"—"Black
Americans, you / wear all the names of the world!"—she speaks in
a conversational tone of the suffering of her people, her struggle to
avoid petty but natural personal interests, the impossibility of
reconciling the traditionally obedient "Nice Young Lady" with the
contemporary liberated "reformer/revolutionary/pioneer! /
'Strongwoman, too.'" She is charged with contradictions, a living
person, monumental but not a monument.

Answering her own question "Do I love Nelson?" Winnie
replies using full rhyme—irregularly metered (in a modern key), yet
rhyme, notwithstanding—as if here the intense lyrical energy de-
manded a more defined music, a song.[17] The prosodic richness,
while relinquishing its imperatives of grand heroic to the intimacy
of the plain, further harvests the latter's opportunity for con-
versation, for the narrative of the griot and witness who is both a
dauntless friend and a guide.

On another level "Song of Winnie" becomes a metapoem that
expresses Brooks's own "some-of-the-time" aesthetic, as she puts it.
Winnie maintains that she is "tired of little tight-faced poets sitting

down to / shape perfect unimportant pieces." A poem, she observes, "doesn't do everything for you. / You are supposed to go *on* with your thinking." Through Winnie, Brooks is also making a didactic, political, and finally a philosophical statement. "My Poem is life, and can grow," she says. Art, its freedom of expression, details organic life and proclaims the liberated human spirit. "This is the time for stiff *or* viscous poems. / Big, and Big"; it is a time for big poems and big humanity. In both parts of this major work, Brooks has attempted to project the Mandelas as figures both real and larger-than-life, idiosyncratic and social, their marriage an emblem of unity in struggle.

Basically an optimist, one who deals constructively with the present and the future, Brooks continues vigorous, peripatetic, engaged in a rigorous schedule of readings, lectures, and workshops throughout the country (usually traveling by train). She is a woman aglow with wit and purpose and informed concern about matters local, national, international, and personal—the last focusing on the welfare of others. She remains an avid reader and follows her own advice to poets by making notes every day—often, she says, in response to "television, radio, newspapers, the street, friends, and meditation."

Early in 1988, when I asked her about her plans, she itemized them: "The completion of 'Winnie'—a short book of poetry about Winnie Mandela. Fiction writing. Further poetry. The eventual publication of 'Report From Part Two,' which is complete except for 'finishing touches' and 'refining.' Also: paperback publication of my novel *Maud Martha*." Since then, *Gottschalk* and *Winnie* have been published; the other work goes on.

In March 1989 Brooks, her daughter Nora, poet Etheridge Knight, and I participated in "A Celebration for Gwendolyn Brooks" organized at Colorado State University, Fort Collins. To climax the event, Brooks addressed a large audience of students, faculty, parents, children, and many who had traveled substantial distances to attend her reading. She invited participation by students and children, and she concluded her presentation with the following poem, published here for the first time. Though she dismisses it as "a jingle," its homey advice, humor, and simple truths suggest the rapport she easily establishes through her natural stance, her essence.

INSTRUCTION TO MYSELF

WATER! WATER!
Air. Air.
Orange, apple,
banana, prune.
These will help
maintain your tune.

Broccoli, carrot,
and cabbage too.
Eat your vegetables.
Good for you.

STRETCH your legs.
Wiggle your toes.
Life is not gone
until it goes.

Love.
Deplore.

Do less.
Do more.

Accept.
Refuse.

Die
in use.[18]

INTERVIEW WITH GWENDOLYN BROOKS

This interview is an amalgamation of both written and oral responses.
The first four questions and answers were exchanged in February 1988;
the rest months later, chiefly in September and December, after I had seen
the manuscript that was published as *Gottschalk and the Grande Taran-
telle*. In response to my question about the term "African American,"
Brooks took special care to answer precisely, since it is a matter she feels
keenly about; I received her written reply, titled "Familyhood," early in
1989. In this, as in all of her written remarks, I have retained her own
eloquent capitalization, punctuation, emphasis, and the like.

DH What leadership role do you foresee for Black poets in the 1990s?

GB I believe Black poets will be *forced by events* into some form of leadership—although not necessarily will they wave their manuscript paper in the faces of the Black "community" screaming "We are now leading you, Black people!" And not *necessarily* will any one of them sit down to desk or table with the self-instruction "I shall now, via this manipulation of language, lead my Black people to salvation."

DH Should the poets continue to direct themselves mainly or exclusively to the Black community?

GB Many Black poets today do not "direct" themselves to the Black community, mainly *or* exclusively. I won't put a "should" on my answer. I'll just say that "essential" Black poets write out of their essence, which does not have to be spelled out at 8 o'clock each morning after coffee and orange juice.

DH Should Black poets be personally as well as artistically involved?

GB Yes—according to their strengths and their compulsion.

DH Where should the emphasis be?

GB On the poet's choice.

DH Looking back on your life, would you change any of your major decisions if you could? Marriage, for example? ·

GB Given old availabilities, I would have married as I married. I married the individual for sound reasons: dignity, volubility, belief in stable decencies (notably a home life and family life with "understood contours": certainly the Norman Rockwell view was "my" view, as I didn't know about African habits), sense of fun, interest in creating and raising children, sociability and an interest in "going out into life," a way-that-matched-mine of looking at Humanity and Eternity; and he, as did I, Wanted To Be A Writer. When you "get to be" my age (71) you have a large eye! You look over your diverse past, and you perceive that the diversities were all tending toward a resolving roundness: blotched, perhaps, nervous, maybe even tumorous—BUT THERE: round. This is not, nor should be, every woman's response. Each woman works with materials to hand or invented.

DH What are the satisfactions of publishing your own work? What drawbacks, if any, have you found?

GB Satisfactions of publishing my own work: "complete"

control over design, print, paper, binding, timing, and, not least, the capitalization of the word Black. Do Blacks realize that they now have—since they got rid of the term "Negro"—NO capitalizations for their *essence*? Publishers refuse to capitalize Blacks. The Johnson Publishing Company of Chicago *does* capitalize Blacks, etc., but insists on capitalizing whites, etc., also. Whites *have* their capitalization: Caucasians. The Caucasians. A Caucasian. The Caucasian. "They spoke of Caucasian matters." Incidentally, the Johnson Publishing Company is Black.

We all happily, even though guiltily, capitalize Native American—which adulteration seems to me an insult to what we used to call "Indians"! I don't know *what* they should be called, but "Native American" suggests that until Amerigo Vespucci emerged, the "Indians" were as nothing. That is: they began to breathe and have being when whites came over to Bless them (and immediately to pollute them).

DH   "African American" has been proposed as a substitute name for Blacks. What is your opinion?

GB   The current motion to make the phrase "African American" an official identification is cold and excluding. What of our Family Members in Ghana?—in Tanzania?—in Kenya?—in Nigeria?—in South Africa?—in Brazil? Why are we pushing *them* out of our consideration?

The capitalized names *Black* and *Blacks* were appointed to compromise an open, wide-stretching, unifying, empowering umbrella.

Some Blacks announce: "That name *Black* does not describe *all* of us." Does the name "white" describe all of the people claiming its services? Those skins are yellow and rose and cocoa and cream and pink and gray and scarlet, and rust and purple and taupe and tan. Ecru. *But* that word "white," to those who wear it, is sacrosanct, is to be guarded, cherished.

Recently, one of our Black Spokesmen listened, with careful respect, to a passionate, sly, strategic white query: "Do you see a day coming when we can forget about EVERYTHING ELSE and just all be 'Americans'?" "Softly" answered our Black Spokesman: "We are *all* aiming toward that day, making progress toward that day—when we can *all* be Americans *merely*."

MEANING? Meaning we are to remember nothing. Meaning we are to renounce *or* forget our culture, our history, all the richness that is our heritage. Our new and final hero is to be Don John *Trump*.

I share *Family*hood with Blacks wherever they may be. I am a *Black*. And I capitalize my name.

DH   You did not mention disadvantages to self-publishing. Have you found any?

GB   Disadvantages? Let's call them "Irks." Disadvantages sounds final, indefatigable. The Irks *can* be defeated, granted a willingness to toil tirelessly—given reliable assistance—and given time.

Irks:

Distribution,
Storage,
Printers.

DH   Your powerful new volume, *Gottschalk and the Grande Tarantelle*, with its social and geographical breadth, presents some new developments in your work. You yourself recognize the poetry as "an advance, an approximation of what I'm aiming for."[19] How would you describe this advance and this aim?

GB   Thank you for saying that *Gottschalk and the Grande Tarantelle*—which contains "Winnie," also available in its own volume—is notable for "social and geographical breadth." (You even said "powerful," D. H.) That pleases me because in this book I have combined what I *have* taught myself about writing with new decisions on what I want language to do for me, for my persuasions, for my compulsions, for my excitements. The title poem, "Gottschalk and the Grande Tarantelle," does exactly what I wanted it to do. There - are - The - Slaves: you are aware of the horror of their crisis *and* you are aware of the fact that human beings *will* break away from ache to dance, to sing, to create, no matter how briefly, how intermittently. Intermittently?—HOWEVER— like an under-earth river, that impulse to beauty and art runs fundamentally, relentlessly. Gottschalk, Elvis Presley, George Gershwin, Stephen Foster, etc., have molded Black exhilaration and richness into money-making forms. Inherent, also, is an ironic, begrudged semi-tribute to the abilities of such people to recognize greatness, to love greatness, when confronted by it. Also, I suspect that you have here a "perfect" snapshot of Louis Moreau Gott- schalk, born in 1829 in New Orleans.

In "Winnie" I display Winnie Mandela talking, more or less, to

America—talking to Outside. I say more or less because she is also talking to herself, she is also "talking" to her husband Nelson Mandela, she is talking to Her People in South Africa (and, to *some* extent, to Black people everywhere); she is also "talking" to Botha-and-such. I have tried to paint a picture of what the Woman must be like. The picture is "built" out of nuance and supposition and empathy. I figure she is composed of womanly beauty, of strengths female and male, of whimsy, willfulness, arrogance and humility, tenderness, rawness, power, fallibility, finesse, a "sweet" semi-coarseness which is the heavy fruit of daily oppression/fury/pain. *And* gloriousness!—glory. She is a glory.

Her Resolution in the last few pages is what it should be. Interestingly enough, although certainly essentially hers, this Resolution is not alien to the impatience, now-shaplier roar, and beautiful self-respect of Today's Woman wherever she may live and under whatever stress she may be striving.

DH   The Black rage expressed in "Gottschalk" seems as vivid as that in "Riot," the poem first published in 1968. Do you see any changes in the Black situation in the United States, for better or worse, since that time?

GB   The "Black Situation" of this time resembles that of the early Fifties, with the Fifties' head-pats and spankings of what were then called "Negroes." With this difference: white power's nervous, irritable wariness. Because white power figures remember what a lot of Blacks don't: the late Sixties, which showed (mirabile dictu) that Blacks working together—or even, in *some* circumstances, just being together—are themselves powerful. Secret acknowledgment of that reality is one of the reasons that the phrase "the Sixties" has been shadowed of late, ridiculed, sometimes spat on: there is a jumpy desire for oblivion of that awareness of Black strength and potential resourcefulness.

There will be betterment when (again) Blacks stop up-staging each other, shrinking away from each other, *selling* each other.

DH   The adoption of Black music by white musicians is an act that parallels somewhat the absorption of African art by modern European art, as in that of Pablo Picasso and his followers.

GB   Right!

DH   With regard to music, what would you suggest as a means of repaying the debt?

GB   I really can't tell musicians what to do. In "Gottschalk" I detailed what one of them *has* done, with the *scheduled* insinuation that other whites have done likewise. I am a reporter.

DH   "Winnie," 377 lines, as you tallied, is your longest work since "In Montgomery," 677 lines. About how much time did you spend writing it? Were there many revisions?

GB   "Winnie"—concept, thought, drafts, completion, polishing—overwhelmed a year. Revisions?—yes yes yes yes yes yes yes yes yes yes.

DH   Do you think that a poem like "Winnie" might influence the partisans of apartheid? Can a Botha be reached by poetry?

GB   The Bothas in this world cannot allow themselves to cry over poetry. They arm themselves against tears. Your official *Nazi* armed self against Jewish suffering. Such people subscribe officially to their arranged dogmas. There are, of course, exceptions to "all" rules. And sometimes it takes only one exception to weaken a prevailing poison, and to—sometimes—overwhelm it. Thus we poets (and here I include all clean pioneers, clean revolutionaries, clean Reporters) must continue our pinpointings, our nudgings, our "revelations."

DH   "Thinking of Elizabeth Steinberg" concerns the martyrdom of an abused child. It mentions the fact that Elizabeth is also your middle name. Were you making a point of your common humanity?

GB   No, I was not. That ought to be assumed, by the humane reader! I wanted to stress my conviction that the torture and murder of children must be stopped. That monsters must be invaded and "finalized."

DH   "Michael, Young Russia," the closing piece in *Gottschalk,* contrasts with the previous poem, "Thinking of Elizabeth Steinberg," by depicting a happy young man of twenty-one. You note that "Michael" was written in 1982 in Kiev, on a visit to that city and immediately after to Leningrad and Moscow. Does the poem's appearance in the new book, instead of in *The Near-Johannesburg Boy and Other Poems* or in *Blacks,* reflect to some extent a response to Mikhail Gorbachev's policy of glasnost, the opening to the West?

GB   Michael seemed to me representative of a fresh, sincere, loving Russia-youth spirit. I wrote the poem in July of 1982, when I knew nothing of Gorbachev, glasnost, or perestroika. When I came back from my trip, I began to read "Michael" to audiences. It was well received. I planned to bring it out in broadside form and then decided to include it in *Gottschalk*.

DH For some time there has been talk—along the omniscient grapevine—of adapting *Maud Martha* for the screen. Such a project is certainly overdue. Are there any literary genres you would like to try that you have not as yet attempted?

GB Yes. An epic. An honest-to-goodness epic.

Gwendolyn Brooks: Works Cited and Suggested

A Street in Bronzeville (1945). In *Blacks*, 1987.
Annie Allen (1949). In *Blacks*, 1987.
Maud Martha (1953). In *Blacks*, 1987.
The Bean Eaters (1960). In *Blacks*, 1987.
Selected Poems. New York: Harper & Row, 1963. Includes "Riders to the Blood-red Wrath." In *Blacks*, 1987.
In the Mecca (1968). In *Blacks*, 1987.
Riot (1969). In *Blacks*, 1987, and *To Disembark*, 1981.
Family Pictures (1970). In *Blacks*, 1987, and *To Disembark*, 1981.
"In Montgomery." *Ebony* 26 (Aug. 1971): 42-48.
Report from Part One. Detroit: Broadside Press, 1972. (Cited as *RPO*.)
Beckonings. Detroit: Broadside Press, 1975.
A Capsule Course in Black Poetry Writing (co-author). Detroit: Broadside Press, 1975.
Primer For Blacks (1980). In *Blacks*, 1987.
To Disembark. Chicago: Third World Press, 1981.
Mayor Harold Washington and Chicago, the I Will City. Chicago: The David Company, 1983.
The Near-Johannesburg Boy and Other Poems (1986). In *Blacks*, 1987.
"Last Inauguration of Mayor Harold Washington." *Chicago Tribune*, Dec. 8, 1987.
Blacks. Chicago: The David Company, 1987.
Gottschalk and the Grande Tarantelle. Chicago: The David Company, 1988.
Winnie. Chicago: The David Company, 1988.

Works for Children

Bronzeville Boys and Girls. New York: Harper & Row, 1956.
Aloneness. Detroit: Broadside Press, 1971.
The Tiger Who Wore White Gloves. Chicago: Third World Press, 1974.
Young Poet's Primer. Chicago: The David Company, 1980.
Very Young Poets. Chicago: The David Company, 1983.

Notes

1. Gwendolyn Brooks, "Paul Robeson," in *Family Pictures (Blacks*, 496).

2. Hortense J. Spillers, "Gwendolyn the Terrible: Propositions on Eleven Poems," in *Shakespeare's Sisters*, ed. Sandra M. Gilbert and Susan Gubar (Bloomington: Indiana Univ. Press, 1979), 233-44.

3. George E. Kent, *Blackness and the Adventure of Western Culture* (Chicago: Third World Press, 1972), 112-13.

4. Gloria T. Hull and Posey Gallagher, "Update on Part One: an Interview with Gwendolyn Brooks," *CLA Journal* 20 (Sept. 1977): 32; D. H. Melhem, "Gwendolyn Brooks: The Social Act of Poetry," *Time Capsule* 7 (Summer-Fall, 1983): 3. Cf. Brooks's comment on her father, "His religion was kindness," in Claudia Tate, ed., *Black Women Writers at Work* (New York: Continuum, 1983), 46.

5. See discussions of "the heroic" and "heroic style" in my *Gwendolyn Brooks: Poetry and the Heroic Voice* (Lexington: Univ. Press of Kentucky, 1987); hereafter cited as *GB*.

6. See the useful analysis by Arthur P. Davis in "The Black-and-Tan Motif in the Poetry of Gwendolyn Brooks," *CLA Journal* 6 (Dec. 1962): 90-97.

7. Nikki Giovanni, "To Gwen Brooks from Nikki Giovanni," *Essence* 1 (April 1971): 26.

8. See the discussion of "American Family Brown" in *GB*, 16-19, 80-83, and of *Maud Martha* in *RPO*, 190-93.

9. Gwendolyn Brooks, "*Black Books Bulletin* Interviews Gwen Brooks," with Don L. Lee, *Black Books Bulletin* 2 (1974): 28-35; *GB*, 101.

10. The term is Brooks's own; see further discussion in *GB*.

11. See discussion of the chanted sermon in Bruce A. Rosenberg's important study *The Art of the American Folk Preacher* (New York: Oxford Univ. Press, 1970), 11-20; and *GB*, 182-83, 215.

12. See Herbert Hill, ed., *Soon One Morning: New Writing by American Negroes, 1940-1962* (New York: Knopf, 1963), 317-19.

13. The poet's comments on my text, indicated by "GB," constitute a kind of dialogue.

14. Safisha N. Madhubuti, in "Focus on Form in Gwendolyn Brooks," *Black Books Bulletin* 2 (Spring 1974): 24-27, aptly perceives the "deep pitch and undulating rhythm of Robeson" as expressed by the poet's "conscious alternation of open and voweled syllables (the long 'o') and closed voweled syllables ('ing')" that "connects, through alliteration, the vowel motifs."

15. See *Performing Arts Annual 1987*, ed. Iris Newsome (Washington, D.C.: Library of Congress, 1987).

16. The special session, "Cultural Approaches to Gwendolyn Brooks's Afro-American Aesthetics," was held at the San Francisco Hilton on December 29, 1987. Organized by Walter B. Kalaidjian, its panel members were

Houston A. Baker, D. H. Melhem, R. Baxter Miller, and Hortense J. Spillers, with respondent Barbara Johnson.

17. Cf. the discussion of "The Last Quatrain of the Ballad of Emmett Till," *GB*, 107-8.

18. "Instruction to Myself," © 1989 by Gwendolyn Brooks. Used by permission.

19. Letter to the author, Sept. 1, 1988.

Leni Sinclair

2. DUDLEY RANDALL
The Poet as Humanist

"I never thought of myself as a leader," says Dudley Randall in his soft, vibrant voice.[1] Yet the historical impact of Broadside Press, begun in Detroit in 1965 "without capital, from the twelve dollars I took out of my paycheck to pay for the first Broadside,"[2] attests to the modesty of his statement. Despite Randall's "silence" between 1976 and 1980, when the Press foundered as a result of over-generous publishing commitments and subsequent debt; despite his depression during those years (he wrote no poetry until April of 1980), Broadside Press—which now continues in the hands of Hilda and Donald Vest—remains his edifice and achievement. It gave opportunity to dozens of unpublished as well as published Black writers (including all the poets in this study except Jayne Cortez).[3] It produced *Black Poetry: A Supplement to Anthologies Which Exclude Black Poets* (1969), the first such anthology to appear under the imprint of a Black publisher. It revived and adapted the concept of the broadside, developed as a polemical device during the Puritan Revolution in seventeenth-century England. Randall's broadsides, many of them printed on oversized paper and decorated as works of art, suitable for framing, often served both aesthetics and rhetoric.[4] But his deep concern was always for the best poetry, "the best words in the best order," as he has stated, invoking Samuel T. Coleridge.[5] An extension of this interest has been the Broadside Poets Theater, a distinguished series of readings inaugurated by Randall in August 1980. Drawing Black poets from across the country, it has become his chief commitment to the arts.

Randall began his career as a writer in 1927, at age thirteen. That year he published a sonnet on the "Young Poets' Page" of the *Detroit Free Press*, winning first prize of a dollar. Music, religion, politics, and poetry were meshed early in his consciousness. Born on January 14, 1914, in Washington, D.C., he is the third (and the sole survivor) of the five children of Arthur George Clyde and Ada Viola (Bradley) Randall. The poet recalls going with his mother to a band concert in Towson, Maryland, when he was a child: "I was so impressed by the big bass drums and the big bass horns that I composed words about them to the melody of 'Maryland, My Maryland,' which the band had played. This is the earliest instance I can remember of my composing a poem."[6] Randall's father, a politically oriented preacher who managed the campaigns of several Black office seekers after the family moved to Detroit, took him and his brothers to hear W. E. B. Du Bois, Walter White, James Weldon Johnson, and others.[7]

In high school Randall developed skill in prosody, which he advises poets to study. Although he writes often in free verse, he does so by choice, not necessity.

> I believe there's an ideal, Platonic line for every thought. The job of the poet is to find it. In traditional verse, it's easier, as there's already a pattern given. Free verse is harder, as there's no given pattern for the line, and the poet has to find the one perfect line out of billions of possibilities. Therefore, the poet who hasn't mastered traditional verse and doesn't know a trochee from a hole in the ground, won't know what to look for or how to select when lines come into his mind. The line I like best in "Ballad of Birmingham" is the line in sprung rhythm, "but that smile / / was the last smile," where the 2 spondees balance each other. Most free verse is bad, as is most traditional verse, but there's more bad free verse than traditional verse. I always scan my free verse, and know what rhythms I'm using, and why.
>
> The spareness of my ballads comes from Black folk poetry— spirituals & seculars—as well as from English folk poetry.[8]

Randall also noted that Henry Wells's *Poetic Imagery Illustrated from Elizabethan Literature* (1924), which classifies images, was an important stylistic influence, as were classical meters and French forms. He has translated some of Catullus into the hendecasyllabics and Sapphic strophes of the original. In translating, whether from Aleksandr Pushkin or Konstantin M. Simonov or Paul Verlaine, Randall tries to render the form as well as the content. His most ambitious project, the "translation" of Chopin preludes and waltzes into "songs without words"—lyrics so totally expressive of the music that they would merge with it—lies ahead. In addition to earning a bachelor's degree at Wayne University (now Wayne State) in 1949 and a master's in library science at the University of Michigan in 1951, Randall has gone on to complete course requirements for a master's degree in the humanities at Wayne State. The Chopin translations may become the thesis for that second master's.

Listening to classical music helps Randall to write. Although he recommends that the poet read widely, "in any language you know," he agrees with Dorothea Brande's suggestion in *Becoming a Writer* (1937) that a wordless occupation, one that is rhythmical and monotonous, helps the creative process. He is not prescriptive about subject matter: "You write what you can," he says.

Randall's feeling for working-class people was deepened by his years at the Ford Motor Company in Dearborn, Michigan (1932-37). "George" commemorates the experience. In 1935 he married Ruby Hands, and soon a daughter, Phyllis Ada, was born. He was employed at the U.S. Post Office in 1938 and worked there—with time out during World War II—until 1951, when he took his first library position. A second marriage took place in 1942. Inducted into the army in July 1943 and trained in North Carolina and Missouri, Randall was sent overseas in February 1944. As a supply sergeant in the headquarters detachment of the Signal Corps, he served in the Philippines and in various islands of the South Pacific. Although he saw no active combat, he was close to those who did. His "Pacific Epitaphs," from *More to Remember*, epitomizes that tragic time.

The poet shies away from the label "pacifist," yet he is strongly antiwar; see especially the title poem of his 1973 collection *After the Killing* and the "War" section of *A Litany of Friends*. Sadly, he likens war to an ongoing family feud and states, "I would say that conciliation is better than revenge." He does accept the designation "humanist." He tells of meeting Arna Bontemps in the 1960s at the Black Writers' Conference sponsored by the University of Wisconsin: Randall, upon asking permission to join a group seated in the cafeteria, was told by Bontemps, "Yes, Dudley, since you're the only humanist here." Like Brooks, Randall sees people in terms of "family" and remains a family-oriented man. Numerous letters to his daughter, correspondence he prizes, contain his own drawings of his Pacific surroundings during the war, including lizards, sand crabs, and flying fish. His devotion to his third wife, Vivian Spencer, a psychiatric social worker whom he married in 1957, is made manifest in later poetry.

When Randall was discharged in 1946, he returned home to go back to school and his post office job. After receiving his master's degree from Michigan, he worked continuously as a librarian: at Lincoln University in Jefferson City, Missouri, from 1951 to 1954; at Morgan State College in Baltimore to 1956; in Wayne County Federated Library System in Detroit to 1969, and at the University of Detroit, where he was also Poet-in-Residence, to 1976. During those years he received many honors, among them the Wayne State Tompkins Award, for poetry in 1962 and for poetry and fiction in 1966, and the Kuumba Liberation Award in 1973. Both the University of Michigan and Wayne State have named him a Distinguished Alumnus, and in 1977 he received awards from the International Black Writers' Conference and the Howard University Institute of Afro-American Studies. The following year the University of Detroit conferred upon him the honorary degree of Doctor of Literature. He is modestly but deeply proud of becoming, in 1981, the first Poet Laureate of Detroit.

The 1960s were critically formative years for Randall, as they were for all the poets in this study. Two stunning events in late 1963, the racist bombing of a church that resulted in the death of Black Sunday school children, and the assassination of John F. Kennedy, inspired the poems that were to become Randall's first broadsides. The "Ballad of Birmingham" and "Dressed All in Pink" began the Broadside Series and Broadside Press in 1965. Both poems were set to music by Jerry Moore; they were later included in Cities Burning.

Another step in the history of the Press was marked by Randall's meeting with Margaret Danner at a party for the late Hoyt Fuller, editor of the journal Black World and then of First World. Danner had founded Boone House, the important Black arts center which, from 1962 to 1964, existed as a forerunner of similar projects later launched with government assistance. The two poets conceived Poem Counterpoem, a unique series of their paired poems that was released in 1966. In May 1966 Randall attended the first Writers' Conference at Fisk University in Nashville. There he met Margaret Burroughs, with whom he developed the idea of the *For Malcolm* anthology (1967). As Randall observes, the press grew "by hunches, intuitions, trial, and error" (*BRM*, 23). At the Conference, he obtained permission from Robert Hayden, Melvin B. Tolson, and Margaret Walker to use their poems in the Broadside Series. He wrote to Gwendolyn Brooks and obtained her consent to publish "We Real Cool." Of this first group of six broadsides, Randall observes, " 'Poems of the Negro Revolt' is, I think, one of the most distinguished groups in the Broadside Series, containing outstanding poems by some of our finest poets" (*BRM*, 23).

The most significant act of confidence accorded Randall and Broadside Press was made by Gwendolyn Brooks when, in 1969, she turned to it for the publication of *Riot*. Randall acted as Brooks's editor and was especially helpful in organizing her autobiography, *Report from Part One*. Brooks, in turn, assisted in the selection of poems for Randall's *More to Remember* (1971), rewriting the preface and eliminating a number of pieces he had planned to include (he now wishes he had excluded even more). The warm friendship inspired both poets. In 1970, Randall dedicated his book *Love You* "to Gwendolyn, an inspiration to us all."

Randall's democratic instincts are offended by what he calls "poet snobs." In a forthright, unpublished poem about the period of his depression, he caustically contrasts some poets' affectation of slovenliness with his own genuine reluctance to care for his body when he was despairing of life itself. With ribald wit he lists the authentic "credentials of dirtiness" and defends his present choice to dress well for public appearances. He feels strongly that poets should be interested in other people. "Shy and self-centered" in his early years, he gradually gained what he refers to as "negative capability" (adapting John Keats's phrase) by thinking of whatever person he meets instead of himself. Randall admires writers in whom he sees this capacity.

Though his humanism remains unaltered, Randall's thinking has undergone some modification over the years, partly as a result of his travels. He still does not "connect" with organized religion (although in *Contemporary Authors*, 1977, he listed his affiliation as Congregational), but his political tone seems more circumspect. "No," he told me in Detroit, as he drew at his pipe and leaned back in a living room chair, "I'm not a socialist. I went to Russia, and I think people are just human beings all the world over." Randall was referring to his 1966 trip with eight other artists to the Soviet Union, France, and Czechoslovakia. He was disturbed about the censorship and treatment of Aleksandr Solzhenitsyn and Osip Mandelstam. In 1970 he visited Togo and Dahomey in Africa and studied African arts at the University of Ghana. That trip enriched his consciousness. Its residue may be seen in his current taste in dress, like his favored orange cap and bright, sometimes African clothing. Yet the impressions revealed contradictions:

> Africa is a very big place. It is very hard to try to sum it up. . . . I think, moreover, that it is very unwise for a person to talk as if he knows a country after visiting it for only a short time and getting only superficial impressions. An instant expert! There were some contradictions. One of them, for example, was being part of an audience that was two-thirds Black, and the African speaker referred to us as "you white folks," which may give you some idea of how . . . this person looked upon Black Americans. Yet I wouldn't generalize and say that every African had this attitude. In the villages that we visited, for example, they said: "We know that you are our brothers who were taken away from us, and now you are coming back to see the land where your fathers lived, and now we welcome you back."[9]

Randall agrees with Haki Madhubuti that whites have been responsible for numerous depredations, but he does not put all whites into the same category. Though he notes wryly that poor whites, who face many of the same problems that Blacks encounter, can be just as prejudiced as those who are more affluent, he continues hopeful that people's attitudes can be altered and that "you can raise anybody's consciousness." Randall maintains his integrationist stance because "we're all human beings." He thinks it important, however, to promote Black solidarity, "to align yourself with those who are like you and in like condition."

Before founding Broadside, Randall was published in various magazines; wider recognition came with the appearance of his work in prestigious anthologies: Rosey E. Pool's *Beyond the Blues* (1962); *American Negro Poetry*, edited by Arna Bontemps (1963); and Langston Hughes's *New Negro Poets: U.S.A.* (1964). It was the Hughes anthology (which bears a foreword by Gwendolyn Brooks) that first presented "The Southern Road" (later reprinted

in *Poem Counterpoem* and *A Litany of Friends*), a brilliant poem
in the strict and now rarely employed form of the ballade. An
important French innovation of the fourteenth and fifteenth cen-
turies the ballade is identified with the poetry of François Villon,
whose work was characterized by intelligence, precision, and real-
ism. Randall's own advice to poets (which appears in *Contempo-
rary Authors*, 1977), begins: "Precision and accuracy are necessary
for both white and black writers." David Littlejohn cites "The
Southern Road" as "a sophisticated rendering of the return-to-the-
South theme."[10]

The ballade, usually in three stanzas of eight lines each plus an
envoi of four, utilizes three end-rhymes and takes as its refrain the
last line of the first stanza. Randall uses a stately iambic pentameter
line, and his skill controls the emotionally charged material:

> There the black river, boundary to hell,
> And here the iron bridge, the ancient car,
> And grim conductor, who with surly yell
> Forbids white soldiers where the black ones are.
> And I re-live the enforced avatar
> Of desperate journey to a dark abode
> Made by my sires before another war;
> And I set forth upon the southern road.

Randall connects "the black river" of Black life with ancient myth:
the "grim conductor" is Charon who, ironically, enforces segrega-
tion. The poet becomes the incarnation and epiphany of his fore-
fathers in a pilgrimage of identity toward life and death.

The second stanza describes the destination, the paradoxical
"land where shadowed songs like flowers swell / And where the
earth is scarlet as a scar." Because the poet's blood has been shed
here, he will claim the land: "None can bar / My birthright." The
dual vision persists in the third stanza:

> This darkness and these mountains loom a spell
> Of peak-roofed town where yearning steeples soar
> And the holy holy chanting of a bell
> Shakes human incense on the throbbing air
> When bonfires blaze and quivering bodies char.
> Whose is the hair that crisped, and fiercely glowed?
> I know it; and my entrails melt like tar

And I set forth upon the southern road.

Darkness and firelight, the sacred and the profane, spiritual immortality and physical death, redemption and murder vie dramatically as the poet, feeling himself ablaze ("I know it"), presses on. The tar simile merges poet with lynch victims, who were often tarred and then set afire. "Human incense" strikes a bitter irony in the religious context. Half-rhyme, used only in this stanza, sharpens the intellectual and visual contrasts among *soar, air, char, tar*.

In the closing quatrain, Randall invokes the land:

> O fertile hillsides where my fathers are,
> From which my woes like troubled streams have flowed,
> Love you I must, though they may sweep me far.
> And I set forth upon the southern road.

Significantly, the earth remains fertile, nourished by the poet's grief and blood, emblems of his people's suffering. The statement passionately affirms Randall's belief in the democratic potential of the United States, his conviction that "conciliation is better than revenge." The poem's refrain gains a semantic increment subtly from stanza to stanza and so transforms from the first, where it functions narratively, to the second, where it asserts a claim, to the third, where it makes a heroic gesture. In the envoi it becomes a measure of love as Randall moves to the simple declarative of the close. The last line suggests the poet as separate yet strengthened by his experience, like Whitman's "simple, separate person" who can "yet utter the word Democratic, the word En-Masse." This poem may be contrasted with the title poem of Sterling A. Brown's *Southern Road* (1932)—reprinted in Randall's useful anthology *The Black Poets* (1971)—which is a blues ballad in dialect expressing a chain gang member's hopeless view of his life.

Cities Burning (1968), the first collection of Randall's own poems, whose cover design and stark colors of red, black, and white resemble those of Brooks's *Riot*, reflects the revolutionary spirit of the sixties. Of its twelve poems, half—including the most polemical—are in free verse; the rest are rhymed. "Roses and Revolutions," written in 1948, sets the tone:

> Musing on roses and revolutions,
> I saw night close down on the earth like a great dark wing,

and the lighted cities were like tapers in the night,
and I heard the lamentations of a million hearts
regretting life and crying for the grave.

The Whitmanic line and inflection draw the free verse to an affir-
mative close. There, the poet's prophetic vision of a future in which
"all men walk proudly through the earth, / and the bombs and
missles lie at the botton of the ocean / like the bones of dinosaurs
buried under the shale of eras," is confirmed by its radiance, in
which will "burst into terrible and splendid bloom / the blood-red
flower of revolution." The coupling of revolution and blossom
invokes the Brooks of the "Second Sermon on the Warpland" and
her counsel to youth: "Conduct your blooming in the noise and
whip of the whirlwind."

Randall's interest in other art forms appears in "Primitives,"
which compares the attempt of abstract art (Picasso is suggested)
and modern poetry, especially the typographically experimental,
to deal with the threat and hideous reality of modern warfare. His
lyrical "Augury for an Infant," addressed to his granddaughter,
Venita Sherron, closes the volume hopefully, seeing the infant as
"infinite possibility." But the strongest poems, apart from the first,
employ the lyrical understatement of Black folk poetry, the ter-
seness of blues, "ballards," spriruals, and seculars, and of old
English ballads like "Edward, Edward," "Lord Randal," and
"The Twa Corbies," where deep feeling compresses into rhythm,
rhyme, and the tragic frame. "Dressed All in Pink" begins quietly,
with a specific reference to John F. Kennedy's ride though Dallas
with his wife, Jacqueline, and Governor John Connally on Novem-
ber 22, 1963, and an allusive one to Camelot, land of the Kennedy
dream:

It was a wet and cloudy day
when the prince took his last ride.
The prince rode with the governor,
and his princess rode beside.

Randall's formal mastery gives a spondaic emphasis to "last ride"
in the only second line of any stanza thus distinguished in the
seven-stanza poem. Having progressed through the shooting, the
piece closes: "and her dress of pink so delicate / a deep, deep red is

dyed." The facts, ordered within the music and noble simplicity of the genre, elevate into myth.

The "Ballad of Birmingham," on the page opposite the Kennedy poem, complements both subject and genre with a similar spare dignity. Like the assassination of the president, the bombing of the Sixteenth Street Baptist Church on September 15, 1963, took place in the year of heightened civil rights protests. This "Negro Revolt" or "Black Rebellion" had culminated in the March on Washington in August by over 200,000 Black and white citizens, who had been stirred by Martin Luther King's "I have a dream" speech at the steps of the Lincoln Memorial. The following month, the Birmingham tragedy took the lives of four little girls at Sunday School and injured other children. The attack aroused nationwide grief and indignation, which the events in Dallas would soon intensify.

Randall focuses upon one child, personalizing both the horror and its context. The girl asks her mother's permission to participate in a freedom march. The mother, fearing the police dogs "and clubs and hoses, guns and jails," protectively refuses and, in searing irony, suggests that her child go to Sunday School instead, where she will be safe. Dramatic tension builds as the mother lovingly dresses the child for church and smiles to think of her daughter "in the sacred place." Then she hears the explosion: "her eyes grew wet and wild. / She raced through the streets of Birmingham / calling for her child." The murder, as if too terrible for description and thus augmented by mystery, powerfully registers in this vignette of maternal anguish. The poem conveys the dreadful lesson: no place is sacred or safe in such a time and place. The name of Birmingham, a city then regarded as the "capital" of segregation, becomes a symbol: "Birmingham becomes any city or town in which the oppressed Black is killed out of racial prejudice."[11]

Publication of the anthologies *For Malcolm* and *Black Poetry*, the addition of Gwendolyn Brooks, Don L. Lee, Sonia Sanchez, Etheridge Knight, Nikki Giovanni, and other important writers to the regular list, along with Broadside Series authors such as Robert Hayden, LeRoi Jones, Margaret Walker, and Melvin B. Tolson, enhanced the prestige of the Press as the unquestioned leader in Black publishing. In *Black Poetry*, Randall reprinted from *Poem Counterpoem* his own popular "George" and "Booker T. and W.E.B." The latter imagines a dialogue between Booker T. Washington, epitome of the industrious, conservative Negro who accepts a subservient position—"Just keep your mouth shut, do not grouse, / But work, and save, and buy a house"—and W. E. B. Du Bois, the intellectual progenitor of the Civil Rights Movement, who disagrees: "For what can property avail / If dignity and justice fail?" Randall clearly and accurately represents both sides, although, as he acknowledges wryly, Du Bois has the last word: "Speak soft, and try your little plan, / But as for me, I'll be a man."

"George," on the other hand, a workingman's tribute in free verse, describes a foundry co-worker who once gave Randall his "highest accolade: / You said: 'You not afraid of sweat. You strong as a mule.' " Years later, visiting the old man in a hospital ward, the poet poignantly returns the compliment.

In 1970, an important year for Randall, he traveled to Africa, and his volume of love poems, *Love You*, was published in London. Of the book's fourteen pieces, a few seem occasionally overwhelmed by ardent felings. Others show the application of his fine lyricism to free verse, as in "The profile on the pillow," and to metrical verse, in which "Black magic" seems to *sing* its refrain of "Black girl, black girl." "Faces" lauds the beauty of ordinary, aging features shaped by experience, "not only crocus faces / or fresh-snowfall faces / but driftwood faces, grooved by salt waters."

"Sanctuary," the last poem, mainly in iambic pentameter with deliberately varied stresses, offers particular interest for its whirlwind imagery, recalling Brooks's "Second Sermon on the Warpland," and its compounding ("nation-death-and-birth"), another heroic device of Brooks. "This is the time of the whirlwind and the fire" also reverts to the introductory poem, "The profile on the pillow," where tender memory remains, despite possibilities that

Perhaps
you may cease to love me,
or we may be consumed in the holocaust,
but I keep, against the ice and the fire,
the memory of your profile on the pillow.

This opening poem may be considered as companion to Brooks's "An Aspect of Love, / Alive in the Ice and Fire" (*Riot*, 1969), a title which alludes in mild irony to Robert Frost's "Fire and Ice."

Brooks, like Randall, offers a tentative hope that personal love will endure.

It should be noted that Randall's use of the strong word "holocaust," which has acquired in this century the connotation of genocide, refers specifically to the widely held belief among Blacks, after the riots of the sixties, that the government was preparing concentration camps for their confinement, even extermination. The poet conveys an awareness of fatal peril that will hurl the lovers "with the other doomed spirits / around and around in the fury of the whirlwind"—an allusion to Dante's meeting, in his *Inferno*, with the lovers Paolo and Francesca, whose passion dooms them to be tossed forever by stormy winds. Brooks, on the other hand, uses the whirlwind as a symbol of social change.

Randall's energies converged in high gear upon a full edition, *More to Remember: Poems of Four Decades* (the 1930s through the 1960s), published by Third World Press the following year and dedicated to Don L. Lee. The collection shows a wide range of interests, prosodic skill, and experimentation, its poems almost evenly divided between rhyme and free verse—the latter featured in polemical pieces and the later poems. The main thrust is political and humane and includes lively commentary on poets and poetics. The book is organized by decades into four sections. The first, "The Kindness and the Cruelty," begins significantly with "For Pharish Pinckney, Bindle Stiff During the Depression," dedicated to the brother of Randall's second wife, Mildred. At one time, the youth had lived as a boxcar-riding hobo who "learned the kindness and the cruelty / of the land that mothered and rejected you." Here the ambivalence of the Black experience in the United States may be generalized to include all those oppressed by poverty (see the expanded version in *A Litany of Friends*). Other poems celebrate youth in forms close to the traditions of seventeenth- and eighteenth-century English poetry. "Shape of the Invisible," a cinquain after Adelaide Crapsey yet showing Japanese influence, effectively measures poetic feet (1, 2, 3, 4, 1):

At dawn
Upon the snow
The delicate imprint
Left by the sleeping body of
The wind.

"Incredible Harvests," the second section, marks an enhancement of poetic power and a life that encompasses fatherhood, love and other problems, wartime service, reflections on police arrest (see the blues ballad "Jailhouse Blues," and "The Line-Up"), and frequently politics. Here the poet attends more closely to visual elements, most notably in "Pacific Epitaphs." The abbreviated and irregular length of these seventeen impressions epitomizes the brief lives of the dead and of their tombs, scattered among Pacific islands. Deep feeling compresses into epigram and understatement, as in "Halmaherra," "Laughing I left the earth. / Flaming returned," and "Guadalcanal":

> Your letter.
> These medals.
> This grave.

Avoiding sentimentality, the poems convey a dignity of grief while employing the restraint of, ironically, the Japanese haiku or tanka. Randall himself points out the additional influences of Edgar Lee Masters's *Spoon River Anthology* and of *The Greek Anthology*, which share a mode that is, in his words, "simple, spare, suggestive."

Yet the poet's lyricism does not fail him. Following "Pacific Epitaphs," "The Ascent" memorably describes an airman's view of the earth as he moves

> Into the air like dandelion seed
> Or like the spiral of lark into the light
> Or fountain into sun. . . .
> . . . .
>
> We poise in air, hang motionless, and see
> The planet turn with slow grace of a dancer.

"Coral Atoll" extends the meditation on natural beauty in the wartime scene and ends with a line that suggests Randall's ideal of poetic form at the time: "Have died into a perfect form that sings." One recalls Keats's "die into life" in speaking of Apollo (*Hyperion*, l. 130).

In several ways, by contrasting form and relating content, Randall emphasizes the senseless recurrence of war and the time-

less fraternity of its dead. "Helmeted Boy" addresses a youth killed
in battle:

> Your forehead capped with steel
> Is smoother than a coin
> With profile of a boy who fell
> At Marathon.

As in "Pacific Epitaphs," the brevity of the lines conveys the brevity
of life.

The third section, "If Not Attic, Alexandrian," is the shortest
yet displays an interesting variety of technique. It represents the
1950s, Randall notes, "when the nation was quiescent under Presi-
dent Eisenhower, and poetry was under the dominance of the Eliot/
academic establishment." It takes its title from "The Dilemma,"
subtitled with a quotation from the late Ray Durem, "My poems
are not sufficiently obscure / to please the critics." In a Shake-
spearean sonnet, the speaker ironically claims that he cultivates his
irony in order to be as confusing as the times. "So, though no
Shelley, I'm a gentleman, / And, if not Attic, Alexandrian." Thus,
tongue in cheek, Randall presents a poem not marked by simple
refinement (Attic) but concerned with technical perfection (Alex-
andrian).

Other sonnets in this section include "Anniversary Words," in
the even stricter Petrarchan form, addressed to the poet's wife:
"You who have shared my scanty bread with me / and borne my
carelessness and forgetfulness / with only occasional lack of tender-
ness, / who have long patiently endured my faculty / for genial
neglect of practicality." Apologia and appreciation, the poem may
be instructively compared and contrasted with "For Vivian," a
more recent tribute (1983), published and then "calligraphized" in
1984, the poet notes, as Broadside No. 94:

> Me, this snoring, belching, babbling semblance of man kind,
> What woman could refrain from laughing at?
> Or, caring more, quietly take her hat
> And leave? Yet, these four and twenty years
> You've stayed, though not without heart wring and tears.
> For which my thanks. And bless your love which binds.

The third section also contains the poet's aesthetic credo

"Aim," which calls for "words transparent as the air, / which hint the whole by showing the part clear." Randall comments that this poem shows his "liking for a classically natural style, without distracting eccentricities and obscurities."

"Interview" presents another technical surprise. In a dramatic monologue in blank verse after the fashion of Robert Browning—its sixty lines constituting Randall's longest published poem—a rich, elderly man (Henry Ford?) explains his tax-exempt research foundation and his life's philosophy to a brash reporter. He grants the interview in order to

> prove to those
> Who could not take the world as they found it
> And therefore lack the power to change it at all
> That one old, greedy, and predacious villain
> Can do more good in the world than all of them
> In all their years of whining and complaining.

The portrait renders the shadowy grays as well as the clear blacks and whites of existence.

The relatively long closing section, "And Her Skin Deep Velvet Night," takes its title from "On Getting a Natural (For Gwendolyn Brooks)," the tribute that ends the volume. Mordantly amusing, "Ancestors" questions: "Why are our ancestors / always kings or princes / and never the common people? . . . Or did the slavecatchers / steal only the aristocrats / and leave the fieldhands / laborers / streetcleaners / garbage collectors / dishwashers / cooks and maids / behind?" The democratic Randall tolerates neither snobbery nor intolerance. In "Aphorisms," written with Blakean simplicity (Randall approves the comparison), he warns, "He who vilifies the Jew / next day will slander you. / / He who calls his neighbor 'nigger' / upon your turning back will snigger," and ends on a religious note: "While he who calls a faith absurd / thrusts the spear into his Lord."

The majority of the remaining poems in this group share a political nexus. "Hymn" expresses horror over "our worship" of the atomic bomb, which may end life on earth. "The Trouble with Intellectuals" and "The Intellectuals" were inspired by the difference between the Mensheviks who talked and the Bolsheviks who acted. A number of the poems scold the excesses of Black

Nationalism and level criticisms of arrogance, extremism, and hypocrisy at some Black activists.

But there are tributes, too. The syncopated "Langston Blues" presents a moving elegy for one who brought "laughter from hell." And the closing poem praises Brooks's adoption of a natural hairstyle and becomes an encomium of her beauty combined in spirit, action, and appearance: "And now her regal wooly crown / declares / I know / I'm black / AND / beautiful."

In 1973 Randall published *After the Killing*, dedicated to the memory of a loyal Broadside worker, Ruth Elois Whitsitt Fondren. The fifteen poems, whose variety of subject matter accompanies the turn to even more free verse (only two are rhymed), show increased versatility in Randall's use of the form, to allow for more lyricism as well as argument. "African Suite," the opening poem in five parts, gives Randall's impression of an Africa still racist and describes his feelings at visiting a Ghana castle that once held slaves. Some pieces apply Randall's critical humor to Blacks as well as to humanity in general, continuing the tact of *More to Remember*.

"After the Killing," the title poem, evokes the Brooks metonymic, heroic style: " 'We will kill', said the blood-thirster, / 'and after the killing / there will be peace.' " Although Randall will not call the poem pacifistic, it does dramatize the absurdity of war, preventive or retaliatory, and of the arms race. "To the Mercy Killers," a Shakespearean sonnet, powerfully affirms life to the end: if ever mercy move you murder me, / I pray you, kindly killers, let me live." "For Gwendolyn Brooks, Teacher," utilizes spondaic energy and a spare meter: "You teach / without talk. / / Your life / is lesson. / / We give / because you do, / / are kind / because you are. / / Just live. / We will learn." Randall ends the book with a translation, an earlier poem, "I Loved You Once" (Ya vas lyubil), from Pushkin, described in an editor's footnote as "the Russian of African descent who is credited for making the Russian language live again."

After emerging from his silence in 1980, in 1981 Randall published *A Litany of Friends: New and Selected Poems*, his first book in eight years. Its moving title poem of dedication, autobiographical, identifies those many poets, friends, and family members who helped him morally, spiritually, and financially during his depression. The long-awaited book, which may be viewed in part as transitional, surprised some, pleased and dismayed others. It comprises excellent selections from previous years and volumes, interfaced with new or newly appearing poems in both free verse and conventional forms. "Verse Forms," written in free verse, defends the sonnet: "A sonnet is an arrow. / Pointed and slim, it pierces / The slit in the armor." (Compare Gwendolyn Brooks's earlier admonition in "The Second Sermon on the Warpland": "not the pet bird of poets, that sweetest sonnet, / shall straddle the whirlwind.")

"A Litany of Friends," also in free verse, was begun April 1, 1980; along with "The Mini Skirt," written on April 4, and "To an Old Man," a sonnet written on Easter Sunday, two days later, it inaugurates the revived creative flow. The three poems, while they reflect the personal emphasis of much of the poetry, Black and white, of the seventies, reveal Randall's psychic energy shaping the two main categories of the new works: humanist concerns (in sections titled "Friends," "War," "Africa," and "Me") and love poetry (in "Eros," which, followed in number by "Friends," contains the bulk of the new poetry).

Part III, "War," offers a distinguished set from *More to Remember*, including "Pacific Epitaphs." Among the new or newly appearing antiwar poems are "Games," a fine Petrarchan sonnet variant on boys' war games transposed into real battle, and "Straight Talk from a Patriot," a satirical quatrain on the Vietnam War. Of two translations from the Russian of Konstantin M. Simonov, the exquisitely achieved "My Native Land (Rodina)," in six rhymed quatrains of iambic pentameter, personalizes patriotism. Randall's translations, for which his skill and temperament seem equally suited, confirm the breadth of his consciousness.

The introductory section, "Friends," reveals the warmth of the poet, who can write with stirring compassion of his dog ("Poor Dumb Butch"); with lyricism of his students ("My Students" is a series of fifteen haiku); and with imaginative appreciation of fellow Black poets ("The Six," from 1975). At times the conventional form strains art into conventional registers, but when it succeeds, it does so notably. Randall comments: "Some of the love poems I wanted to sound simple and naïve: 'For love converts away from sad,' using the adjective *sad* as a noun; 'And never mind receive,' using the verb *receive* as a noun, the object of the verb *mind*."

What has disturbed some readers more than the uneven quality of certain pieces is their content. Part II, "Eros," has incurred the

most criticism, partly for its unabashed indulgence in sensual
appreciation and its occasional Elizabethan inflection (as in
"Maiden, Open" and "May and December: A Song"). But Ran-
dall replies: "Poets strain against barriers. Wordsworth attacked
Pope's 'poetic diction.' Now, no contemporary poet would be
caught dead using 'poetic diction' like 'maiden,' 'bower,' 'sigh.' It's
this new interdiction that I fight. Call it 'The New Romanticism,' if
you will. I fight for the right to use 'romantic' diction as much as the
Black poets of the 1960s fought to use street language."

    "The Mini Skirt" typifies the relaxed, Rabelaisian mode.
Health of both ego and libido return here in force as the poet
delights in his own recovery. The mischievous iconoclast appears in
"The New Woman," a reply inscribed "to M.H.W. and D.H.M."
(Mary Helen Washington and me), "who said that my poem
'Women' was sexist." Hence, from the mildly amusing "I like
women they're so warm & soft & sweet / Touch one & her skin
yields like the flesh of a peach" of the older poem, "The New
Woman" shifts to "I like women they're so hard & tough & strong
/ Feel their muscle it's hard & hairy as a coconut," and charges on
to a hilarious reversal of the first poem's images and values. An
intriguing found poem, "The Erotic Poetry of Sir Isaac Newton,"
convincingly adapts *The Motion of Bodies* (1687) to free verse.
"Translation from Chopin"—Prelude Number 7 in A Major, Opus
28—the first published sample from Randall's intended project,
seems to dissolve into the poignancy of the piece when read accom-
panied by the music.

    Some of Randall's friends and fellow poets had expected stir-
ring political broadsides, calls for justice, and exhortations to Black
unity. Several wondered, as he observes in the militant apologia "A
Poet Is Not a Jukebox," "But why don't you write about the riot in
Miami?"[12] In this rebuttal, forthright in free verse, Randall admits
ignorance of Miami because of his immediate needs to revive his
economic and creative life. But his defense turns into a spirited
offense. He warns that

Telling a Black poet what he ought to write
Is like some Commissar of Culture in Russia telling a poet
He'd better write about the new steel furnaces in the Novobigorsk
    region,

Or the heroic feats of Soviet labor in digging the trans-Caucasus
     Canal,
Or the unprecedented achievement of workers in the sugar beet
     industry who exceeded their quota by 400 per cent (it was later
     discovered to be a typist's error).

Randall's unfailing humanity empathizes with the Russian poet
who may be devastated by his mother's dying of cancer, or by other
personal matters. Further, states Randall, as the broadside becomes
an aesthetic manifesto,

I'll bet that in a hundred years the poems the Russian people will
     read, sing, and love
Will be the poems about his mother's death, his unfaithful
     mistress, or his wine, roses, and nightingales,
Not the poems about steel furnaces, the trans-Caucasus Canal, or
     the sugar beet industry.
A poet writes about what he feels, what agitates his heart and sets
     his pen in motion.
Not what some apparatchnik dictates, to promote his own career
     or theories.

Randall maintains his freedom to choose, in his own time, his
own subjects, those which move him personally, including Miami.
He goes on to defend writing about love and, with extravagant
seriousness, offers love as a sociopolitical prescription. He sar-
donically notes that "If Josephine had given Napoleon more loving,
he wouldn't have sown / the meadows of Europe with skulls." In
closing the poem and the book, Randall insists:

A poet is not a *jukebox*.
A poet is *not* a jukebox.
A *poet* is not a jukebox.

So don't tell *me* what to write.

The revolutionary action of poets has ever been freely to create
from their deepest psychic sources. Defending himself, ably and
with humor, Randall affirms his own center, his humanist core.
One anticipates that as the poet retrieves and reshapes the exten-
sions of his daily life, he will again articulate the range of interests
that have made him, in the words of R. Baxter Miller, "one of the
most important Black men of letters in the twentieth century."[13]

The reader will welcome his courageous heart, its wit, lyricism, and humane expansiveness.

INTERVIEW WITH DUDLEY RANDALL

DH   I think of you as a political person. I was wondering whether you considered yourself a socialist or socialistic?

DR   No, I'm not a socialist. I went to Russia, and I think people are just human beings all the world over. And wherever you have human beings, you're going to have tyrants and bosses. You have a socialist state, and you'll have tyrants and bosses and everybody. I saw the pecking order.

Just in our entourage there were nine artists, Black artists, touring Russia. We had Igor to be our interpreter. And Anna, the guide, and Igor would lord it over the waitresses at the Hotel Warsaw in Moscow. Igor didn't have to eat with us, because he lived in town, but he ate with us because he could get better food. He would demand his mineral water—"Give me some mineral water!"—to the waitresses; "Give me some more chicken!" [*Chuckles*] And one waitress, when he wasn't looking, pointed at him and looked at us and drew the knife across her throat. Then on the other hand, Anna, who had a higher rank, would lord it over Igor. And we couldn't understand Russian, but just by the tone of the voice and the rhythm, we could tell. When we went somewhere, he had to take care of the baggage, and by the body action, we got that she was telling him off and telling him what to do, and he better do this and better get this right.

So no matter, you could have a kingdom, you could have a so-called democracy, you could have a socialist state, but there will be people, people will be people. And you may give them different titles—he may be comrade Igor and she may be comrade Anna—but they'll still lord it over, they'll still cheat, and yes, I guess there will still be good people, too.

DH   You've used the expression "production for use instead of for profit"—

DR   Yes.

DH   —Which was your conception of Broadside Press. I wonder whether you still have that perspective and whether that could be related to any kind of socialistic view.

DR   Oh, you take the book situation over there. They were artists and they talked mostly about painting. We went to art museums and studios and had seminars on Russian artists. You know how in a socialist state, you see how they do with the writers. A good writer, a very brave writer by the name of [Aleksandr] Solzhenitsyn is silenced. They don't publish him. He had to smuggle his books out. You talked to me about censorship yesterday, about self-censorship, which comes about from pressures from other people—"You shouldn't write this kind of poetry." "You shouldn't write poetry with four-letter words"—and that's a kind of censorship. But in a socialist state, the censorship is official. This is unofficial, personal censorship. But there it's official. And the best writers—who was that poet that died in a concentration camp, [Osip] Mandelstam; his wife memorized his poems. That's all that made his poems never die, because she memorized his poems. But that's official censorship.

DH   So then you would be against censorship of either kind.

DR   Yes. Here we don't have censorship except in extreme cases, like during World War I and after World War I, when they had purity raids. Because the way it is now, any poet that can get a mimeograph machine can mimeograph something or type up something and staple it together, take it to the Eighth Street bookstore or sell it on the street.

DH   Do you think that's good for poetry, the proliferation of the interest?

DR   Sure. Yes.

DH   Because there are people who say, "Well, there's too much poetry beging written."

DR   Don't worry. Most of it will die.

DH   I feel that it is better to have more poetry, because out of that abundance will come the best, and the greater the abundance, the better.

DR   I think so, too.

DH   The more potential.

DR   I think about an audience for poetry, but I'm afraid the audience for poetry is other poets.

DH   Do you think the audience has grown? How would you compare the audience with the audience in the sixties?

DR I don't think it's grown from the sixties, because there were a lot of people in the sixties who were political.

DH Do you think it has diminished?

DR Yes, I think so. I think it's diminished. Since people are not so interested in politics, the audience has shrunk. But I'm for looking upon poetry as entertainment, as you've heard me at the church expostulate.[14] And I think it can be done, because I think poetry has so much to offer people, once they listen to it, without the inhibitions and without being intimidated that they have to look on it with a certain awe and respect. Maybe these bawdy poems are the type of poem that people will say, "Boy—I really enjoyed that."

DH Do you think that the entertainment is a means of attracting people to the content of what you're saying?

DR Yes. Of course the entertainment poems are just entertainment. So I'm interested in reading to you the first poem I finished after I started writing again, April 4 [1980]. [Reads "The Mini Skirt"]

DH What do you think of my perspective, if I have expressed myself clearly enough to you, which possibly I haven't, about the poets as carrying on the leadership, as it was in the sixties—

DR I never thought of myself as a leader. I'm pretty sure Don Lee does, because he explicitly said so. He says that young people in the colleges where he reads are looking for guidance and direction. The title of one of his books is *Directionscore*. And I think Gwen [Brooks] feels that way, too.

DH I think she feels that way about him and about herself.

DR And about me. She doesn't want me to write this kind of verse. When I read her something like this ["The Mini Skirt"], she says, "Yes, Dudley, but what about Miami? When are you going to write about Miami?"

DH I think you have written so much and you have done so much, I see you as a very modest person. And I think you are undeniably a leader. You have a position of leadership, and there are different kinds of leadership, of course. You mentioned Haki Madhubuti and his sense of leadership. It is a very different kind of leadership than what you offer. It's a different kind in that you say different things. I was wondering, for example, about your opinion of his perspetive in *Enemies*, of seeing opposing forces, Black and white, and sort of putting all white people together as a kind of common enemy.

DR Well, a lot of what he says is right. Because it seems that wherever whites have gone, they have destroyed people and destroyed cultures and looked upon the people that lived there with contempt, destroyed those people's self-respect, made them feel inferior; they treated them as if they were inferior creatures. . . .

They seem so acquisitive. They're always into taking something. I wrote a poem—I didn't know whether you've read it or not—about colonizers. Wherever they go they think about making money. They see an island, and immediately they think about dividing it up into real estate subdivisions—"How can I make some money on this?" And they see the natives there, living and loving, and they put them to work. They make them work and work for them, to make more money for them. They just seem to be that way.

DH Um-hum. But that is colonialism, which is an aspect of racism. I wonder whether you agree that it makes sense to group all white people in the same category. Because there are many white people who feel they have the same enemy. I mean, would Black people and white people who feel they have the same enemy, wouldn't they have more in common in facing, let's say, an oppressive system, an exploitative system?

DR That's the crucial dividing point. He [Madhubuti] looks on the struggle between Black and white as some people look on it as a struggle between classes.

DH Which is your view?

DR Well, in the oppressed white classes, you'll find just as much prejudice. Take a poor white—a poor white workingman will be just as prejudiced, or even more prejudiced than a middle-class white or an upper-class white, because he feels more threatened.

DH I guess you might say that that would be the white person whose consciousness, whose social consciousness, has not been raised. But there are white people who have that and are aware of economic forces working upon them.

DR Yes. I know that there are good white people. I'm not like Haki, putting everybody into the same class. What I'm saying is that a lot of what he says is right. You can raise anybody's consciousness. If you raise anybody's consciousness, he'll probably change. But the consciousness has not been raised to a point where it is effective, or generally prevalent.

I gave a talk last week at a motel, Holiday motel by the airport. Melba Boyd's class for gifted children was having a sort of graduation exercise. The parents were there. And I talked about how the parents could help the children, not only by just giving birth to them—because they were not really responsible for that; they just happened to have those genes—but by the way they nurtured them and bought them books and read to them, the kind of conversation they had around the dinner table and in the living room. And there was one woman, she must have been a poor woman—it's a lower-middle-class neighborhood; they're working people, factory people—she looked at me with this cold, blue-eyed stare that I'm so familiar with. I made no impression on her. She was just thinking, "What is this nigger up there talking about?" [*Laughs*] And that's the way so many of them are. That look of cold hate. . . . So, in a way, a lot of what Don Lee says is right.

DH   He speaks about power. He feels that essentially it is a question of power and consolidation of power. And there seems to be—from the criticism, for example, that I have read of his *Enemies* and his attitude toward the Sixth Pan-African Congress—there seems to be a division between those who have followed Du Bois and those who follow Garvey and the separatist-nationalist position, versus the integrationist and socialistic class perspective.

DR   Yes.

DH   Do you see it that way? Do you see that this is the alignment?

DR   There's that alignment, and in that last Pan-African Congress the socialists won out. I guess they look on people from the United States, Blacks from the United States and Blacks from South Africa, as being very radical. But the Blacks from South Africa and the Blacks from the United States have really seen them [whites] and they know what it's like, whereas in some other countries—maybe there 95 percent of the people are Black and you have a few merchants in the towns by the sea. It's very different from a country where it's just taken over by the whites, like South Africa, or here, where the country's controlled by the white majority.

DH   If you see things in terms of power, do you think that one can have enough power in a kind of enclave of a group, of a racial group, without seeking power in a much broader perspective, in a class—according to classes rather than according to a small group? Aren't you really dividing your potential strength that way?

DR   Yes. That can be called an enclave, like the Armenians in Fresno, wherever they settle. Many of them are wealthy and civic leaders, and they're not trying to spread the Armenian power all over the United States.

DH   Do you see your position as shifting or having shifted or potentially changing at all? Because from what I've read of you in the past, I have seen a more integrationist perspective and more of a class view.

DR   I think I'm an integrationist in that I believe Blacks are part of this country, and whatever is to be done in this country, I believe Blacks should take part in it: go where you want to go, live where you want to live, marry whom you want to marry, love whom you want to love, just because it's your right as a person.

DH   Yes. So actually your basic philosophy—

DR   We're just human beings. We're all human beings. You should have the freedom to develop the way you want to. Part of the way to marshal your strength is to align yourself with those who are like you and in like condition. Blacks—for instance, this neighborhood is almost all Black, so why shouldn't Blacks organize? That's the way we elected a Black mayor [of Detroit]. The Blacks voted together.

DH   What do you think of [Amiri] Baraka's view of the—

DR   Baraka changes so much. I don't pay much attention to his changes. I think that anybody that follows him, the next minute he'll find Baraka at his throat, because Baraka will have changed to an entirely different position. Suppose a man followed Baraka into Greenwich Village, married a white woman, had two or three children—and then Baraka went back to Harlem, then went back to Newark, and was so Black, and this man would be left stranded in Greenwich Village with his white wife and his three half-white children, just from following him. So I wouldn't follow Baraka. He changes. The next minute he'll be something else.

He attacked Don [Lee]. I was so hurt by that. He spoke here, so I went to him after he spoke and said, "I'm very sorry to hear about you and Don. Don admires you and he's imitated you." And he says—he didn't speak harshly, he has a soft voice—he says, "Well, that's the way it is." So that's the way it is. So anybody that follows him will probably find himself being attacked by Baraka the next minute when Baraka has another one of his changes.

DH   Well, their views are antithetical at this point.

DR   Yes, because Baraka has gone into socialism.

DH   He's very strongly committed to that.

DR   Yes, but he might change again. You never can tell. He might be a feminist or a banana eater, the way he changes.

DH   One of the poems you have in *After the Killing*—it's the title poem—I interpret it as a pacifist poem.

DR   "After the Killing?"

DH   Yes.

DR   I don't give it any label. All that I'm saying is that people go on killing each other, like the Hatfields and McCoys. Somebody in this family is killed or this group is killed. So in order to get revenge, this group kills somebody in the other group, and then the other group, in order to get revenge, kills somebody in the other group. And it just goes on and on and on and on and on.

DH   So do you think war is senseless, by and large?

DR   Yes. Sure it is. I think these people ought to make friends, say, "This has happened in the past. Forget it. Let's go on from here and be friends."

DH   So would you say your tendency is toward a pacifist view, or do you shy away from the label?

DR   I shy away from the label. I would rather describe people by what they do. I would say conciliation is better than revenge.

DH   You've really written some wonderful antiwar poems. I love your "Pacific Epitaphs." You told me that the inspiration for those poems was your own experience, right?

DR   My own experience when I was hit in the ribs by a chair, and that was enlarged, exaggerated, made death. And what I saw happening to others. Like the fellow in our outfit that was hanged for rape. Some of it I just imagined, I guess.

DH   Were you in action in World War II?

DR   Not really in action. I was with the Signal Corps outfit. They put up telephone lines betwen airports, and I was in the headquarters detachment. The headquarters detachment didn't even do that. They kept the records and sent out reports in quintuplicate.

DH   I was wondering about some of the new work that you're doing, and whether you view it as transitional or just something you're doing now, and the question that Gwendolyn Brooks or perhaps some other poet may have had about your more personal current work. Do you see it as just something you're doing now, that is not necessarily going to detract from any of the more political stuff you may be writing now and in the future?

DR   Well, you write what you can, and you write what you feel an urge to write and what you enjoy writing. I get these ideas. Like before I left, I got the idea to write an answer ["The New Woman"]. And I put it down, just so it would be down on paper. And I did it.

DH   Good. I agree. I think that you should just do what's right for you at that time: write an honest poem, and then you'll write another honest poem about something else. [*Laughs*]

DR   Yes. Something else. It'll come. . . .

DH   Absolutely.

DR   This is just in ink. Maybe I shouldn't show it to you, because it's just a first draft. [*Randall shows several new poems in manuscript.*]

DH   I am very impressed by your new work. Not only do I like the poems, but I am impressed by the variety and the openness. For example, your "translation" from Chopin. And then you have a found poem from Sir Isaac Newton, the love poems, and the great variety.[15] Do you feel anything special going on? Do you feel that this is a particularly fruitful period, a productive period?

DR   Yes, I think so. I don't know when I've written so much, except maybe when I was a kid just starting. A kid—he'll do anything, sit and read Shelley's "The Cloud," and then go in and write a poem with internal rhymes; he just sits down and writes them. I had those poems in a notebook, but I lost it.

DH   Do you revise much?

DR   Yes.

DH   I notice that you have two versions of the translation from Chopin. The first version was in October of '54, and you revised it in June this year.

DR   I couldn't remember exactly what I wrote. The first version was more like the first stanza. The first stanza is really the whole poem, because it's a very short piece, just two bars. But finally I said I'd better sit down and write this. I'd been listening to Chopin a lot, sometimes staying up all night listening.

DH   Do you find that classical music inspires you?

DR   It doesn't inspire me; I enjoy it. But I think, on another

level, it may help me to write. Because I think I've told you that
Dorothea Brande's book [*Becoming a Writer*], this red book, dis-
covers that what often makes poets write is some occupation that's
wordless, rhythmical, and monotonous. Some people scrub, some
people take a long walk, and they don't know what it is except that
they find that it works for them, and they have to do it to get them to
write. And maybe it's the wordlessness.

After listening to music all night or till very late at night, I go to
sleep. Then, when I get up early in the morning, the house is quiet
and I have no disturbances. Then those words, having been sup-
pressed in that wordless occupation, and the rhythmical and mo-
notonous occupation which hypnotizes you, the words come out of
the unconscious.

DH   That makes a lot of sense. I am especially impressed by
revision. I revise my work a great deal. One thing that endeared
Yeats to me was knowing that he revised "Fergus and the Druid"
over a period of thirty-four years. [*Laughs*] And he had all these
different versions published, which is a kind of deterrent to people
who want to be published too soon, because all your sins are in
print forever.

DR   That's true.

DH   I want to ask you about a few specific poems. For exam-
ple, you have a poem called "Poet," in *More to Remember*. (I have a
few questions about *More to Remember*.) This sloppy, white,
Anglo-Saxon poet about whom you write rather endearingly—I
was wondering whether you had someone in mind.

DR   No particular person. I had an image. I'd seen a play at
Wayne State University, *Cyrano de Bergerac*. I believe there's a
scene in the play where the poets are going to a cafe, and Cyrano
wears a big hat and fine clothes. I think that image was in my mind,
besides my image of poets in blue jeans and barefoot, long hair
hanging down over their shoulders. Did I show you that poem?[16]
Maybe you'll enjoy that. I'll read it to you.

DH   Okay.

DR   [*Looks through notebook*] I'll have to find it. I think I
read it to John and Mary Doe. James and Mary Doe. Relatives.
They liked it.

DH   Doe? D-o-e? Doe? Did you say Doe?

DR   Yes. Didn't I tell you at the writers' convention I put on
my name tag "John Doe," because I didn't want people asking me

for my autograph, or saying, "Are you Dudley Randall?" So Herb [Boyd] went along. He said he was my brother James, and his wife Melba was Mary Doe, and we had left our Brother Doe Doe back in Detroit. [*Laughter*]

So we had a lot of fun. The first night I talked with a woman. She approached me. We were sitting down in the hall. And she asked if I was there for the writers' convention, and I said yes, and I asked if she were there, and she said yes. I asked what she wrote. She said she wrote short stories. She started writing because her aunt had committed suicide. Then she asked me what I did, and I said, "Why, I'm a retired librarian, and I try to write poetry." So we talked a little about writing. Then we went into what they call the Off Broadway Theatre and saw a play, and we were both very tired. She had come down from Milwaukee on Amtrak; I had driven from Detroit. So we were both nodding. Finally she got up and didn't say good night, but just went on to her room. Then the next day she was in my poetry workshop, and after that she was telling people, "Well I spent the whole evening with Dudley Randall. He didn't even tell me who he was. He just said he was a retired librarian!" [*Laughter*]. . . .

But here is this poem. Herb and Melba say I show a kind of anger about the way some poets dress. I had "I hate," but that word was too strong. So I said: "I abhor snobs, and most of all / poet snobs. . . ." [*Reads the poem, written on June 17, 1980.*]

DH   When did this very productive period start? Was it the past few months, would you say?

DR   It started the fourth of April, when I wrote "The Mini Skirt." That was my first poem in five years. . . . And I followed two days later on Easter Sunday with "To an Old Man." I think I used to be very shy and self-centered. I would think about myself. If I met a new person, I would think about myself. But do you know what I do now? I meet somebody on the street, and I look at that person, and I think about that person instead of myself. . . . So I start talking about that, and I don't think about myself. I'd be riding around for the [U.S.] Census, and I'd see a man walking on the street. I'd wave to him, and he'd wave back. And because I go out of myself—and I use a census term. You know the circle that you're supposed to blacken? And if you don't blacken it all the way, then it doesn't register on the computer.

So instead of saying, "Be universal," which is fraught with

emotion—you make some guys angry if you say anything about universality—I just say, "Blacken the FOSDIC circle."[17] The FOSDIC circle is the other person or the object. It may be a bird, it may be a sparrow. And you forget about yourself. You obliterate your ego and your personality, and you go out to the other person, to the other person's mind. Forget about yourself.

DH   Do you connect your feeling to any particular religious or philosophical belief?

DR   No.

DH   Or do you feel it's a more personal kind of energy?

DR   I don't connect it with religion. When you get old, you think about life. In these last few months, I think the purpose of life is life.

DH   That sounds very young to me. That doesn't sound old at all. I think you'e a very young man, Dudley Randall! [*Laughter*]

I heard a wonderful thing on television a few weeks ago. People were talking about age, and this woman got up and said, "I've met two kinds of people. There are young people and there are old people. The young people are young all their lives, and the old people are old all their lives." [*Laughs*] And those are the two kinds of people.

DR   It may be the way they look at life.

DH   I think you are one of the young people. I think Gwen [Brooks] is.

DR   She's so strong—vigorous. Although she doesn't have this conscious theory, she doesn't do it consciously, she's the kind of person that goes out to the other person. Because I was telling her this theory; I don't think I had formulated it so much then, but I gave as an example a poet to whom I came, very excited. "I had a poem translated into French!" And the other poet, instead of going into me and trying to find out all about my experience, put me down. He said, "Oh, yeah? I've had a poem that was translated into French, Spanish, Italian and German and Urdu." So that just puts me down and turns me off. Especially the Urdu. [*Laughter*]

And I told it to Gwen, and I said, "Now, you, Gwen, if you saw me coming, you wouldn't even have to wait. You would say—because you would notice not yourself, but me—you would say, 'Oh, Dudley, you're smiling and you look so happy. What is it?' And I would say, 'Gwen, I had a poem translated into French.'"
And then she would enter into the experience, and she would say,

"Isn't that wonderful. Who translated it, and where did it appear, and what do you think of the translation?" You see, she would blacken this circle, going into the circle of me more and more . . . until the circle was completely blackened.

But this is an example of how far she goes: She even went into the mind of this poet who turned me off. She would say, "Well, you have to understand the poet who turned you off. Maybe he felt insecure. He was insecure, so he had to boast about something to make himself feel more secure." You see, she went a step further. She—even such a reprehensible person as that—she could go into his mind.

DH   Yes. She has enormous compassion and understanding. And of course, that poet had a serious problem, a poet whose ego gets in the way of his vision, his or her vision.

DR   There are poets like that, though.

DH   Yes, and it's too bad, because—

DR   It limits them.

DH   It limits their poetry, and that's what they have to live with.

DR   Yes. But a poet like Shakespeare, Shakespeare or Keats, that universal type (to use that phrase), they could become a horse or a bird. Tolstoy was that way. He became a dog. Do you remember that passage in *Anna Karenina*, when Levin goes hunting with his dog Laska [Part II, chap. 15, "Birdshooting"]? Tolstoy enters into the thoughts of the dog. Levin tells the dog to go over here, and Laska thinks, "That's the wrong order. There's a . . . snipe over there, but I'll make believe that I'm obeying him." So Laska walked over there, and sniffed around as if she were obeying him, then walked around to where the snipe really was. Tolstoy forgot himself and became a dog. . . .

Tolstoy had all these theories about the noble Russian peasant, but when he wrote his book, he had one scene showing the peasants working in the fields all together and the women dancing, but yet he had other scenes where he showed that the peasants looked on people like Tolstoy, nobles that tried to improve their condition, as fools, and they would cheat them, and they were always suspicious of them. They were not going to let these nobles outwit them, and they thought they were shrewder than the nobles, and they would break their tools, and they wouldn't use the improved agricultural methods that Levin proposed. So he saw the other side that just came out of him because he was so realistic, no matter what theories he had or what ideology he had. If you're a universal person, the truth will come out.

That's why I don't like ideology. Because when you look through ideological glasses, no matter what you see, you have to distort it so that it could fit your theories. "This may not be so, but I have a theory or Marx had a theory, so somehow we have to twist things so that they fit into that theory." And that's why I don't like ideology, because it makes you twist life so that you don't see life. You see life through the glasses of this theory.

But as I said, a really universal writer will be universal in spite of that, in spite of your ideology, if you have one. You may have an ideology like Tolstoy about the noble Russian peasant, but yet the truth will come out. You could see it if he cheats and malingers and breaks the tools and kills the horses and misuses the horses, because that's the way it is. And that's because you can enter into that peasant. He probably wasn't criticizing that peasant. He just entered so completely into the peasant, he became that peasant. And [chuckles] that's the way they act.

DH   You seem to have a great admiration for Tolstoy.

DR   Yes. I read *Anna Karenina*. It's a good book.

DH   Do you recommend, to writers or people who want to write, to read all literatures?

DR   Yes. I say read anything in any language you know: Spanish, Chinese, Arabic, French.

DH   You have a poem called "Hymn" in *More to Remember*.

DR   Yes.

DH   I was puzzled by the subject. It begins, "Squat and ugly in your form."

DR   That's the atomic bomb.

DH   I thought you were talking about a bomb, and I wasn't sure whether you had a particular bomb in mind.

DR   Well, it could be any kind: hydrogen, one of those superbombs, not just a dynamite bomb. And I made it appear religious, because we seem to put our faith in the bomb. That was at the time when they were discussing bomb shelters, and whether you should have a right to shoot your neighbor if he tried to get into your shelter. People take the bomb for granted now. They forget all about it, but at one time they were conscious of it. People would have bomb shelters and would store food in their bomb shelters.

DH Well, I think they may be a little more conscious of it lately again because of the discovery that our systems have been giving us misinformation about attacks, and we may start a war by mistake. People are worrying about that again.

DR There was a failure in an airport, I heard, too—some kind of a system that warns planes that are about to crash into each other. They say there have been several near-crashes, near-collisions in the air.

DH Oh, there have been quite a few, quite a few.

DR But this happened specifically because the machinery went on the blink for a time.

DH And also, they say, there are too many planes up in the air.

DR Yes. Especially our own planes don't follow the rules. . . .

DH You have a poem called "An Answer to Lerone Bennett's Questionnaire On A Name for Black Americans." First of all, was there a questionnaire?

DR I don't remember whether it was in the form of a questionnaire, but he had an article discussing both sides. He said Du Bois and others used the term "Negro." To me it seemed silly when they were talking about using "Black" instead of "Negro," because "Negro" is just Spanish for black. And *black* is an Anglo-Saxon word. And Anglo-Saxons treated the Blacks worse than the Spaniards did. So why should they have such affection for an Anglo-Saxon word?

DH So you feel it's not really a logical argument.

DR No, it's not logical. It didn't make any difference. "Black" came in; I use "Black" now.

DH You also have a poem called "The Militant Black Poet." Did you have anybody in mind?

DR That was me. I read at Grosse Ile, which is an island in southwest Detroit, near the Detroit River. These people may not be wealthy, but it's an isolated community with a bridge, and they have their lovely homes there. And I guess it was in the sixties when a Black poet was a curiosity. I worked at the Wayne County Library, and Isabella Swann, our assistant librarian, had a home out there, and I think it was through her I was invited to read to this Tuesday Club—genteel, white-haired women. And I read some poem, and a little old white-haired lady, she was more militant than I was: "Yes,

that's right! I believe you're right." So I said, "What am I doing
here?" to myself. "I should be reading this poem to Black folks, not
to these wealthy white folks." That's what I thought. I exaggerated
that. I said the poet went home and hanged himself—

DH   Yes, I remember that.

DR   —at finding a little old wealthy white woman more mili-
tant than he was.

DH   You have two poems about intellectuals, "The Trouble
with Intellectuals" and "The Intellectuals." Did you have anybody
in mind for those poems, or was that a general—

DR   Yes, sometimes you write two poems on one subject. As
you think about it, different facets come to your mind. I was at a
party, and everybody there was very bright. They knew all the
answers. Me and this fellow's wife, we were sitting in a corner not
saying anything, and we looked at each other and smiled at all these
people that knew so much, and nothing was really done. So I wrote
that poem "The Intellectuals" and how they just talk. The trouble
with intellectuals is that they talk too much. They just talk and talk
and talk.

DH   Do you think they should act more?

DR   Yes. The second poem is about that. Of course you know
the reference there.

DH   You mean "The Intellectuals"?

DR   "The intellectuals talked." Well, I don't mention the
details. The details may be right, but during the Russian Revolu-
tion there were the Mensheviks and the Bolsheviks. The Men-
sheviks were the more moderate party, and they believed in
parliamentary procedure. And while they talked, the Bolsheviks
just surrounded the hall and shot the leaders, arrested the others,
whom they later hanged. They were not the intellectuals that talk-
ed. They were the intellectuals that did something. Not that I
approve of the Bolsheviks, but that's what happened.

DH   You have a poem "Ancestors," which I like very much.
You have such a sane view—Your judgments are solid and com-
monsensical. And in this poem you talk about the poets needing to
have ancestors who are all kings and queens, and why can't they
have some ancestors that are from the common people.

DR   And they talk about warriors, too, there. They were just
ordinary people. I guess it is kind of a romanticism to say, "She's an

African queen; the blood of African queens runs in her veins," when she's probably descended from just an ordinary person.

DH Do you think there was a value in that?

DR Probably there was an exceptional person, like this famous [Joseph] Cinque.[18] If a person wants to believe that and the person becomes what he believes, it may have a certain value. But there's a certain value in just being an ordinary person. In our own West, nobody asked a man what his ancestors were. They judged a man who walked into a saloon by what he could do. If he could use a six-shooter and say, "I'll shoot you," it was okay. He didn't have to say, "My uncle was Mayor of London" or something like that. He was judged by what he was.

DH I'd like to ask you just a little bit about your attitude toward form. First of all, do you think it's a good thing to study forms? Do you feel that forms are a basis of craft, at least an understanding of what they are?

DR Yes. Although I've been reading in that book *The Poetics of the New American Poetry* [1973], edited by Donald Allen, some poets are against that. Robert Duncan says that form is something that stifles people, because people are afraid of their subterranean impulses and emotions and afraid of a straitjacket.

DH Well, Duncan was a follower of [Charles] Olson, of course, and I find Olson makes a great deal of sense with his theory of Projectivism and Robert Creeley's—

DR I can't understand what they're talking about.

DH Creeley formulated Olson's poetics in a very simple way, and Olson quotes Creeley, actually, in his essay on Projective Verse. He says that Creeley's formulation is that form is never more than an extension of content. And I think that the best poets unconsciously are aware of this, the way I notice in your form: for example, in some of your poems where you showed me this reaching out, this very—

DR The long lines—

DH —erotic or loving poem where the lines are really reaching out, the way Whitman's lines are reaching out to the country, and there is this horizontal extension. The form really expresses the content. And then you have other poems that are very pithy or the lines are short, and they lie a certain way on the page.

DR Yes.

DH You showed me a poem in which the word "self" is isolated on the line in a beautifully precise way, because the self was isolated, indeed. And so I think that is a generally useful philosophy.

DR It's been around a long time. It's not new.

DH Yes. You're right.

DR Content dictates form.

DH Sure.

DR But the reason I was a formalist was because when I was in high school, we were studying scansion. I was not graceful, I couldn't dance, I stumbled when I walked, and I didn't do so well in scansion, although I had been reading poetry and liked it and had been writing it since I was nine. I started seriously writing it when I was thirteen. When I was about thirteen, I was in this teacher's class, Miss Helene Sooey, and when I expressed some difficulty about scanning, she said, "Well, it'll come easy if you're graceful and know how to dance." And that was just striking to the heart of me, because I wasn't graceful and I couldn't dance.

So, as a result of that remark, I consciously studied versification. I went to the library in school and got books on versification and studied them and learned how to scan. But later I learned that I was right to begin with, because all accented syllables don't have the same weight. And my ear was delicate enough to know that, and I couldn't put the heavy thump on a word: For instance, "quantity," where you have a light *y* at the end—that accent is not really as heavy as *quan*. And it was words like that that I was kind of weak on in my actual scansion. The teacher saw only the formal pattern, but I heard the actual, varying weights of the syllables in my ear. So later I discovered that I was right, after all.

But anyway, I made a study of versification, and was very interested in it by the time I met Bob Hayden. He was interested in diction, in metaphors, and I was interested in sound. So he would tell people, "Dudley knows more about how to write verse than I do." But he introduced me to something, or anyway he got me interested in images, so then I started studying images, too, as well as the sound. One time I wrote a little in classical meters. I wrote some hendecasyllabics, that Catullus wrote in. And I wrote something in the Sapphic stanza, translated a couple of poems in the Sapphic stanza. And I translated some of Catullus into hendecasyllables: "To Lesbia and Her Sparrow."

DH   So then you translated from various languages.

DR   Yes. And Pushkin. And Chopin, the language of music. I want to play that, and then I want you to read it and see how it goes with the music.

DH   Yes, I'd like to.

DR   Let's see. I tried to do something in French, but didn't. I think I translated one line from Verlaine.

DH   Would you like to do more?

DR   Well, that was my project for humanities. I would have a master's in humanities, because I've done all the work, the book work. But I didn't do the thesis which was to translate from Chopin into words. The collection I would get from that I would call "Songs Without Words." And that would be because the words, ideally, would be as delicate as the music of Chopin.

DH   What do you think of Stephen Henderson's view in *Understanding the New Black Poetry*—

DR   It's interesting.

DH   —the use of Black music and speech as referents?

DR   It's interesting. I think a lot of Black poets are influenced by music. They play a lot of jazz, a lot of Black music. If you go into Don's house, he may have a record on, a Black record, or tune to a Black station or a station that plays Black music.

DH   I hear music in Black speech very often. I hear music in the speech.

DR   You do?

DH   I hear often a kind of syncopation in the speech pattern itself.

DR   Yes. Probably you'd be more conscious of it than I. Just like [Ezra] Pound said that it helps to read in a foreign language or to translate, because then, not being familiar with the language, it doesn't mean so much to you and you hear the sound more.

DH   Yes.

DR   Then I was interested in French forms, too. I think I wrote a term paper on classical meters and French forms like the ballade and the villanelle. The poem "Southern Road" is a ballade. And that's why I'm critical of critics, because they don't seem to notice that. None of them have said, "This poem is a ballade." The person that noticed it was this fellow [David Littlejohn] who wrote *Black on White*. People like Hoyt Fuller really hated him because—are you familiar with that book?

DH   Yes.

DR   Because Hoyt says he [Littlejohn] doesn't understand Black poets, and he writes from a sense of guilt. But I believe he's not too bad. Of course he doesn't know much about Black poetry. Because, from the book, one gathers that he wanted to write or maybe he had an assignment to write it, so he went just consciously and with a superior attitude that a lot of whites have, that they could learn all about Black poetry by reading some anthology. He read Langston Hughes's anthology *New Negro Poets*, where that poem appears. But his criticism was pretty good. He gave credit to the good poets, like Gwendolyn Brooks, Langston Hughes, Robert Hayden, and he pleased me by saying, "Of the young poets, Dudley Randall has a sophisticated form"—he didn't say "ballade." He probably didn't even know it was a ballade, because I didn't want to be obvious and say "Ballade of the Southern Road." But that surprised me, because I'm so awkward and ill at ease socially, that finding somebody calling a poem of mine sophisticated—[*Laughter*]

DH   You don't seem awkward or ill at ease. I don't know which Dudley you're talking about. It must have been a long time ago.

DR   At one time I was. The old Dudley at that time, in the sixties. So I'm not as angry with him as Hoyt Fuller is.

DH   Hoyt Fuller may be angry about his magazine, which was a great loss. Do you feel that the loss of *Black World* was important?

DR   Yes. A great loss. It represents so much that was in there, some of the symposiums he would have on different subjects—on Black power, for instance, or literary lives.

DH   Yes. I miss it myself. It was unique, of the highest caliber.

DR   Of course, that's *First World*, now. Do you get that?

DH   No.

DR   It's a quarterly out of Atlanta. He's gone to Atlanta. He says he's staying in Atlanta, although he teaches at Cornell and commutes, because his aunt, who raised him up and is very close to him, lives there and she's old. So he stays in Atlanta. I've been urging him to make up an anthology of the work—you know, one big anthology of poetry that appeared in *Black World*, and of the fiction and of the essays or criticism. And all the writers would gladly just donate the work. It wouldn't be expensive. He could publish it himself or get a big company to publish it. With a big company, probably, the writers would expect to be paid. Double-day—they have enough money. But it would be a very good anthology, because he's published all the best poets—Baraka and Hayden and Brooks, and all the younger poets.[19]

DH I'll ask you one last question. Do you plan another book? I imagine you do.

DR Yes. The book will be *A Litany of Friends*. I'm trying to get a grant for it. All I've done is inquire about the procedure, and I have the applications, but I just haven't had the time to sit down and fill out all those papers, ask for references, say how I'll spend the money, and what the procedure will be: Number one, I'll do this; number two, I'll do that. And I'll collect poems from books that are out of print, so that they will stay in print; I'll put them in there. It's going to be a big book.

DH So it will be selected and new poems?

DR No, just a new collection. I won't even mention that, because some of the poems in there are in the other books, like "The Profile on the Pillow," that will be in there, and "W.E.B.," "Ballad of Birmingham." There will be a section called "Eros"—I think I told you this before—where I'll put the love poems and the bawdy poems.

DH Then it will have quite a scope.

DR And a section called "Me," where I put poems that are more, I would say, like Horace. You know, Horace would walk around Rome and talk like personal essays. Like the poem, for instance, "A Poet Is Not a Jukebox"—I might put that in a section called "Me," which would show my personality.

DH So what are the different sections you have?

DR Well, first would come "Friends." There will be poems in there like the one I wrote to Margaret Danner on opening Boone House; "To Gwendolyn Brooks, Teacher"; "On Getting a Natural" [for Gwendolyn Brooks]; and this long poem "A Litany of Friends," naming all the friends who helped me when I was in that depression, what they did. Like one girl—"To Susie, lover of dolphins, who sent me a Christmas card at Christmas." She was a little girl, then—I never met her—from Chevy Chase, that exclusive suburb of Washington. So I know she's white. When she was in high school, she was writing a paper on me and Baraka, and she asked for information about me and I sent her information. I asked her to see the term paper, and she said Baraka just sent a mimeographed form, but I wrote her a letter. Then she sent me a poem that showed she was a talented girl. I praised her poem.

So every Christmas she would send me a card and I'd send her a card. She's gone now—she loves animals—she's gone into marine study. She's gone to college, and she's studying dolphins. That's some place near the ocean.

DH Dolphins know how to live in peace with each other. And then will you have a political section?

DR No, I wouldn't have a section called "Politics." The first will be "Friends," and "To an Old Man" will go into that section of friends. And then I'll have "Eros," the love poems and the bawdy poems. Then there will be a section "Africa," and that will start with "African Suite" from *After the Killing*. And then we'll be able to stand into America—African America. And those, I think, will clinch the political poems. We'll have some nonpolitical poems about Blacks, like "Old Witherington" and "George." They're not political poems. "George" is about an old Black man who worked in a factory. Although he could be in "Friends," because that poem's message is not only Black; it's about an old man. And then there will be a section, "Me."

Then I might have a section called "Juvenilia," which Gwen doesn't approve of. She doesn't want the juvenile poems. But I guess it's kind of a prelude to show that when I was a teenager, I had kind of a skill with words. Like one poem that had appeared in the *Free Press* "Young Poets' Page" was written in ottava rima, which a sixteen-year-old doesn't usually write.

DH Oh, that's a difficult form.

DR Not so difficult. It's just *a b a b a b c c*. But it's in pentameter. You usually don't write in pentameter.

DH Well, it's hard to use such a strict form and keep it interesting. It's basically two rhymes with a third thrown in as relief.

DR Yes, a couplet at the end. And I wrote a dizain, with its alternation of iambic lines and trochaic lines. I was very interested in Milton's "Il Penseroso" and "L'Allegro" and to find how he would alter, according to the thought and the mood, his iambs and his trochees. And in that poem I tried to do that. [*Reads a pastoral poem, commenting on its meter.*] I did that one when I was a teenager. Usually teen-agers don't have that metrical skill.

DH How old were you when you started to write?

DR Seriously, about thirteen. And I sent a sonnet to this "Poets' Page," and it won the first prize of one dollar. At thirteen, in 1927.

DH That was in the—

DR *Detroit Free Press.*

DH [*Pause*] Well, Dudley, thank you very much.

DR Let me play you that Chopin. First we'll listen to it, and then [*searching*]—where is that verse translation from Chopin?

DH I've got to hear it.

DR And then we'll see how the words fit the melody. It's kind of intricate to do.

Dudley Randall: Works Cited and Suggested

Poem Counterpoem, with Margaret Danner. Detroit: Broadside Press, 1966; rev. ed. 1969.

For Malcolm: Poems on the Life and Death of Malcolm X, coedited with Margaret G. Burroughs. Detroit: Broadside Press, 1967.

Cities Burning. Detroit: Broadside Press, 1968.

Black Poetry: A Supplement to Anthologies Which Exclude Black Poets. Detroit: Broadside Press, 1969.

Love You. London: Paul Breman, 1970.

More to Remember: Poems of Four Decades, Chicago: Third World Press, 1971.

The Black Poets (anthology). New York: Bantam, 1971.

After the Killing. Chicago: Third World Press, 1973.

Broadside Memories: Poets I Have Known. Detroit: Broadside Press, 1975. (Cited as *BRM.*)

A Capsule Course in Black Poetry Writing (co-author). Detroit: Broadside Press, 1975.

A Litany of Friends: New and Selected Poems. Detroit: Lotus Press, 1981.

"For Vivian." *BALF* 17 (Winter 1983): 170. Reproduced as Broadside No. 94 by Broadside Press, 1984. Other new poems also included in *BALF* issue, pp. 168-70.

Notes

1. My interview with Dudley Randall took place at his home in Detroit on July 3, 1980. Unattributed quotations from Randall are taken from my

conversations with him in 1980 at his home, at the Broadside Press offices, and in New York. For more on Randall, see the University of Detroit *Varsity News*, Sept. 1969, and reference works such as *Contemporary Authors*.

2. Dudley Randall, "Broadside Press: A Personal Chronicle," *Black Academy Review* 1, no. 1 (1970); rpt. in Floyd Barbour, *The Black Seventies* (Boston: Sargent, 1970), and in *BRM*.

3. See Leonead Pack Bailey's useful *Broadside Authors and Artists: An Illustrated Biographical Directory* (Detroit: Broadside Press, 1974).

4. The Press encouraged and utilized the talents of many established and unestablished Black artists in designing its broadsides. Noteworthy examples include Shirley Woodson, whose work appears on Randall's "Ballad of Birmingham," Broadside No. 1 (Sept. 1965), and "The Six," *Broadside Series*, Poster No. 6 (1975); Cledie Taylor, who designed Gwendolyn Brooks's "We Real Cool," *Broadside Series* No. 6 (Dec. 1966), and illuminated Robert Hayden's "Gabriel (Hanged for Leading a Slave Revolt)," *Broadside Series* No. 3 (Sept. 1966); and Talita Long, the designer for Etheridge Knight's "For Black Poets Who Think of Suicide," *Broadside Series* No. 36 (1970).

5. Charles H. Rowell, "In Conversation with Dudley Randall," *Obsidian* 2 (Spring 1976): 36.

6. Gwendolyn Fowlkes, "An Interview With Dudley Randall," *Black Scholar* 6 (June 1975): 87.

7. "*BBB* interviews Dudley Randall," *Black Books Bulletin* 1 (Winter 1972): 23.

8. Letter to the author, Dec. 15, 1980.

9. A. X. Nicholas, "A Conversation with Dudley Randall," *Black World* 21 (Dec. 1971): 32-33.

10. David Littlejohn, *Black on White* (New York: Grossman, 1966), 95.

11. John T. Shawcross, "Names as 'Symbols' in Black Poetry," *Literary Onomastic Studies* 6 (1978): 152.

12. The Miami riots of May and July 1980 were sparked by an all-white jury's acquittal of four white policemen after the fatal beating of Black businessman Arthur McDuffie. The victim's offense was driving through a red light. Eighteen lives were lost in the subsequent civil disturbances.

13. R. Baxter Miller, " 'Endowing the World and Time': The Life and work of Dudley Randall," in *Black American Poets Between Worlds, 1940-1960*, ed. R. Baxter Miller (Knoxville: Univ. of Tennessee Press, 1986), 77.

14. Broadside Press was housed in the basement of the Alexander Crummell Memorial Church (Episcopal) for several years. I visited the offices with Randall before our interview.

15. Poems mentioned here later appear in *A Litany of Friends*.

16. Randall had revised the poem, updating it by changing a word. In *More to Remember*, the poet is "bearded, hatless and graceless" (l. 3); in *A Litany of Friends*, he is "bearded, shoeless and graceless."

17. Randall worked for the U.S. government census that was taken in

1980. On the census form, the FOSDIC circle (film optical sensing device for input to computers), which indicated a choice of responses, was to be completely blackened in pencil in order to register on the computer.

18. Joseph Cinque (1811-52) was an African slave who, in 1839, led a violent mutiny aboard the Amistad, a ship bound from Havana, Cuba, for Puerto Principe (Port au Prince), Haiti.

19. Hoyt W. Fuller died at age fifty-seven of an apparent heart attack on May 11, 1981, in Atlanta. *Nommo: A Literary Legacy of Black Chicago (1967-1987)*, ed. Carole A. Parks, published in 1987 in Chicago by the Organization of Black American Culture (OBAC) Writer's Workshop, which he cofounded, was dedicated to him. It contains many tributes, including those by Gwendolyn Brooks, Haki R. Madhubuti, and George E. Kent, Brooks's biographer.

Dudley Brooks, *The Washington Post*

3. HAKI R. MADHUBUTI
Prescriptive Revolution

Clarity of purpose directs the life of Haki Madhubuti. "I am a Black man, a man of Afrikan descent who writes. Writing picked me. I am not a born or trained writer. . . . I use writing as a weapon, offensively and defensively, to help raise the consciousness of myself and my people."[1]

The introduction to *Enemies: The Clash of Races* (pp. iii-v) gives a moving account of the poet's early years. Madhubuti was born Don Luther Lee on February 23, 1942, in Little Rock, Arkansas; he grew up on Detroit's Lower East Side and Chicago's West Side, in severe poverty. Most of the time the family was on welfare: "Our lights and gas were seldom on at the same time." He and his younger sister Jacqueline were usually clothed in hand-me-downs; even when he could buy his own clothing, it was customarily secondhand, from a Chinese laundry. The poet began working at age ten; he acquired his own paper route, shined shoes, delivered groceries, collected junk, and assisted the janitor. "I also learned to hustle and steal (liberate) needed items very early. My education was provided by the Detroit and Chicago public school systems, the streets, the U.S. Army, and Chicago's Jr. College system which was at best an advanced senior high school."

Madhubuti and his sister were raised by their mother, Maxine Graves Lee. His father was "trying to survive"; briefly, there was a stepfather. His mother, an attractive, fair-skinned woman, influenced the poet's love of literature (especially Richard Wright's *Black Boy*)[2] and of Black secular music (mainly jazz); and she quickened his racial consciousness. Mrs. Lee won the title of Miss

Bar Maid of 1948 and worked desperately to maintain her family. A succession of jobs included grocery cashier, building caretaker ("it was very painful watching her carry gabage cans down and up three flights of stairs three times a week"), barmaid, and, finally, prostitute. "These latter two occupations soon drove her to drinking and she died an alcoholic at the age of thirty-five. At her death, I was almost too hard to cry," the poet notes with bitterness. He loved his mother dearly.

Maxine Lee's tragic life and premature death forced early responsibility upon her sixteen-year-old son: his sister, two years younger, had a year-old baby at the time. Madhubuti developed an antipathy toward alcohol. He learned to see liquor, drugs, and religion as deliberate tools to control populations. Constant uprooting, never living in one apartment for more than two years, made the brother and sister fearful of making friends. "We became like the cities, the *people of concrete;* hard, full of cracks. Unproductive." Education beyond high school was never suggested; a "good" job at Ford or General Motors represented the future. What mattered was mere survival, centered on pleasurable weekends that dissipated the meager paycheck. Privacy was a luxury the poet did not experience until 1960, when he entered the army at age eighteen. He remained in the service until 1963; he was married that year, and in December his son Don was born.

Madhubuti cites his early spiritual impoverishment as critical. "There was little joy and much pain in our lives and this, as far as I can see, was not the exception but the norm in Urban Black America." As David Llorens has pointed out, Madhubuti's "rather ascetic" nature, expressed in his world view, is not the result of an unemotional process. "It is his witness."[3]

Upon returning to civilian life in Chicago, the poet attempted to survive within a white framework. He loaded trucks and railroad cars, operated an elevator, worked at Montgomery Ward and the post office while he furthered his education at Kennedy-King, Roosevelt University, and mostly, as he puts it, "by self-study." He succeeded in becoming a junior executive in a mail order house (see "The Only One" in *Black Pride*). But poetry became more and more his overriding interest. In 1967 he ventured to have his first volume printed, *Think Black!* "I started selling at the El stop along 63rd. I sold 600 copies in a week. It scared me a little—people were actually reading me."[4] Later that year he entered Gwendolyn

Brooks's workshop; their initial aesthetic conflict turned to mutual admiration and respect. He also met Dudley Randall, who published his second book, *Black Pride*, the following year and subsequent, enlarged editions of *Think Black!*

With Carolyn Rodgers, a member of the Brooks workshop, and Johari Amini, Madhubuti founded Third World Press, its conception dating to August 2, 1967. As publisher-editor, he produced 130 titles in twenty years, including works by Gwendolyn Brooks and Amiri Baraka (post-LeRoi Jones). In 1969, Broadside published his *Don't Cry, Scream*, which attracted a national audience. That year he made his first visit to Africa and participated in the First Pan-African Festival, in Algiers. Afterward, with four co-workers, he founded the Institute of Positive Education, of which he is the director, and in 1972 the New Concept Development Center, the educational arm of the Institute. That year he also began publishing and editing the social and literary journal *Black Books Bulletin*. The New Concept elementary school is headed by his present wife, Safisha, a teacher and critic, whom he married in 1974. A daughter, Laini Nzinga, was born to the couple in 1975, and they have two sons, Bomani Garvey, born in 1977, and Akili Malcolm, in 1980.

Madhubuti's seamless concern with family, education, culture, and sociopolitical structures is epitomized in *Kwanzaa* (1972). This useful chapbook describes "the only 'indigenous non-heroic Black holiday in the United States' " (p. 4), quoting Maulana Karenga, who created Kwanzaa in 1966. The two final *a*'s distinguish the term from the Swahili word *kwanza*—"which means first and is part of the phrase *Matunda Ya Kwanza* (first fruits)"—and set it apart as the name of an African American holiday that links ideology with culture. Madhubuti actively links both elements further with education and health. As part of the national Black Wholistic Retreat Foundation, he has conducted since 1984 an annual retreat in various locations.

Madhubuti is a widely traveled man. In 1974 he attended the tumultuous, divisive Sixth Pan-African Congress in Dar es Salaam, Tanzania,[5] and in 1976 was a guest of the Senegalese government at Encounter: African World Alternatives. Three years later, he journeyed to Israel to investigate the status of a group called Original Hebrew Israelites (Black Jews). As the author of fourteen popular books of poetry, essays, and criticism, he is highly sought as a dynamic reader and lecturer; he has presented his work at more than a thousand colleges, universities, and community centers in Africa, Asia, the Caribbean, South America, and the United States. He has served as writer-in-residence at Cornell University (1968-69), Morgan State College (1972-73), Howard University (1970-77), and Central State University (1978-79). After receiving his master of fine arts degree from the University of Iowa in 1984, he joined the faculty of Chicago State University where he now serves as professor of English.

The single most important influence on Madhubuti's career has been Gwendolyn Brooks, who gave him moral, artistic, and economic support, particularly with his *Directionscore* (1971). In "A Further Pioneer," her introduction to *Don't Cry, Scream*, she views him as "a positive prophet," a writer "at the hub of the new wordway" whose toughness "goes right through to the bone." His poetry has been praised by white critics, as well as Black. Helen Vendler, in a laudatory review of several Broadside poets, writes: "Lee's poems, written in a rapid, jerky, intense speech rhythm in almost Morse shorthand, have sold over 100,000 copies without any large-scale advertising or mass distribution, a phenomenon which (like the success of Ginsberg's "Howl") means that something is happening. . . . In him the sardonic and savage turn-of-phrase long present in black speech as a survival tactic finds its best poet."[6]

Although Madhubuti's work is dynamic and positive, he appraises his deep conflict as follows, recalling Du Bois's concept (in *The Souls of Black Folk*) of "two warring ideals in one dark body": "Most of all I am a product of America's *whiteness* and *Blackness:* these two forces penetrate every cell in my body and like fire and water have become antagonists and are not able to occupy the same space at the same time without one being master and the other slave" (*Enemies,* i). He sees the struggle as both individual and social, a basic reality for Black-white relations today.

Madhubuti's creative and sociopolitical philosophy is central to his work and life and epitomizes an aspect of the Black Nationalist-separatist position. From his earliest work he has revealed unmistakably his political priorities. In *Think Black!* he attempts to define Blackness and separate it from whiteness. His introduction begins, "I was born into slavery in February of 1942," and he dedicates the book "to all Black People—**Where-ever** you are." He sets his musical ear and acerbic humor to social purposes, as in "Education":

My teacher taught me other things too,
Things that I will be forever looking at;
  how to berate
    segregate,
    and how to be inferior without hate.

In "Understanding but not forgetting (for the Non-Colored of the World)," an autobiographical meditation, a progression of personal and quasi-personal observations condemns "the American System" and the "negative images" it offers Black children. His ability to compress idea and image serves both the poetic and didactic elements of his work. He uses words as weapons, for example, breaking "white" into two syllables; the sarcastic enjambment of the line terminus "whi" with "te" in the following line or the hyphenation on the same line, "whi-te," suggests the pronunciation "whitey."

Black Pride (1968), dedicated to "brothers Malcolm X, Langston Hughes and John Coltrane: All innovators in their own way," carries an introduction by Dudley Randall, who notes that Madhubuti "writes for the man in the street and uses the language of the street, and sometimes of the gutter, with wit, inventiveness, and surprise." Here the theme of Black pride becomes more sharply focused. In the widely anthologized first poem "The New Integrationist," the unequivocal vertical of univerbal lines suggests both an individual and a political placard:

I
seek
integration
of
negroes
with
black
people.

Madhubuti's eye is as sharp as his ear. For emphasis and patterns that enhance meaning, he frequently liberates the stanza from conventional left-alignment. Lowercasing, which conveys an internalized effect, appears in the more personal polemics. There are poems about an incompatible marriage; the death of his mother, whose tragedy was reduced by others to "why was i present / with / out / a / tie on"; "The Self-Hatred of Don L. Lee," a frank acknowledgment of his proud, Black inner self at war with his hated light skin, identified with oppression; "In the Interest of Black Salvation," a vitriolic attack on commercialized Christianity, in which "Jesus saves—S & H Green Stamps." At times the anger overrides poetic shaping, as in "The Black Christ." But the beautiful tribute to his mother, "an ebony mind / on a yellow frame," in "The Death Dance," powerfully combines surrealistic imagery with a realistic account of his life: The youth absorbs strength from his mother's love and faith—"son you is a man, a black man"—as she descends past "sadtalk" toward alcoholic oblivion, "until pains didn't pain anymore."

"The Wall," asserting the heroic identity of the "mighty black" Wall of Respect, differs from the majestic Brooks poem (see Chapter 1) in presenting as polemical reportage the attitudes and vernacular speech of common people in the audience at its dedication. "Only a Few Left," dedicated to Langston Hughes, makes the point of this study: that bravery is no longer the province of the soldier, "not he / who is abundant / with heroic deeds / for the state." Bravery now lies in the truth told by a "little black man" surrounded by people: "they say / he's / a / poet."

Don't Cry, Scream (1969), which gave Madhubuti a national reputation, appeared while the poet was teaching at Cornell, at the time of an armed takeover of a building by Black students. It takes its title from his mother's early words to him: "nigger, if u is goin ta open yr / mouth **Don't Cry, Scream.** which also means: **Don't Beg, Take.**" Its crackling intelligence expands Madhubuti's use of puns and visual effects. In the first poem, "Gwendolyn Brooks" (which introduces Brook's Caedmon record), for example, he notes that "time magazine is the / authority on the knee/grow," using the pun on "Negro" attributed to Baraka (see Interview, Chapter 6). After describing Brooks's "total-real" makeup and sarcastically listing her credits as "a fine negro poet," he defines the word "black" in a jazzlike improvisational stream of unpunctuated compounds, "black doubleblack purpleblack blueblack beenblack . . . " of increasing sophistication until "black blackisbeautifulblack i justdiscoveredblack negro / black unsubstanceblack." Having deni-

grated and replaced the term "negro," Madhubuti finally acknowl-
edges Brooks as a "blackpoet." The title poem, dedicated to the
great tenor saxophonist John Coltrane, employs brilliantly a vari-
ety of technical effects: punning, visual and aural attempts to
reproduce instrumental music (scatting), and a jazz singer's inter-
mittent riffs.

> into the sixties
> a trane
> came/ out of the
> fifties with a
> golden boxcar
> riding the rails
> of novation.

The sound of train wheels, a gold boxcar antithetically suggesting
precious freight or a hobo—not a passenger but someone *outside*
the regular car—merges with the sound of the music, so that
novelty, "novation," becomes absorbed into the poem's content.
The poet identifies jazz with blackness, affirming it over the blues:
"we ain't blue, we are black." Continuing to extend his lexical
range and flexibility, the poet adapts some of the Brooks com-
pounding-metonymic mode:

> soultrane gone on a trip
> he left man images
> he was a life-style of
> man-maker & annihilator
> of attache case carriers.

Poems on the assassination of Martin Luther King, Jr., on
Malcolm X, and on Black war heroes who were awarded medals
posthumously praise Blackness and attach *black* as prefix to nouns
and to the qualities of the race; other works excoriate "negroes"
who emulate whites as betrayers of their people. "A Poem to
Complement Other Poems" is a lyrical exhortation to personal
growth: "change. / life if u were a match i wd light u into something
beauti-/ ful. change."

At this point, one may remark upon Madhubuti's poetry as
performance. His work shares the aim of Brooks's "preachments,"
but its path lies at a different level. He is on intimate terms with his

audience, speaking their language, rising directly out of their midst as primus inter pares. His fiery delivery communicates a jazzy rhetoric of urgency. His record albums *Rise Vision Comin* and *Rappin' and Readin'*, unequivocally convey this musicality within the direct appeal of vernacular language and its often syncopated rhythms.

We Walk the Way of the New World (1970) is dedicated to thinkers, leaders, and people in the arts who "helped create a New Consciousness." The epigraph "your enemy knows his enemy" suggests the view of racial polarity that Madhubuti develops later in his prose. The introduction, "Louder but Softer," advises: "Remember *a leader is not only one that leads but is the best example of that leadership.*" It ends with a stirring poem of exhortation, "Blackman / an unfinished history." Tracing the experience of Blacks in the United States from the days of slavery to the present rhapsodic promise of fulfillment, the poet dramatizes the progression by means of jazzlike, onomatopoeic exclamations:

> HEY   blackman look like
> you'd be named something
> like. . . . *earth, sun*
> or *mountain.*
> Go ahead, *universe*
> Zoommmmmmmm. Zooommmmmmmmmm
> Zoooommmmmmmmmmmmmmm   click   click.
> be it,
> blackman.

"Zoom" and "click" suggest photography and film, focus and enlargement, a grand scale of subjects bigger than life-size. "Zoom" further implies a shooting upward, outward—to the stars.

Outstanding in "Blackwoman Poems," the first section, is "Big Momma," the poet's courageous grandmother who, at sixty-eight,

> moves freely, is often right
> and when there is food
> eats   joyously with her own
> real teeth.

More lyrical are the exquisite images of "Man Thinking About Woman":

> your beauty: un-noticed by regular eyes   is
> like   a blackbird resting
> on a telephone wire   that moves
> quietly with the wind.
>
> a southwind.

Annette Oliver Shands, writing of the poem "Man and Woman," points out that the poet's frequent use of the prefix *un*-changes negative ideas to positive ones—"soft voices / that undoubtedly are heard unconfused through / their walls"—and relates to masking, "the Black man's enduring protective manner of concealing and revealing the truth simultaneously."[7]

A group of "African Poems" conveys impressions of Madhubuti's African trip in 1969 and his worry that the continent's integrity may be compromised by Western influence. The section is pervaded by a sense of exile. As witnessed by the opening poem, "A Poem for A Poet," addressed to Mahmoud Darwish ("Darweesh"), the renowned Palestinian poet, and one to Ted Joans, the Black jazz poet who moved to Timbuktu. "New World Poems," the last section, contains an elegy, "One Sided Shoot-out," for Fred Hampton and Mark Clark, Black Panther leaders "murdered 12/4/69 by Chicago police at 4:30 AM while they slept." The book's title poem stresses exemplary status for the Black male:

> We walk in cleanliness
> the newness of it all
> becomes us
> our women listen to us
> and learn.
> We teach our children thru
> our actions.

"Directionscore," the last and title section of his 1971 volume, is a slight group of five poems that suffer from a haste to get through to the messages, essentially the crimes of whites and the hope for Blacks, without the careful shaping typical of Madhubuti's previous work. It bridges what the poet refers to as his "conventional" free verse and the work that appears in *Book of Life* (1973).

Book of Life is dedicated to "my son and his sons, and their sons." The Swahili inscription: "Sifa Zote Ziende Kwa Maisha Afrika" translates: "All praise is due to African life." The introduction, "Discovering the Traitors," charts the direction of Madhubuti's thinking, discerning as "enemies" Black artists who have been seduced by white culture. The first of the book's two parts comprises poems that resemble short speeches—criticizing, praising, exhorting. It ends with "Spirit Flight into the Coming," a kind of long rap about the need for identity, purpose, direction, which calls Black people to work toward nation-building. It defines contemporary "slavery" to white values and closes with a call to Amiri Baraka and the Congress of Afrikan People[s] to lead the Black endeavor.[8] The paean to work is reminiscent of Thomas Carlyle's "The Everlasting Yea" in *Sartor Resartus*, "Work while it is called Today; for the Night cometh, wherein no man can work" (itself an adaptation from Ecclesiastes and the Gospel of John): "All that is good and accomplished in the world takes work / Everything else is Jive."

The volume's second part attempts the simple, didactic mode of the aphorism or proverb, with its venerable ancestry in African and Asiatic cultures and in the sacred writings and oral traditions of many peoples. Madhubuti's experiment mediates between poetry and later prose works like *Enemies,* as if he were exploring means of communication that might serve his purposes. The first of the ninety-two numbered precepts (see Interview), which range from three to thirty-eight lines, states: "the best way / to effectively fight an / alien culture / is to live your own." At times sacrificing freshness of statement for accessibility, the poet presents an impressively ambitious array of topics. In addition to emphasizing Black pride and African heritage, he deals with proper eating habits (vegetarian, moderate) and health; self-knowledge ("self-definition is the first step toward / self control"); family ("the family will live and endure because / the nation is families united"); pedagogy ("best teachers / seldom teach / they be and do"); thought ("you / are nothing / as long as / nothing is on your / mind"); cooperation as preferable to competition; the interdependence of nations—among other observations and advice.

Madhubuti's dedication to concrete action and substantive change sparks his judgment of the Harlem Renaissance as deficient because "no lasting institutions were established" (*Directionscore,*

12).[9] This haunting failure impels his quest for construction and stability. *From Plan to Planet* (1973), a prose work published jointly by Broadside Press and the Institute of Positive Education, charts this direction, subsequently expressed in *Enemies* and other works. His records, his critical examination of 1960s Black poets in *Dynamite Voices* (1971), and (with Gwendolyn Brooks, Keorapetse Kgositsile, and Dudley Randall) *A Capsule Course in Black Poetry Writing* (1975) reveal this basic tendency in his thought. The Institute, the New Concept Development Center, Third World Press, *Black Books Bulletin*, Third World Press Book Store (1967), the African American Book Center (1983)—his ongoing projects—along with his pervasive concern for family cohesion all continue to support the dynamic Black edifice, whose cornerstone is Madhubuti's active trust in its capacity to strengthen and grow.

Poetry took a "back seat", as he once put it, for about ten years, but it still generates the energy of his vision. *Earthquakes and Sun Rise Missions* (1984), winner of the Du Sable Museum Award for Excellence in Poetry, reveals the development and expansion of the poet's sensibility. Like Sanchez, Cortez, and Baraka, Madhubuti shows an increased awareness of the Third World and—also joined by Brooks and Randall—the Pan-African relation to freedom struggles outside the United States. His ongoing amalgamation of poetry and prose tends to liberate both the style and the message. In a prefatory note to *Earthquakes,* Madhubuti states that he has deliberately "positioned" two essays at the beginning and the end of the book in order to provide the poetry with "a cultural and literary heritage to dance in. Words cut and heal. I am not a doctor; however, I would like to think that *Earthquakes and Sun Rise Missions* is preventive medicine" (*ESM*, 11).

The prominence of rhetorical and polemical prose is supported typographically. Both in the essays and the poetry here, one notes the use of bold type (seemingly adopted from the interviews of *Black Books Bulletin*) for emphasis.

The first essay, "Black Writers and Critics: Developing a Critical Process without Readers," discusses the decline of reading among Blacks, which Madhubuti attributes mainly to faulty education, the dissolution of the Black family unit, and the deleterious impact of television. He sees the critic's function as that of a mediator between book and reader, as an educator open to new ideas, and as a "fighter and visionary." He cites Addison Gayle, Sherley Anne Williams, George Kent, and Darwin Turner as prime examples of such "creators." In his view, "The critic, along with publishers and writing institutions, must establish a means of rewarding and recognizing the contribution of Black writers" (*ESM*, 28-29).

The second essay, "Remembering the Middle Passage: Culture as Motion," is a thoughtful critique further subtitled "Why Life in America is Not Working for Black People and What Needs to be Done to Change the Future." Instead of the present short-term "culture of survival," Madhubuti calls for a long-term "culture of development" (*ESM*, 148). While the first may riot, the second plans revolutionary change. The poet itemizes twenty-two aspects of each mentality and predictably prescribes the latter for Blacks. He admires the Japanese for their industriousness, their sense of themselves, their respect for elders, their literacy, and what he sees as a more even distribution of wealth that deemphasizes class differences.

The essay also demonstrates Madhubuti's appreciation of wo-men, an important feature throughout the book. He praises their role in culture, commenting, for example, "The women build the churches and the men run them" (*ESM*, 157). He discusses crime: Black on Black, white on Black, and white-collar crime. He ties Black disparity with whites to a worldwide power imbalance. He digests current writing—such as John Naisbett's *Megatrends: Ten New Directions Transforming Our Lives* (1982)—and abstracts main ideas, both to provide information and to encourage like readings on a variety of subjects. He concludes with practical suggestions for a moral and healthful daily life. His call to action, evoking the Black diaspora, uses the rallying cry "REMEMBER THE MIDDLE PASSAGE!" He had dedicated *Enemies* "to the Memory of the 250,000,000 and more Black men, women and children murdered by White people during the Euro-Asian trade in Afrikan slaves," and for him, the whole history of slavery is murder: both physical and psychic. "I don't see too much difference if you're dead mentally and you're still walking around. . . . Africa would be the heaviest-populated continent if the slave trade had not taken place. The number of Africans that were murdered during the Middle Passage is still being debated," he remarked in our inter-view.[10]

Madhubuti's concern with the Middle Passage and the blight of slavery pervades his philosophy and reflects in his thought about Jews. Like many Blacks, he grew up seeing Jews merely as whites, with conditions and interests undifferentiated from those of other whites. His objective, however, in his writings, has been to distinguish Black interests from those of Jews as well as of others. During a recent discussion, I asked him to clarify the position he had taken in the interview. "I am pro-Black, not anti-Semitic," he emphasized. "My position expresses the statements and actions of a people who are under continuous siege. Our people are still at war today in white America. It belittles our whole movement to reduce it to anti-*anything* instead of a movement for liberation."

While Madhubuti's approach is both intellectual and emotive, his strongly paternal appeal complements Brooks's maternal one. By precept and example, he seeks to inspire intellectual growth. Brooks's awards promote writing; Madhubuti's writing promotes reading. Both poets uphold the integrity of the Black family. Both seek to instill cultural pride and encourage creative accomplishment. Madhubuti's long-standing impatience with Black malfeasance—a part of his general social critique in this essay—now permits his affection to gleam through. Like Brooks, although more systematically, he offers guidance to all elements of the Black community, its children and adolescents, as well as its adults.

In the first poetry section of *Earthquakes,* Madhubuti presents several of what may be called "speech poems," fusing rhetoric and polemics. "Everything's Cool: Black America in the Early Eighties" makes the point "that the one / undeniable freedom / that *all* agree exists / for Black people in america / is the freedom / to / self destruct." International awareness dominates poems such as "The Shape of Things to Come," in which the poet responds to the profit-seeking scavengers who capitalized on grief following an earthquake in Naples, Italy, in December 1980. In "Beirut Massacre (September 1982)," expressing outrage at the massacre of Palestinians at the Sabra and Shatila refugee camps, he warns of the "lesson in creating pure, / pure hatred."

The section titled "The Women" is often lyrical, as in two poems for his wife, Safisha. "Winterman," an extraordinary prose poem, describes, with sympathy and humor, a mistreated Black woman who finally turns from Black men to celibacy and "winterman" Jesus. It allows acute insight into Black self-hatred. Although some of his work reveals impatience with gays, in "My Brothers" the poet champions Black women who "have not been / loved enough," and writes, "my brothers i will not tell you / who to love or not to love." "Struggle," addressed to Black men, is a poem on battered women. Madhubuti adapts his technique to appeal to a variety of listener/readers: rhyme cedes to a prose poem followed by a speech poem. Lyrical and yet akin to the Brooks heroic style, "A Mother's Poem" offers a fine, touching tribute to Gwendolyn Brooks in which the author thanks her "for / saving a son." The group ends with the passionate eulogy of Black womanhood, the lyrical "Rainforest." Speaking as an adoring lover, the poet employs symbols from Nature to the need of Black men and women for each other.

The section "Men" offers more criticism than praise. "The Destruction of Fathers" effectively contemplates the emptiness of a divorced man's life. "The Damage We Do" and "Rape: The Male Crime" scourge the abusive Black male. In "Black Manhood: Toward a Definition," Madhubuti again tries to prescribe codes for an ethical oasis in the dominant culture's moral desert. His forthcoming collection of essays, *Black Men: Obsolete, Single, Dangerous?* assesses the current situation.

The last section sounds a prophetic tone. The concluding poem, "Destiny," whose rhetoric lacks the freshness of the other pieces, reiterates the theme of two essential Black needs: "land and selfhood." It exhorts to "reverse destruction. / capture tomorrows." The book's title poems, "Earthquakes" and "Sun Rise Missions," are significantly dedicated to Frances Welsing and Hoyt Fuller respectively; like the views of the writers they celebrate, their radical positions remain steadfastly Nationalist.

Killing Memory, Seeking Ancestors (1987) steps further into an international dimension. The first section, portentously called "Who Owns the Earth?" begins with the major speech poem "Killing Memory," dedicated to Nelson and Winnie Mandela. In this important melding of the genre with the prosody of Brooks's heroic mode, Madhubuti surveys American trivial pursuits (with a fillip to the obsession with Michael Jackson), then shifts his polemic to El Salvador, South Africa, Afghanistan, Lebanon, and Ethiopia. Alluding to Ronald Reagan, he scores "decisions / made at the washington monument and lenin's tomb / by aged actors viewing / *red dawn* and the *return of rambo part IX.*" His critique anatomizes a whole society, including Blacks, whites, and all who destroy the proletarian, egalitarian dream.

Firmly stating his poetics, Madhubuti invokes a poetry of leadership, a poetry of "fire erupting volcanoes," of music and the healing of "dumbness & stupidity / yes, poets uttering to the intellect and spirit, / screaming to the genes and environments, revitalizing the primacy of the word and world—recalling the Gospel of John, "In the beginning was the Word," and the concept of *nommo*, a term of Bantu origin, meaning "the magical power of the word to make material change."[11]

"In Moonlight and After" is again a section of praise to Black women. "Poet: Gwendolyn Brooks at 70" pays a fine tribute to his mentor and acknowledges her pervasive influence:

> artfully you avoided becoming a literary museum,
> side-stepped retirement and canonization,
> gently casting a rising shadow over a generation of
> urgent-creators waiting to make fire,
> make change.

In the last section, called "Findings," an admirable poem titled "The Great Wait" excoriates with wit and passion the "waiters," those numerous Blacks who are addicted to waiting for social change, and the "movers," those who "say that waiting is an ancient art form / perfected by negroes waiting on something called *freedom*." Here is Madhubuti at his acerbic best, incorporating humor and incantatory and jazz rhythms into his speech poem. "negro: an updated definition part 368" catalogs a series of "definitions" punctuated by a line from the popular Bruce Springsteen song "Born in the U.S.A." It mercilessly attacks Blacks corrupted by American values: the ethos of success and the love of money. One recalls Ezra Pound inveighing against "usura" (Canto XLV).

The book ends with a critique and call. "Seeking Ancestors," a five-part poem, was written for the First Annual Egyptian Studies Conference, held in Los Angeles in February 1984 (organized by Maulana Karenga and Jacob Carruthers). The poet begins with an emotion-filled prophetic vision of the United States. Next, he identifies a proud African cultural heritage; he cites needs and recalls ancestry; he scores cultural plunder that cannot truly copy the original. He concludes with a dual quest: for the lost records of a people, and for the rise of Black artists and intellectuals "to / recall the memory / to / recall the tradition & meaning / to rename the bringers / genius."[12]

In the introductory essay to *Earthquakes*, writing of the need for critics, publishers, and writing institutions to recognize and reward Black writers, Madhubuti calls for "an annual recognition feast." Two salient examples of his own contribution in this respect occurred in 1987. First, he edited and published a tribute anthology to celebrate Gwendolyn Brooks's seventieth birthday; *Say That the River Turns: The Impact of Gwendolyn Brooks* was presented to her at a festive book party at Third World Press. Six months later, on December 11 and 12, Madhubuti organized the lively and important Twentieth Anniversary Conference on Literature and Society to celebrate "Third World Press: Twenty Years and Beyond." Dedicated to "the memory and work of Mayor Harold Washington, John O. Killens, and James Baldwin," the conference presented several exciting and valuable workshops conducted by distinguished Black cultural figures,[13] and the publisher distributed more than three dozen awards, including thirty-two "Builder's Awards" for writers, social activists, and Black organizations.

Third World Press received several awards of its own, including the Robert Hayden Award from Broadside Press and the National Council of Black Studies Award. "For the cynic," Madhubuti commented, "twenty years of publishing represents nothing more than a teardrop along the long pendulum of time. For the optimist, twenty years of running a book business is like walking through fire drenched in oil and coming out with a minor sunburn. However, for the realist, and I consider myself an optimistic realist, twenty years with Third World Press has been revelation, condemnation, and renewal. In a few words, it has been one of the greatest challenges and battles that one could fight."

In 1988 Madhubuti himself received an award from the National Council of Teachers of English for his contributions to Black literature and publishing, the third annual Sidney R. Yates Arts Advocacy Award from the Illinois Arts Alliance Foundation, and (with Sonia Sanchez) a citation from the African Heritage Studies Association "for distinguished leadership in the presentation and transmission of African-American cultural traditions."

Madhubuti's example of courage and determination in maintaining his press, his support of other writers, his teaching, readings, lectures, and, most critically, the vigor and social direction of his poetry all contribute to his major status in our country's literary and social landscape. His writing growls, crackles, and sparkles with anger, wit, and love. As Darwin T. Turner writes in his excellent afterword to *Earthquakes*, "Madhubuti's powerful message will shut off some television sets, redirect some minds, and may invite book burning in some quarters" (*ESM*, 189). This poet's voice will continue to make a difference in how Black people view their present situation and approach their future lives in the United States.

INTERVIEW WITH HAKI R. MADHUBUTI

DH   I notice that you used to lowercase "don l. lee," and now it appears in upper and lower case. Does this have any significance?

HM   The lower case was basically keeping consistent with the poetry. Much of the earlier poetry used mainly lower case. It came out of more or less disrespect for the language, and trying to reshape a language which we could communicate in. Also the lower case in the name—I did not and still don't know what "don l. lee" means, in terms of its literal meaning, and that was another reason it was used in lower case.

DH   Dudley Randall says in *More to Remember*, in his poem "An Answer to Lerone Bennett's Questionnaire on a Name for Black Americans," "the spirit informs the name and not the name the spirit." Would you agree?

HM   Right. Well, partially. I think that everything has a meaning to it or behind it. For instance, I did not name myself "Haki." The name was given to me by people at the Institute [of Positive Education]—our Naming Committee. People who wish to change their names submit reasons why, and a biographical sketch either written by them or by somebody else, and then generally the committee looks into the person's background, and names are given according to how the name might fit the current personalities and what they feel the people are. And so the reason we named our children the names we did—for instance, the first girl born to my current marriage, Laini, Laini Nzinga—of course "Laini means precious, and "Nzinga" is after the Queen Nzinga of Angola. And Bomani Garvey is our second son. "Bomani" means warrior and "Garvey" is after Marcus Garvey. And our current—we just had a son April the eighth—his name is Akili Malcolm. "Akili" means understanding and "Malcolm," of course, after Malcolm X. So, the names have not only a spirit behind them, we feel, but also a literal meaning which, if understood properly, will give direction to those who take the name. And so I honestly try to live up to the name that was given to me, so that it would be in the context of both spirit and literal meaning. ["Haki R. Madhubuti" translates from Swahili as justice, awakening, strong; also precise/accurate.]

DH   The title of your book *Enemies: The Clash of Races,* implies a future conflict. Is this what you see ahead, and isn't it a kind of self-fulfilling prophecy?

HM   Well, the conflict exists and has existed, and I don't see it abating anytime soon. I feel that basically the struggle is for two things: one, land, and the other, power over people. Black people in this country are moving toward becoming a landless people. In fact, by 1984, the way things are going now, we will be landless. Black people are losing approximately somewhere between eight to ten thousand acres per week, and it is estimated—by the Emergency Land Fund—that Black people in America will be completely landless by 1984. So we find ourselves basically in this country and much of the world—as consumers only. We don't produce things of value, and consumers have never been equal to the producers. Those things that we do produce are not of real value in terms of what we consider life-giving, life-saving.

In *Enemies,* I was dealing internationally, but I always try to focus back in on what's happening to Black people in this country, in that we are being boxed into a situation where it will probably come down to—probably a shooting war, the way things are going. I think Miami is indicative of what I mean.[14] You see, people thought that once you left the sixties, and you've come through the seventies without any major incidents, that things have been cleared up and that things are better, but they're not. In fact, as I see it, things have gotten progressively worse. What has happened is the elevation of a few people, and these people are not really in decision-making positions. They are in positions where they make choices within the parameter of other people's decisions. Andy

Young is a good example of that.[15] Many people saw Andy Young as being an example of what could happen or what can happen if people would study, be educated, and so forth. But Andy Young, in many cases, did not fulfill the promise of what people, Black people, felt generally at the community level he should be doing. And even though, because of his background, he spoke out, he made mistakes, and so forth, and of course was in a leadership position. And then with [Donald F.] McHenry getting in there, who was nothing but a diplomat—I mean a trained diplomat—he's going to follow the line just as Andy did. We see that as being very superficial, because it really does not begin to speak to the needs of Black people in this country.

DH   You're talking about a shooting war between white and Black people?

HM   Well, I don't know if you saw yesterday's *Sun-Times*. . . . There was a two-page spread on the superpatriots who were meeting in downstate Illinois. And basically, their thing is that they feel that once the depression hits its bottom, the cities are going to go, and people will be spreading out into the countryside, trying to survive and maintain themselves. And what they are teaching—and these are all white people—they are teaching people the art of self-defense, the art of survival. Now at one point these people were being called "crazy," and of course they pointed out in the article that now they are just being called "half-crazy." Because, as things get worse, people begin to look for survival networks; and the cities, in many cases, will be the last place that anyone will want to be in a real crisis, because the support systems are not such that they can support a large group of people—you're talking about millions of people—if the outside is cut off and you don't have the regular flow of food and water and things like that.

Now we see ourselves basically at the bottom. We are the ones that firstly suffer any shortage, any cutoff. It seems as though now in Chicago would be a good example of that. For instance, in Chicago you have young Black men—I'm talking about, say, from sixteen to around twenty-seven—about 40 percent out of work. If you're talking about the general Black population, you're talking about 16 or 17 percent out of work. And so there's a real depression in the Black community again, and we see basically no hope. And it gets to the point, what do you do when people continue to push you back with your backs to the wall? And in many cases they want you to react, because by reacting then, of course, they are able to come down in force.

Miami was just an example of being pushed to the back. You bring in 110,000 Cubans or more, and here Black people have no work whatsoever. You can absorb that many people coming into the country, and at the same time you cannot meet the minimal needs of the citizens of the country.

DH   What are you going to do with the white people who feel they share the same enemies that Black people share? I mean, for example, poverty, war, unemployment. There are a lot of white people who are afflicted by these enemies; who have the same kind of people, fascistic people, whom they would oppose—and *fight*. So are you going to forbid them to share forces with you simply because of the color of their skin?

HM   Well, it's not my job to forbid anybody to fight against that which is incorrect. I think that people will essentially do what they feel is best, in any circumstance. Now in terms of telling whites who see injustices what they should do about them—I mean, that's their decision. I'm only saying, D. H., that I can only go from history. And if I look at the Civil Rights Movement with an eye of one who was a participant and at the same time understanding the history of it, I feel in many cases we were used. Black people were *used* basically in the Civil Rights Movement, and really, the benefits of that have been negligible—other than being able to stay at the Palmer House, to sit in the restaurant, but in terms of long-term benefits, other than the right to vote, I see very few. But in terms of whites, my position always has been—I think that white people of good will need to be with other white people, you see. I just don't feel at this point that, for instance, I could have any real effect upon the Klan, or the major right-wingers in the country. I think that at least by being white you have the entrée to begin dialogue with negative white forces.

DH   Well, my own perspective—I mean I agree with you that it is a question of power, and my experience in the Peace Movement of the sixties reinforced that belief. Only when we were able to marshal masses of people against the war, then we were able to have a voice and eventually stop the war. I don't think that my being white is going to have any effect on a fascist, on a member of the Klan. I think that if I were part of a powerful group, a coalition of Blacks and whites and anybody else who cared to join, I think the power of the group is what would influence the Klan, not the color of my skin.

HM   Well—

DH   That's my perspective.

HM   I respect your perspective. I'm still not convinced that whites and Blacks can work together as partners. History has shown that basically when those two elements came together, whites ended up trying to run the show, or if not, moving in very key positions. For instance, look at our so-called key political figures. Generally, the staffs and especially those who are making some of the key policy decisions are basically white. And then—okay, you read the piece I did on Blacks and Jews?[16]

DH   Yes.

HM   I am not against Jews specifically. I just want people to stop thinking of us as naïve in terms of our relationship with the world. Jews in this country represent about 25 percent of the lawyers. I think that's important. I mean, people always have to think in terms of their own survival. I have nothing against that. But don't at the same time think it naïve of me to say that we need 25 percent of our people to be lawyers, too. Don't begin to impose quotas on me when the quotas one time existed with Jewish people and they moved to cut them down. . . .

DH   The tone of the article seems to imply that Jews are the enemy of Blacks. Is that a correct appraisal?

HM   Yes. Pretty much so. But I'm talking about *all* white people. It's not just Jews. Coming from historical evidence, Jews that were involved in the slave trade, just as Anglo-Saxons, just as the Portuguese, just as the Spanish, and Arabs—

DH   What about Blacks, too?

HM   Right. Right. One of the major reasons that we are in this position that we are is that we have been betrayed by our own people. No doubt about that. I'm not for excusing anybody, and I think one of the problems now in terms of a lack of movement and development is that our leadership has failed drastically. Black leadership—for the most part—is corrupt. A great many Black leaders have been bought off—not only by money and pseudopower but by privilege. I think that there exists, for all practical purposes, no real national Black leadership. Yesterday's paper pointed out that Benjamin Hooks of the NAACP—they just raised his salary to $125,000. How can you accept a salary of $125,000 when Black people are in such a position that we are in now? I don't consider that leadership at all. . . .

DH   Do you think that the fact that there are "traitors"—that the motivation may have some connection to the economic basis of the system, that it may indeed be a function of an acquisitive, capitalistic system, rather than simply that these are individuals who are betraying, that they reflect—that people tend to reflect a system of competition or a system of cooperation?

HM   Oh, I don't doubt that. I think that capitalism has had a disastrous effect upon most of us. I have no doubt about that at all.

DH   You talk about "communalism." How is that different from communism?

HM   Well, we basically see that the ownership of property, where there's real property or what I call "transient property," that the ownership must be by those persons who do the work. One of the ways that the Institute works so well is that if I were to leave tomorrow, or something happened to me, Third World Press, the *Black Books Bulletin,* the Institute of Positive Education, our Land Development Corporation, the school, the food co-op, the bookstore would continue. It's not based upon one person. You do not buy your way into IPE; you work your way in. It might take a year, it might take a year and a half to two years for you to work your way in, but once you work your way into the structure itself, you become not only one of the owners—it's more like a cooperative—but a decision-maker, which is even more important. No major decisions about what we do with the moneys that come in from what we produce can be made without the workers' input. You feel part of that. But at the same time we do say to people that, for instance, if you're an artist in that cooperative, you have the right to paint or to produce whatever you do and to sell it. All right? And that becomes your money. Now, all we ask for is that if you're working jobs outside the Institute, that you donate to the Institute 15 percent of your annual salary.

DH   So it's sort of midway—

HM   Right. It's a mixture.

DH   —between individualism—

HM   Correct.

DH   —and a group sense.

HM   Right. And I think that what we're trying to always do is to make sure that people's initiatives are not squashed because they do not see any concrete monetary return from their labor. Because that's fantasy. We do not believe in monopoly capitalism. We do not believe in large corporations. We feel that they are detrimental.

DH   You talk about the acquisition of land. Are you referring to land in the United States or buying land in Africa, or both?

HM   Land anywhere. I think this is a concept that Black people have to take internationally. But Black people in this country—we are basically citizens of this country, and by and large, Black people are not going any place. Therefore, wherever you are, you need to have land. So I think that, rather than invest in gold and silver or in other things of less value, the major investment should be in land, since land is the only thing that nobody nowhere is making any more of, and everything of value comes from land.[17]

DH   The goals that you seek for Black people—do you see Black Nationalism as an end in itself? Or do you think that ultimately there is some way that all the people in this country could somehow participate in the organization?

HM   That's a very difficult question when you haven't gotten to first base. . . . I guess the most current parallel would be Jews in Israel. Is that an end in itself? Even though the Israeli government has very close economic contacts and relationships with this country and of course, other parts of Europe, it is, in itself, autonomous. It is an entity in itself and makes its own governmental decisions. So I think that basically what we're saying is that we want what other people have in terms of a nation-state, and that nation-state within the context of this country or the world. You cannot isolate yourself. You have to work with other people. That's realistic.

DH   In a kind of United Nations?

HM   Right.

DH   Do you think the United Nations is something that should be strengthened?

HM   Yes. I think the United Nations should be strengthened, mainly because I think that anytime you have a vehicle where people can begin to express themselves on somewhat of an equal footing, that's good. I think that you should be able to talk first and try to resolve problems in a civilized way, rather than going directly to the gun. I think that the United Nations, for the most part, has given a voice to those nations who are not as powerful as the nations in the West. And so, therefore, that's a help in many ways, and I do think it should be strengthened.

DH   In *Enemies* you talk about the "accountability" factor
and the necessity of force, and the "accountability force" as a kind
of group. Would this force operate to patrol Black people, and to
whom would the force itself be accountable?

HM   Well, when you talk about any kind of people who
consist in themselves, a self-determining people, they have a police
force. That's what I'm talking about, essentially. . . . For instance,
you look at the Italian community in the city—there is no drug
problem. There's no real problem of Italians raping Italian women.
The problems are kept at a minimum, and generally, when some-
thing happens, that community takes care of it. That's what I'm
talking about.

DH   That's true in New York, too. They say that Little Italy is
the safest place to be because the Mafia is in control.

HM   Right.

DH   After World War II, the intellectual crisis identified itself
with the division between Jean-Paul Sartre and Albert Camus, the
Communist movement as primary versus the individual conscience
as primary. I think a parallel may be drawn between the attraction
of W. E. B. Du Bois, who late in life became a Communist, and
Marcus Garvey, the Black Nationalist and separatist. Now do you
think it is necessary for Blacks today to choose one or the other, or
can they follow both to some extent?

HM   Well, to be perfectly frank, the great masses of our
people have not chosen either one. However, I do think that the
majority of our people, given the choice, would choose Garvey. The
reason I say that is because the record proves that. Du Bois, for the
most part, was an intellectual who did not appeal to the masses. He
worked with the NAACP and edited *Crisis* for many years, but in
terms of speaking for or representing a great mass of Black people,
he himself never did. However, Garvey did. Garvey built the first
real Black mass movement in the Western Hemisphere. And this is,
of course, why he was taken off the scene, because he was seen as a
real threat, on the same level of a Martin Luther King or a Malcolm
X. But of course, Garvey had gone beyond either Martin Luther
King or Malcolm X, or even the Honorable Elijah Muhammad.
Now that's not to say that Du Bois and the ideas which he espoused
are not important. I wouldn't want to say that. I think they are. I
think that what he did in his life was tremendous and cannot be
belittled by anybody. And there's always a place within our move-

ment for our intellectuals and scholars. I think that you become very shortsighted when you do not allow people to study and to produce and to theorize. Du Bois was both: He was not only a theoretician; he was an activist, too. He was one of the major motivators of the First Pan-African Congress. And so credit must be given, at the same time realizing that Garvey and Du Bois were working under very serious difficulties, and it's a different historical time. So whether either/or, we have to understand that both contributed mightily to the development of Black people.

DH   I am struck by the amount of suffering that appears in your work and in your early life, which you presented so honestly and movingly, I think, in *Enemies*. And you mention the terrible fear of whites. Was physical fear your experience, and if so, is this a typical experience for Blacks, still?

HM   Well, yes. I think anybody who's got any sense would fear whites in this country, not only in terms of looking at what whites have basically done to Native Americans, Blacks, and other people but the current, day-to-day situation that exists in the country. I can go to my file—I have a very good file system documenting the Black men that are killed on a daily basis around the country. And so I'm saying you'd be crazy not to fear that. I'm only coming from the point of view that you recognize a fear, and then you've got to begin to deal with it.

DH   Right.

HM   Force has been one of the prime movers in the Western ethos, like the Western movie—shoot first and then talk later. [*Laughter*] That becomes more than a joke if it's reality.

DH   Yes.

HM   Now as a result of that, several things have happened to us. One is not being able to deal with that fear, not being able to deal with that violence. In any case, we psychologically turn inward, and because of the frustration that many men have in this country, Black men, we turn on each other. You see, when you cannot deal with the enemy—Fanon talks about that, Frantz Fanon, the psychology of the oppressed—when you cannot deal, even at the same level the enemy deals on you, at the violent level, you turn that violence inward, and you essentially destroy yourself or those closest to you. And that, of course, speaks to one reason for the high level of Black-on-Black crime. But very few people talk about the *white-on-Black* crime that perpetuates the Black-on-

Black crime. I have personally experienced the violence from whites. I have seen much of it coming up on the streets, in Detroit and Chicago. I grew up on the Lower East Side of Detroit and many times was thrown up against the wall and searched for no reason, as well as physically beaten.

DH   By individuals or a gang?

HM   Individuals, mainly so-called "legal"—police.

DH   Oh!

HM   Well, we did not have too much of a problem with white gangs or white people, because I lived in an all-Black community. They didn't come into our community, and we didn't go into their community. It was mainly the legal forces that were dominant in terms of the violence in the Black community, as it is today. You don't find too many white people coming into the Black community on their own, to be violent, because basically the legal forces, police, were violent.

DH   Do you think that different urban centers project different kinds of experiences? For example, I happen to live on the Upper West Side of Manhattan in New York. It is a peacefully integrated neighborhood.[18] We take great pride in it, as a matter of fact. I think we live in a most interesting and varied and intellectually alive area. Do you think that perhaps there may be a difference between, say, Chicago and New York, as far as integration goes, or the feelings that Black people may have?

HM   Yes. You see, again, one of the reasons why the New York you live in is so interesting and, quote unquote, "integrated" has a lot to do with the Jewish population which, by and large, are people who have suffered a great deal and have a certain moral responsibility to see that, at least at a certain level, they don't perpetuate on other people what has been put on them. I really feel that one of the reasons you might have that type of community is because it's a high level of Jewish community and there's no place else to run to. So you make it work. Whereas here, on the South Shore where I live, it used to be a predominantly Jewish community, but they're gone. They left. But in New York, where you have a very large, a very—and I put "secure" in quotes, because I don't think anybody is really secure—secure Jewish community, there's no place left to run, so you stay and you make it work.

DH   Well, where I live, we have Jewish people, Blacks, and a very large Puerto Rican population—

HM   I don't doubt that.

DH   —and a marvelous mixing. There are lots of community issues that come up, but if we have problems with the schools or whatever—sure, there are conflicts, but they're intellectual conflicts, and they're always resolved in some democratic way.

HM   I'm not doubting that. I'm saying it probably does exist. But see, again, in New York you've got Harlem, you've got Bedford–Stuyvesant.

DH   Yes. Right.

HM   You've got those poles. Just like where you are here, you may have uptown and Hyde Park, but these are little enclaves, and the thing that holds Hyde Park together is the U. of Chicago. If the University of Chicago were not there, then you would not have that community as it is. There's always something that holds that community together. But the University of Chicago, by and large, has been detrimental to the existence and development of Black people who surround it, not only in terms of its bigness and the direction in which it is going but you can't even get Black people into the institution itself. It's a lily-white institution right in the middle of the Black community. You've got the lake on one side; then you've got, I'd say Forty-seventh down to Twenty-second, which is all Black—well, not all Black. Starting around Twenty-seventh to Thirty-sixth they're beginning to build a lot in the city, you know, bringing whites back into the inner city. But you have very few communities, genuine communities, where you have whites and Blacks interacting, Puerto Ricans and West Indians interacting at any really qualitative level.

Integration, as far as I'm concerned, has been a real farce. It's been, you know, like a joke that people mouthed. Because we are the ones who really believed it and really tried to move toward a genuine integrated society. No doubt about it. If I, personally, wanted to move into an area where it was predominantly white, or there was a "mixture," there would be no problem for me, being light-skinned and intelligent and able to do things that are not thought of as "odd" by white people. But in terms of the great majority of Black people—that's the question that's always on my mind: What can we do? And we know that that question becomes a farce by the mere fact that economically the great majority of Black people cannot move out of the community that we now live in. And please don't have any children. Once you have children, that's almost like a slap in the face, because landlords don't want any children. It puts us in a very difficult and dangerous position.

DH   Of course, a lot of white people—the poor white people—have trouble moving—

HM   I don't doubt that.

DH   —anywhere. As a matter of fact, people now find it very difficult to move anywhere because the society seems to be moving towards a division between a few very wealthy people and a broad base of poor people. So the people are pretty much stuck where they are—

HM   Yes.

DH   —with inflation and higher rents, and all. It seems to be a pretty general problem, exaggerated in the Black community, no doubt.

HM   Right.

DH   You write of *Ujamaa* [oo-jah-MAH]—is that the correct pronunciation?

HM   Right.

DH   That beautiful conception of the extended family as an ideal, as opposed to the nuclear family.[19] Now at what point, logically can you set a limit and say, "Well, this is the family," and not permit that conception to extend and include the family of—humanity?

HM   Oh, I see. Well, we recognize the nuclear family of biological contacts. But what we are trying to do is to say that there are values, there are communal values, human values that go beyond just your biological union. For instance, within the context of the Institute, those persons, those men and women and children who are involved in that—we see ourselves in extension of each other, in this family where I'm responsible for all the children, not only my own but the other children who are not biologically mine. Now you say, how can you talk about that and not extend it to the human family? Well, "humanism," "universality," these are fine words; even the concepts are laudable. But I'm dealing with reality. And people get tired of being slapped in the face for trying to be good, for trying to go beyond and extend themselves, and what you begin to see is everybody looking out for number one. Everybody is looking out for their thing first. And people are only respected to the level that they can develop a base. One of the problems with communication within the Civil Rights Movement was that Black people were willing to join everybody else and all kinds of coalitions and alliances, but there had not been a real base developed in the Black community.

You know, people want to criticize me and maybe others for just working within the context of our community. But the same criticism is not given to other people who decide that the development of the Italian community is their utmost responsibility or the Jewish community or the Polish community in a city like Chicago. So that it becomes a joke to just step out of the community in which one lives and have not developed a base and talk about alliances and coalitions—that's funny and should not be taken seriously. Now once a people are strong within themselves, not only in terms of population but economically and otherwise, then that people can talk about humanity; you can talk about universality. But otherwise, people are not going to take you seriously. It's just like the United States or the U.S.S.R.—they don't go around the world talking to nobody; they will talk *at* you and you listen. [*Laughter*] And until all people can respect each other at the level of human values and universal values, then such concepts become veritable jokes, and weapons in the hands of the strong to use against people who are weak, economically and otherwise.

DH   So in other words, your position may be modified as the conditions change and as power of the Black community becomes consolidated and Black people can speak from a position of strength—

HM   Right.

DH   —rather than weakness.

HM   Right. You know, there are few permanent positions. Even though I see white people as the dominant enemy of Black people—I'm talking about basically the white race—now within that race there are individuals who possibly could not be considered enemies. It's not like 100 percent. Just say it's 85 percent. All right, say you have 15 percent of the white population that truly are trying to move toward that which is good and just and correct— then, I don't see it being my responsibility to find them. You see?

DH   Yes.

HM   My responsibility basically is to try to continuously make our community aware of what is happening to them. And for that 15 percent to make itself known to the world, it will be done only through good deeds.

DH   In *Enemies* you suggest polygamy as a possible solution to the fact that there is a greater number of Black females than males. I think the statistics you quote are 1.5 to 1. I wonder whether you had any reaction to the idea from Black women, and what reaction do you have from Black men?

HM   In *Enemies* I did not suggest polygamy. What I tried to do was chronicle what exists. I was talking about the quality of sharing and essentially saying that this is what exists. Now what do you do about that? How do you begin to legitimize that, or is it illegitimate, and so forth. But since *Enemies* I have gone on and done other work in the area in a piece in one of the issues of *Black Books Bulletin*. The title of the piece was "Not Allowed to Be Lovers," dealing with Black male-female relationships.[20] What is happening, D. H., is that the ratio is greater than that. I use a very conservative figure. Robert Staples, in his latest book on singles, talks about the ratio of Black women to Black men as something approaching ten to one.

We come to a very complicated question when we talk about available Black men, because even within the ratio of ten to one—or let's just say five to one; I know that we are within realistic boundaries when we say five to one—that "one" does not actually exist, because we're taking into account basically "one" being the male that is alive, that will move toward some type of heterosexual relationship. But in fact, when you start talking about "one," you're talking about a very large prison population: Black men compose essentially, nationwide, something like 82 percent of the prison population. And there's a wide number of Black men who are just going crazy and are now incarcerated in mental health institutions, especially between the ages of twenty-five and thirty-five, young Black men. And you're talking about the Black men who have been caught up in alcohol and drugs, who are not good for anybody, even themselves.

Then you're talking about the Black men who essentially have been turned into white men, who do not have any allegiance to the Black community, who basically see themselves as watchdogs for the white establishment. And then finally you're talking about Black men who have been effectively turned into homosexuals. We have a very large Black homosexual community. And so therefore, when you're talking about conscious Black men who are concerned about the development of family, who are concerned about

Black women, who are concerned about children, then that ratio is just totally out of proportion.

Now there are really only two or three ways to deal with that problem. I didn't speak to the homicide rate of Black men. For every 100,000 people in this country—you're talking about white women: 2.3, white men: 7 something—I used those figures in *Enemies*. The figure I used in *Enemies* for Black men was far below the actual figure that exists today. It's like 160-something per 100,000. Black men are just being taken off the earth.

When you talk about the conscious Black men, what we see as being one of our major problems now is the breakup of the family, the destruction of the family. Of course, [Chancellor] Williams talks about this and how we begin to destroy that family.[21] It is very easy to see the destruction of any people, because the family becomes the organizing mechanism, the socializing mechanism. And when you have young Black men coming into the world without fathers, it puts a very terrible and very heavy burden on the women that have to raise them. In many cases, they can't do the job at the level that it should be done, because any time a young man gets to be thirteen on up, he don't want to be Momma's boy anymore, not in the Black community, and once he steps off there, he's got to deal with his peers. So he is going to continue to challenge her from that point on. And the streets, in many cases, are going to win out on that. So if you don't have a man around, you have very little control over the young men coming up, and during that period from thirteen to twenty-six, the psychosexual energies are at the highest.

One of the reasons countries send young men to war is that that's when they're ready to fight somebody. You see, when you can't channel that energy in a constructive manner, then it's going to be destructive. That is essentially what is happening within the context of our community. This is the first time since Blacks existed in this country that you have a serious problem of Black-on-Black crime. But again, you have to look at the reasons why, and the core of the reasons is white–on–Black crime. When you begin to wipe out the male, when you begin to wipe out the men in any community, within any people, then that people cease to be a real threat.

This is what is happening in terms of white-Black relationships in this country, because white men who run it realize that at the bottom line the greatest threat has always been Black men. And so you deny a lot of that element to be organized. And you begin to move against it very subtly and very systematically. White men do not fear white women. They are concerned. They are going to make some changes. White men don't fear Black women. Black women basically have been sexual objects to white men. But the key fear has always been with Black men. Now when you destroy the male population of an enemy—and that is how we have always been in regard to white men; I mean, white men basically run it, and the slave master, or the master-slave relationship, has never really been wiped out of the psyche of most Black men.

So in order to deal with that, with the Black men who are coming on strong, who seem to be coming on strong, then you begin systematically to wipe them out. You wipe them out physically and you wipe them out mentally and you neutralize them. All right? Now, when you neutralize the male population of any people, then the rulers don't have to worry about that population. Because essentially what you have left to fight are the women. And generally, men don't fear women, especially if they've got the gun. And that's essentially what's happening in this country. The problem is that people don't want to deal with that. They don't want to recognize it. They want to speak around all kinds of other issues but don't want to look at how essentially the Black male population is being wiped out whole scale in this country. And it's a very serious problem.

Now the other question that you pose, about polygamy, or extended family, or what we call polynuclear family—we talk about functional families, where, say, you have a man in what is called a nuclear family situation, and all the other women out there with children, who have no father image for the children, and so forth. When we say "functional families," we're saying essentially a man and a woman—because it would have to be a dual decision to bring another woman into the family with her children, all right? Now bringing that other woman into the family does not necessarily mean that man will have a sexual relationship with that woman. All it means essentially is that you will compose a family, which would give a father to the children. Okay? Now that's one way.

The other way is that there is a possibility that you would or could bring another woman or women into the family, and they would essentially be wives of the male. Now that exists, but what exists now, D. H. is what I call "illigamy." That is, you have a male possibly dealing with one, two, or three other females, but there is no responsibility to these females and the children that may have resulted from the relationship. And so that's the quality of sharing that exists now. What I'm saying basically is, how do you clean that up, to bring it to the point where the community recognizes that a legitimate relationship exists, and that the children are taken care of, and so forth? I'm personally against the older men with families adding other women to their families if they cannot satisfy the needs of their current family. It becomes a great mistake to say that if you cannot satisfy the economic, the sexual, the educational, the cultural needs of a woman in that family, that you can satisfy the needs of two women. You see what I mean? That becomes a real contradiction.

So that's just one answer to it. The other answer, in terms of the question posed, is that you stop the destruction of Black men. That's long term as well as short term. But the ratio is so out of proportion now that you have to begin to do something that's going to clean up the relationships as they now exist. You see, there are two things that everybody in this world goes after: food and sex. So therefore they've both got to be put into their proper perspective. And then, with the whole sexual question, what I'm saying basically, at least in the work I'm doing now, is that men in their thirties and beyond leave the young women alone. Because the young women and the young men should get together. Young women will go after or deal with the older men because they have more to offer, and they are more attractive in terms of their stability and what they have. But that's incorrect, because it takes from the young men. If we see that multiple wife structure, it's necessary that the older men should, if they're really concerned about the development of the family, deal with women who are alone and who have children, and who essentially are looking for honest, open companionship.

DH   So you really want to prescribe roles and determine even the kind of mixing that's going to take place. I wonder how a certain kind of feminist, for example, might view this. And there are women who say that, well, women have alternatives. They can turn to other women.

HM   Well, I am against that if you are talking about homosexual activity as an accepted movement among Black people. I am against women turning to other women and men turning to other men as sexual substitutes. We don't see that as productive or life-giving or life-saving.

DH   But it happens.

HM   So it happens. To say that we're against it doesn't mean we're going to wipe it out. You see, in a society like this you have so many options, positive and negative options. So if that's your choice, there's nothing I can do about it.

DH   Let's talk about your poetry. Do you write as inspired or because a poem is needed?

HM   Generally, if I see a need in a certain area, I'll just try to compose a poem around that theme.

DH   Like Miami?

HM   Right. The new book of poetry [*Earthquakes*] that will probably be out toward the end of 1982—most of those poems are dealing with specific situations. I don't work too much out of inspiration.

DH   You might say—

HM   It might take a long time to come. [*Laughter*]

DH   Well, I guess you might say that your beliefs are your inspiration.

HM   Right. You just try to do what you can and work on that.

DH   When did you begin writing, and what poets or other people influenced you?

HM   Well, I guess writing started around 1962—'61, '62. And during that period I was in the army and going through a lot of problems. Talking about the violence, there was a lot of physical violence in the army between whites and Blacks. Where I was situated, there were only three Blacks in a company of about three hundred men—white men. And it was a real problem all the time.

DH   Supertokens.

HM   So I began to research and to study more during that period and just really try to find out about myself. Even though my mother had read Richard Wright and I had read Chester Himes— that was my starting-point; I had read *Black Boy* at thirteen and *Cast the First Stone* around that same time. Once I got into the service, it was so isolated, I just began to look and devour the library, and so forth, and that's when I began to visit used book stores. Every place I would go and visit I would look at the used book stores. And I would write the poems and began to write because I felt that in many cases the poets I was reading did not totally reflect what was in me. The major early influences were basically Gwendolyn Brooks, Langston Hughes, Claude McKay, Jean Toomer. The book *Cane* by Jean Toomer was very important.

DH What a beautiful—

HM It had a tremendous effect on my poetry.

DH —a very experimental book.

HM Right. Margaret Walker, *For My People.* Those were the poets. But the major writer, really, I mean in a long term, that had the greatest effect, other than Gwen—but Gwen was in different ways, because I met her personally. And it was not only in her work but her personality, and then I began to appreciate the total person. But I guess the single most important writer that had a great effect upon me, that I did not meet, was Richard Wright. Because *Black Boy* was the single most important work. And then, after reading *Native Son, The Outsider,* and the other works of Wright, I began to get a total picture of the man, plus his world view. Of course, "Black Power," the piece he did on his visit to Ghana and dealing with Nkrumah, was very important in terms of just beginning to open me up to a larger world.

Baraka came in a little bit later as an influence, a poetic influence.[22] It was maybe around '65, '66. I had read his work but I wasn't terribly impressed with *Twenty Volume Suicide Note* and stuff like that. Because, see, I had never had a white influence in terms of the writing at all. . . . There wasn't any, even though in junior college I did take a couple of creative writing courses. But they were not poetry; they basically were prose—short stories, stuff like that. Even though I was aware of what many white poets were doing at that time, the white influence was not a major one.

DH As a poet, I was wondering whether you are a reviser, or does it just come out a poem and you let it go?

HM Oh, no, I'm a reviser. Gwen taught me that. And you see it more and more in the later works, I guess from *Don't Cry, Scream,* on up.

DH You seem to have a very healthy respect for craft, for the craft of writing. And I notice that in your criticism, especially *Dynamite Voices* and *A Capsule Course in Black Poetry Writing.* What training in craft and in reading would you advise for a beginning poet?

HM I think the key thing, at least in terms of my development, has been workshops, as a part of OBAC [Oh-BAH-see], Organization of Black American Culture. Hoyt Fuller, who was one of the founders of OBAC and, of course, the managing editor of *Negro Digest*, later to become *Black World*, was a major influence on my work. He, Dudley Randall, Gwendolyn Brooks were about the major living influences, especially in terms of discipline and in terms of trying to be specific about what I was going to say, and the use of concrete words. Hoyt and Gwen, and Dudley (as my editor), played a very important part in shaping my work. Not in a heavy manner—just a suggestion here and a suggestion there. And generally I listen to people. Now my advice to young poets basically would be the workshop experience, especially with other writers who are serious and who are not necessarily going to bite their tongues around criticism. The other two things would be to write *regularly* and *to read*. When I was in the army, I learned to read. At that time I was reading about four or five thousand words a minute. . . . I would read easily two books a day. For about four years I read on the average at least one book a day.

    DH   Did you study speed reading?

    HM   Right. And—

    DH   Do you recommend that?

    HM   I do. On some work.

    DH   On some work. You miss out on style if you're reading poetry or something—

    HM   Well, you couldn't do it with poetry. But it's important that new writers read everything. I think that you have to be keenly aware of what is happening in poetry. But my greatest ideas and the development of ideas came basically from reading nonfiction and other Black writers. The reason I say you have to read a lot is that I think it is important to become aware of good writers. They may not be saying too much, but in terms of style and craft, you can see that they have the ability to put words down on the page. And I think that's important.

    The only thing I say to most young Black writers is, never forget who you are, that you're not a writer who happens to be Black, but you're a Black person who writes. I think that's the key; I think that's the key for any people, not just for Black people. And I very seldom find any people—the Jewish Nobel laureate [Isaac Bashevis] Singer—all he writes about is Jewish people. And somehow people accept that as being legitimate and having validity within the context of their own lives, which I think is correct. But any time you can talk about Ernest Gaines, one of the best short story writers we have, and novelist, somehow people don't think that his work, or even Gwen's—you know, Simpson's making that idiotic statement about Gwen in terms of writing about Negroes and that's not necessarily important—

DH   I mention that in my book.[23]

HM   Yes. So I'm just saying that it is important to read everything and everybody and to realize that no single people have a corner on knowledge at all, and that the beauty of the world, I think, I feel, is that you do have different cultures, different languages, and different people. And I would hate to see all of this be destroyed by trying to—everybody's trying to become alike. I'm totally against that. I don't think that's wise. I think when you do that, you really destroy the flavor of the world, and that the key to world understanding is to have a living and honest respect for differences, and that your differences should not be imposed on anybody else, and that communication becomes—I think the study of languages is very important, even though I'm not proficient in any language other than English myself.

DH   Stephen Henderson, in *Understanding the New Black Poetry* [1973], refers to Black speech and music as basic referents in the poetry. Your work seems to be a fine example of that, and I was wondering to what extent you think that Black speech and music have influenced you.

HM   Well, it's the major influence, especially the music. I grew up with the music.

DH   Which music would you say particularly inspired you?

HM   We called it "Black secular music," which other people would refer to as "jazz." But Black secular music was always in my home. And then the spirituals, too, because I grew up in the Baptist Church. But I more or less rebelled against the spirituals, because it seemed to me that they were not always dealing with reality. The Black secular music, everything from the early Miles Davis, Ella Fitzgerald, Billy Eckstine—I mean all that was always being played around home—Louis Armstrong. And at the same time, when I began to deal with the music myself, the early groups that came out of Motown—the Supremes, the Temptations, the Four Tops, of course early Stevie Wonder, Ray Charles—were all very important in terms of my development.

DH   What about African music?

HM   Not until later—

DH   Because I see that, also—I *hear* it in your work.

HM   —until I had become an adult, of course. I began to travel a little bit more and study more. I didn't get to Africa until '69, and before that everything about Africa was either taught to me by Africans from the continent or came from what I had read, so it was basically secondhand.

DH   I believe it was Larry Neal in one of his essays who used the expression "destruction of the text," meaning reconstruction of the text, considering the poems as scores to be interpreted. Do you consider your poems as scores to be interpreted ad lib by different poets, or do you want your poems read a certain way?

HM   I really don't even think about it. No, it's not really that important. I do try to write clearly enough, where the general meaning of what I'm saying is obvious, but the way you read it and the way you interpret it ultimately—that's up to you. That don't even bother me sometimes, because everybody has their own interpretation of the music. That's what poetry is to a large extent—just music with words.

DH   Well, you read so distinctively, I really can't imagine anybody else doing justice to your work the way you do.

HM   I've heard other people do—at least for me—do it much, read much better than I, some of the poems.

DH   I notice that you and Gwendolyn Brooks have both written excellent poems about the Wall of Respect. I was wondering whether the poems were connected or whether you were both inspired by the same event.

HM   I think that was it basically; we were inspired by the same event. We were there and took part in the dedication of the Wall. And it was during a period, I guess around '67, that there was a lot of activity in Chicago around the reemergence of Black culture. So we were both intimately involved in that. And the Wall was a very important pivotal point.

DH   What did you think of the destruction of the Wall? It was eventually torn down, I understand.

HM   Well, what happened—the city had proposed to destroy it several times, and there were large demonstrtions to stop it. And it really did not get destroyed until the seventies, like the middle seventies. And it was just done, overnight. Nobody knew anything about it. The next day it was gone. But by that time, I think, in many cases—you see, when the Wall of Respect came into existence, there were very few Black cultural institutions in existence. And when the Wall was destroyed, there were other institutions that essentially—not necessarily took up the slack from that, but we were so involved in trying to keep these other institutions open and making them live in reality that our energies had been dissipated in doing that, rather than trying to react to the city tearing down that wall. Because what was happening was that they were renovating that whole area, and the Wall, of course, stood for something very important, but we just couldn't do anything about it. We had to put a twenty-four-hour guard, and so forth, and that was beyond our capacity.

DH It seemed to me an act of vandalism.

HM Yes. Right. "Legal" vandalism.

DH I thought it was a desecration.

HM Well, even the city could have taken it and preserved the Wall itself as a piece of community art.

DH The last line of the poem seemed to imply a kind of immortality, the reference to someone still "layen there." Is that what you intended? As a kind of tomb of a spiritual figure?

HM I don't really put too much store in physical structures. You mentioned earlier the spirit; I think the spirit is very important in terms of what lives on and what is actually real. Even my own work: I think I've done some important work, but it's not like all of it's going to last. And believe me, it really doesn't affect me that much whether it lasts or not. I think the key thing, at least with me, is to continue to be productive, and people will make a decision of whether it's important or not in the long run. But if people are so concerned about whether their work is going to last for prosterity, or whether they are "universal," I think that hampers the work. If you are so concerned about that, how other people are going to judge your work, it's going to color your work. What's important to me is the spirit in which the work is developed and which can now be transmitted through the work, and if that spirit is legitimate and if it has meaning in speaking to the times and speaking to some clear direction, then it's going to be around. At least for a while. That's good. But the spirit is the most important thing.

DH You use the word "spirit" and you are, obviously, a spiritual person. I was wondering whether you connected the spirituality any longer to a conventional religion. At one time, you were drawn towards the Islamic faith.

HM I think many of us during the period of the sixties were drawn to Islam, mainly because of the Honorable Elijah Muhammad and the Nation of Islam. And I rejected Islam when I went to North Africa and began to see what was happening there. I had never become a Muslim, but in terms of spirituality, basically my feelings are expressed in the *Book of Life*. I think that the spiritual connection or the conscious connection between people really comes down to the point of how can we relate, and if we really like each other, and are we trying to move toward a common good. That's what's most important to me. Ideologically, if we, say, are both nationalists, that may be fine, but if I don't like you or you don't like me, then regardless of our ideological makeup, whether we care about each other is going to have the utmost say-so about our relationship. So, what I look for in a person, man or woman, are those qualities that would allow us to meet and develop on a person-to-person level.

DH You're talking about Black—

HM Right. Most of my relationships are with Black people. In fact, all my relationships are with Black people. I don't have any relationships with white people. And that's by choice. Let me put it this way. We do business all over the country and other parts of the world, and basically I deal with white people the way they deal with me, on a business level. In terms of socializing, there is absolutely none in my life. So in the relationships I've developed, I'm looking for how we can connect up as people who are trying to do some good, first and foremost. Whether we agree ideologically or not, philosophically or not, then those words will be tested as the relationship develops or not develops.

At this time in my life I'm not as dogmatic or self-righteous about my positions, and recognize that there are other variations and there are other positions that have got to be respected; that in a country like this where the options are many, mainly negative options, that's all you can do. You can't force people to take your position.

DH I have one last question. You seem to be moving from poetry to "rappin' and readin'," which is the title of one of your records, and from there to reading with jazz, and now to a more directly political mode, in prose. Do you see your commitment to poetry receding or just developing into another form?

HM   That's a good question. I think the poetry will always be important, and I do not do a lecture or a program without including the poetry. The poetry definitely has taken a back seat in the sense that in trying to communicate specific ideas and concepts, basically they are communicated better in prose, in terms of total explanations. Now at the same time, the reason I wrote *Book of Life* and numbered the poems is that with each poem I was trying to deal with a concept, and that has worked very well. *Book of Life* probably is approaching the sales of *Don't Cry, Scream,* because it hits all eyes. You can deal with small children with it, and of course you can deal with adults.

DH   You're really a teacher in that book.

HM   Well, I was trying to be. *Book of Life* was written for two reasons. One, coming out of the sixties and coming out of a whole lot of death and pain, and seeing a lot of people just totally, spiritually drained and going into a whole lot of negativism and drugs and alcohol and other things, what I was saying and trying to say, at least, was that there is another way. We just have to keep pulling from the best of us and not let other people or other situations destroy our will to do what is best. And knowing that within whatever situation we find ourselves, any people who understand their roots, who understand themselves, have the capacity to move out of any situation. So this is what I was trying to convey in *Book of Life.* But yes, the work has moved toward a more definite political stance, for the very reason that just about everything in this country is political, and that even though I would never run for office or be involved—unlike Pablo Neruda; didn't he hold office or become an ambassador?

DH   Yes—

HM   And others—well, Mao Tse-tung was a poet. I do not see myself in that capacity. I would not want to be that, but I would much rather be behind the scenes, trying to offer constructive criticism and trying at some level to be an example of what can be. The only reason that we built a publishing company and the school and these other things is that I feel that instutitions, much more than singular persons, will be what's going to last. Now you will still be embodied in the institution, undoubtedly, but the institutions essentially determine the strength of the people, because they become the place where you gather and you grow and you become stronger. And you look at any people—if you have strong people, you have strong institutions.

That is the one thing that's missing among our people. The only institutions that we've had that have any strength, unless it's qualitatively compared to other people, would be our church. But see, when you looked at other people, you not only saw the church; you saw the military, you saw the educational institutions, the medical institutions, and so forth, the publishing companies, things like that. And that's what I see as my job; to help try to build these institutions, more than trying to be out there and deal with trying to be in politics. But you can't build institutions unless you're aware of politics, especially in a city like Chicago. So therefore the work, as you pointed out, has definitely taken on a political flavor. But at the same time, I have been involved politically, but more or less as an organizer rather than as a leader.

DH   Well, this is exactly what John Milton did during the time of the Puritan Revolution. He wrote prose, and he worked very hard with it. In a way you're responding to the needs of the times, the urgencies of the times, and perhaps, when the times change and call for something different, you will respond.

HM   The new book—the title is *Earthquakes and Sun Rise Missions*—has a long essay dealing with culture as the guiding force of any people and, of course, dealing with Black people too. And energy comes from, essentially, your culture, whether it's language, whether it's art, whether it's economics, and so forth. Part Two of the new book will be the poetry, unlike *Book of Life*. *Book of Life* had a short introductory essay, and then it had two parts of poetry. In *Book of Life*, the first part is what I call traditional poetry—the heavy use of language and the words, the similes and metaphors that grow directly out of our community—and Part Two is more quiet, introspective, and personalized.

DH   I wondered about the aphorisms—the style of that, whether there was any particular influence.

HM   My style?

DH   Yes, in *Book of Life*. The short sayings and precepts.

HM   That's an African influence, African proverbs influence on Part Two. But in the new book—it's unlike much of the poetry I've ever written. A lot of it is completely different. Some prose poetry. The lines and structure in many cases are different from other poetry that I've written. It will be the first book of poetry since '73. There will be about seventy-five poems.

DH   You said the lines and structure are different. In what way and from what influence?

HM   Well, again, influence is always what's the best way to communicate. And so where I would, maybe, start a poem off with the traditional way—maybe one stanza would be the traditional poetry, free verse poetry—maybe the next stanza or two stanzas would be prose poetry, where I might use the paragraph form and still try to construct the words in a poetic manner.

DH   In other words, the form is an extension of the content.

HM   Right. And the content varies but of course is dealing with the whole struggle. But a lot of poems are a lot more personal than I have been in the past. I didn't get personal about myself, really, until the introductory essay in *Enemies*, and maybe a few of the poems throughout the earlier books. But otherwise I stayed in the background.

DH   (Pause). Well, I want to thank you very, very much.

HM   You're welcome.

Haki R. Madhubuti (Don L. Lee): Works Cited and Suggested

Poetry

Think Black! Detroit: Broadside Press, 1967.
Black Pride. Detroit: Broadside Press, 1968.
Don't Cry, Scream. Detroit: Broadside Press, 1969.
We Walk the Way of the New World. Detroit: Broadside Press, 1970.
Directionscore: Selected and New Poems. Detroit: Broadside Press, 1971.
Kwanzaa. Chicago: Third World Press, 1972.
Book of Life. Chicago: Third World Press, 1973.
Earthquakes and Sun Rise Missions: Poetry and Essays of Black Renewal, 1973-1983. Chicago: Third World Press, 1984. (Cited as *ESM*.)
Killing Memory, Seeking Ancestors. Detroit: Lotus Press, 1987.

Prose

Dynamite Voices I: Black Poets of the 1960's. Detroit: Broadside Press, 1971.

From Plan to Planet: Life Studies, The Need for Afrikan Minds and Institu-
tions. Detroit: Broadside Press; Chicago: Institute of Positive Education,
1973.
A Capsule Course in Black Poetry Writing (coauthor). Detroit: Broadside
Press, 1975.
Enemies: The Clash of Races. Chicago: Third World Press. 1978.
Say That the River Turns: The Impact of Gwendolyn Brooks (editor).
Chicago: Third World Press, 1987.
Black Men: Obsolete, Single, Dangerous? Essays in Discovery, Solutions,
Hope. Chicago: Third World Press, 1989 [forthcoming].

Recordings

Rappin' & Readin'. Broadside Voices, 1970.
Rise, Vision, Comin. Institute of Positive Education, 1976.

Notes

1. *Enemies: The Clash of Races* (1978), introd. ii. Cited as *Enemies.*
2. In a recent interview with Kevin Johnson, Madhubuti observed that
he had wanted to be a jazz musician until *Black Boy* "introduced me to
myself" (*Chicago Tribune,* Dec. 23, 1987, sec. 5, p. 3).
3. David Llorens, "Black Don Lee," *Ebony* 24 (March 1969): 74.
4. Brent Staples, "A Third World Bookstore," *Chicago Journal* 4, no.
25 (Feb. 27, 1980): 6.
5. See n. 21 below.
5. Helen Vendler, "Good Black Poems, One by One," *New York Times*
Book Review, Sept. 29, 1974, pp. 3-16.
7. Annette Oliver Shands, "The Relevancy of Don L. Lee as a Contem-
porary Black Poet," *Black World* 21 (June 1972): 35-48.
8. Baraka and Madhubuti both participated in the Congress of Afrikan
Peoples (CAP), which was inaugurated in 1970 in Atlanta. The Institute of
Positive Education was originally conceived as a chapter of CAP.
9. John A. Williams, "The Harlem Renaissance: Its Artists, Its Impact,
Its Meaning," *Black World* 20 (Nov. 1970): 17-18, makes a useful distinction
between "Renaissance I" of the 1920s and 1930s and "Renaissance II" of the
1960s, seeing the first as cultural, the second as political.
10. The interview with Madhubuti took place at the Palmer House in
Chicago, July 8, 1980. The poet articulated his ideas—even the most radical
and controversial—with a reflective candor, attending carefully to each topic.
On Sunday, June 11, 1989, we spoke by telephone about a number of ques-

tions I had posed regarding this chapter. One of his replies appears in the next paragraph.

11. See Parks, ed., *Nommo*, Chapter 2, n. 19. See also Paul Carter Harrison, *The Drama of Nommo* (New York: Grove Press, 1972, which perceives *nommo*, a oneness with the life force, in all phases of Black life.

12. Cf. Baraka's major poem "In the Tradition"; see Chapter 6 below.

13. The following workshops and participants were scheduled: "The Writer and His/Her Social Responsibility" (Gwendolyn Brooks, Sonia Sanchez, Mari Evans, Sterling Plumpp); "John Killens and James Baldwin: Their Legacy, Their Work" (Acklyn Lynch, Eugenia Collier); "The Art and Business of Publishing" (Haki R. Madhubuti, Eugene Redmond); "Racially Motivated Attacks" (James Turner); "Perspective on Sex Socialization" (Vivian Gordon, Useni Eugene Perkins); "Afrocentricity" (Molefi Asante); "African-American Theatre: Its Meaning for Writers" (Woodie King, Jr., Ruby Dee, Kalamu Ya Salaam); "The Problem of White World Supremacy" (Frances Cress Welsing).

14. The 1980 Black riots in Miami (see Chapter 2, n. 12) were very much in the news at the time of this interview.

15. Andrew Young served as ambassador to the United Nations, 1977-79; from 1981 on he has been mayor of Atlanta. Donald F. McHenry, appointed by President Jimmy Carter to succeed Young at the U.N. in September 1979, served until the end of Carter's tenure in 1980.

16. Haki R. Madhubuti, "Anti-Semitism as Weapon and the Jewish Mis-Use of Blacks in Their Struggle for Power and Maximum Development," in "Blacks and Jews" issue, *Black Books Bulletin 5* (Winter 1977): 24-29, 72-74.

17. This view pervades Madhubuti's thinking and his prose writings. See also his article "Land and Survival," *Black Books Bulletin 7* (Winter 1982): 4-7, 35. He continues to feel that Black people do not own the significant amount of land needed for production and that, for all practical purposes, they remain landless. He reaffirmed his assessment in a telephone conversation, Feb. 28, 1988.

18. Since this interview, however, rapidly increasing rents and the rush to replace low-rise commercial and residential buildings with expensive, high-rise cooperatives and condominiums have been developing a socioeconomic stratification that threatens integration.

19. In *Enemies*, Madhubuti cites *Ujamaa* as one of the seven principles (*Nguzo Saba*) of Kawaida, which he, like Baraka, refers to as a "Black Value System" (p. 120). Madhubuti adapts the economic principle to represent "Cooperative Economics and Extend Family." (See Chapter 6, n. 19, below.)

20. "Not Allowed to Be Lovers: Black Men and Women in the Struggle for Meaning, Family, and Future," *Black Books Bulletin 6*, no. 4 (1980): 48-57, 71. Madhubuti also refers to Robert Staples, *The World of Black Singles: Changing Patterns of Male/Female Relations* (Westport, Conn.: Greenwood, 1981).

21. Chancellor Williams, *The Destruction of Black Civilization: Great*

Issues of a Race from 4500 B.C. to 2000 A.D. (Chicago: Third World Press, 1974).

22. Although Madhubuti's thinking as well as his poetry had been, in the 1960s, allied with and influenced by Baraka, the Sixth Pan-African Congress, held at Dar es Salaam, Tanzania, in 1974 and attended by both poets (Baraka as the chairman of CAP), marked what may be called the "great schism" among Black intellectuals. The Congress called for an end to both colonialism and neocolonialism and proposed "class struggle in the African world," as Baraka pointed out in *Black Scholar* (Oct. 1974, p. 44); it marked the struggle as to the direction Black destiny should take—toward "Nationalism, Pan-Africanism, or Socialism," as the choice was put by Maulana Ron Karenga in the same issue (pp. 21-31). As the debate raged, Madhubuti and Baraka were among the chief post-Congress antagonists.

23. *GB*, 245, n. 8 (the book was in progress at the time of this interview). The reference is to Louis Simpson's review of Brooks's *Selected Poems*, expressing doubts that a Negro can "write well without making us aware he is a Negro," and stating that "if being a Negro is the only subject, the writing is not important" (*New York Herald Tribune Book Week*, Oct. 27, 1963, 27).

Gordon R. Robotham

4. SONIA SANCHEZ
The Will and the Spirit

Dynamic: the word immediately describes Sonia Sanchez and her art. Petite, attractive, on the stage she seems to become physically larger. Born to Wilson L. and the late Lena (Jones) Driver on September 9, 1934, in Birmingham, Alabama, Sanchez was named Wilsonia after her father, who had wanted a boy. She has an older sister, Patricia; her half-brother, Wilson Driver, Jr., died in 1981.

At the age of nine, Sanchez moved with her family to New York, where she attended elementary school, junior high, and George Washington High School. She was graduated from Hunter College in 1955. Selected for a poetry workshop, she studied at New York University with Louise Bogan, for whom she has the highest respect. Her daughter, Anita Sanchez, product of an early marriage, was born on May 24, 1957. Twin sons—Morani Meusi ("Black Warrior" in Swahili) and Mungu Meusi ("Black God")— were born on January 26, 1968.

Sanchez has taught at several colleges, beginning with San Francisco State (1967-69). There she helped to introduce the first Black studies program in the United States; it was chaired by Nathan Hare. Sanchez brought Amiri Baraka to the campus as the first Black invited to do cultural work, which chiefly involved producing his own plays. She has also taught at the University of Pittsburgh (1969-70), Rutgers University (1970-71), Manhattan Community College (1971-73), and Amherst College (1972-75). Since 1977 she has been teaching at Temple University, where she offers courses in creative writing, Black literature, and women's studies. Currently, she is the Laura H. Carnell Professor of English—the first Black to hold a chair at Temple—and the university's first Presidential Fellow.

The poet has also taught at Graterford Prison as part of a community writing program since the fall of 1980, and she has lectured at more than 500 U.S. colleges and universities. "I get a lot of joy out of teaching," she told me during our interview.[1] "I think it is important for those who have vision to be around students and see what this country is about and have them see their relationship to their parents. . . . A teacher can give them a sense of reality, a sense of the future, of what can be, what they can be. It makes them take chances, bring new ideas and new possibilities into the curriculum."

In the 1970s, her reputation grew as a figure in the new Black poetry and in the drive to establish college-level Black studies programs. For three years Sanchez gave a poetry workshop at the Countee Cullen Library in Harlem and later for another three years at the Afro/American Historical and Cultural Museum in Philadelphia. The anthology *three hundred and sixty degrees of blackness comin at you* (1971), culled from her Countee Cullen students' writings, includes poetry, short stories, and plays.

In 1972, as part of a cultural tour, Sanchez traveled to Guyana, Bermuda, and Jamaica; the following year she visited the People's Republic of China. She went to Cuba in the summer of 1979, on a tour sponsored by the Venceremos Brigade, and she has also read her poetry in England, Australia, Nicaragua, Norway, and Canada.

Sanchez's honors and awards increase. She was recipient of a National Endowment for the Arts fellowship in 1978-79 and the Lucretia Mott Award in 1984; the following year she won the American Book Award in poetry. In 1988, she received the Pennsylvania Governor's Award for Excellence in the Humanities, an honorary doctorate from Trinity College in Hartford, Connecticut, and the Peace and Freedom Award of the Women's International League for Peace and Freedom. The next year she was chosen to receive the Paul Robeson Social Justice Award.

Introducing her first book, *Homecoming* (1969), Haki Madhubuti (then Don L. Lee) notes: "Black people's reality is controlled by alien forces. This is why Sonia Sanchez is so beautiful & needed; this is also why she is dangerous" (p. 7). He sees her poetry as love poetry, "the love of self & people," negating negative influences, inspiring pride and hope.

The book's title poem tells of her daily return to Harlem from a college situated on luxurious Park Avenue:

i returned tourist
style to watch all
the niggers killing themselves
3 for oners
with needles
that
cd
not support
their stutters.

Stuttering becomes a metaphor of weakness. The poet's renewal of Black identity is a "home-coming,"[2] but she sees the self-destructive anger in her people and seeks to reverse its path. In "nigger," she scores the use of the word among Black people and points the way to pride: "i know i am black. / beautiful. / with meaning. / nigger. u say. / my man / you   way behind the set." The last phrase conveys being behind the times, not keeping up with the "set," the music being played; the term has come into general use at poetry readings. (Sanchez also favors the word *gig*, originally meaning a jazz musician's job, in referring to her reading engagements.) There is a sense of colloquial, up-to-the-minute speech in her verse, together with the quickness of speedwriting ("cd" for "could," frequently) and other unconventional, attention-getting devices: words fully capitalized; words scattered on the page in relation to breath and emphasis; change of pace. The poem "to CHucK" parodies the style of e. e. cummings ("i'm gonna write me / a poem like / e. e. / cum / mings to / day."). It shows to advantage Sanchez's humor, admits of self-parody, and defends her lyricism while it acknowledges her model's liberating features.

Her poetic technique may be experimental, but Sanchez's moral canon is a stern one, issuing from self-discipline. Like Madhubuti, she is a vegetarian who neither smokes nor drinks alcoholic beverages, and she too views love as properly heterosexual and family-oriented. While she does not share his impatience with homosexuality, she can, as she says in "to a jealous cat," "jokingly" chide her man "that jealousy's / a form of homosexuality." She differs radically from Madhubuti, however, in favoring interracial coalitions to organize political action.

The personal poems in *Homecoming* are self-revelatory: full of anger and compassion for her sisters, edged with loneliness and melancholy introspection. The touching lyric "poem at thirty" reflects upon her childhood, when "i walked two / miles in my sleep," and depicts a poet who is still "traveling. i'm / always traveling." In a powerful image of isolation, the speaker describes nights spent "on a / brown couch when / i wrapped my / bones in lint and / refused to move." Then, in a gesture to another isolated being, she calls:

> you you black man
> stretching scraping
> the mold from your body.
> here is my hand.
> i am not afraid
> of the night.

The poem, begun in solitude, at midnight, in a time of decision, at thirty, looks past early youth and struggles out of the self that "no one touches" anymore toward the maturity of loving.

Again in first person, "summary," "a poem for the world / for the slow suicides / in seclusion," describes an unhappy "stuttering self" that projects its misery onto a perfidious American culture. Poems "to all brothers" and "to all sisters" attack Black stereotypes of white women as desirable or as exemplary. Sanchez assures her Black sisters that the white woman has no advantage except her whiteness; that Black men are superior and worth loving, even though love may bring pain: "hurt ain't the bag u / shd be in. / loving is / the bag, man." The poet seeks to elevate the pride of both sexes, thus turning them to each other.

Of the political pieces, some address heroic figures: Malcolm X, Bobby Hutton of the Black Panthers, saxophonist Pharaoh Sanders. Others are general, like "small comment," a lesson in compulsive inquiry.

> the nature of the beast is the
> man or to be more specific
> the nature of the man is his
> bestial nature or to

bring it to its elemental terms
the nature of nature is
the bestial survival of the
fittest the strongest the richest.

The "man" is, of course, the white man.

Like many elegies by Black poets for the slain leader, "mal-
colm" elicits some of its author's most moving lines and images. Its
anger reflects Malcolm's own ("he said, 'fuck you white / man. we
have been / curled too long. nothing / is sacred now' "), yet it
articulates an overwhelming sorrow. The poet, who will "breathe /
his breath and mourn / my gun-filled nights," knows that she too
will die and asserts with delicacy that "violets like castanets / will
echo me." As she merges with the fallen Malcolm, "what could
have been / floods the womb until i drown." But the womb con-
notes procreation and continuity. Though the grieving poet main-
tains "death is my pulse," she has assured us from the beginning
that she rejects martyrdom: "i don't believe in dying."

Another political poem, "the final solution," ironically sub-
titled "the leaders speak," asserts that sending Black men to fight in
Vietnam is America's version of genocide. A triptych, "Memorial,"
comprises "1. the supremes—cuz they dead," a rebuke to the
singing group as "bleached"; "2. bobby hutton," an angry elegy
that ranks the Black Panther leader, martyred by policemen's bul-
lets, with Denmark Vesey, Malcolm X, Marcus Garvey; and "3. rev
pimps," a poem that mocks the translation of Black revolutionary
fervor into sensuality: "ain't nothing political / bout fucking," the
poet admonishes.

Two poems—"definition for blk/children" ("a policeman / is a
pig / and he shd be in / a zoo") and "poem (for dcs 8th graders—
1966-67)," the latter exhorting the capital's children to consider
their proud history and Blackness—target the thinking of Black
children. The volume concludes with "personal letter no. 2,"
another cry of loneliness that ends, nevertheless, with courage:
"but i am what i am what i / am. woman. alone / amid all this
noise," yet aware of realities and willing to face them.

We a BaddDDD People, published in 1970, was criticized for
its "noisy exhortation."[3] Haki Madhubuti found fault with its
shrill sixties rhetoric; like Dudley Randall, who wrote the intro-
duction, he preferred her more personal poems.[4] Randall's intro-

duction comments: "Some of her poems are political, but I think the most moving are those in which she talks of man and woman, of women and of drug addiction. It is apparent that she has suffered during the writing of this book. Her suffering has moved her to song, sometimes to inarticulate screams" (p. 10).

Suffering, much of it related to her marriage to Etheridge Knight (who had a drug problem), and political fervor mark this volume. It is dedicated to "blk/wooomen: the only queens of this universe." A breathless racing to uplift reveals most of the poems as rescue attempts that sometimes grasp quickly at facile rhetoric—as does "221-1424 (San/francisco/suicide/number)," which opens the first section, "Survival Poems." Yet its monologue dramatizes the ironic situation: a Black expressing rage, then feeling better and advising the "honky" at the suicide prevention number to "hang it up." The most personal, "a poem for my father," exposes a young woman's chagrin at the love affairs and six marriages of her father.

The main thrust of the book, however, is political. In "blk/ rhetoric," she asks:

> who's gonna give our young
> blk/people new heroes
>   (instead of catch / phrases)
>   (instead of cad / ill / acs)
>   (instead of pimps)

pointedly marking the syllables and words with a solidus: The automotive symbol of luxury and American capitalism is broken into "cad," "ill," and "acs"—negative images ("acs" suggests "aces," gambling, "acts," "axe").

In the first section, personal poems commingle with public ones. Her "hospital/poem (for etheridge. 9/29/69)" expresses the poet's feelings about her husband's immortality, despite medical predictions that he will die of drug abuse; "blk/chant" ("we pro-grammed fo death /") and "in the courtroom" attack the falsity of white justice for Blacks. Personal and social converge in "summer words of a sistuh addict," which movingly interprets a young girl's history, then asks, "sistuh. / did u / finally / learn how to hold yo/ mother?"

The second section, "Love/Songs/Chants," reveals Sanchez's ample lyric gifts. In her personal struggle with the man she loves, who is "on shit" (heroin), she mourns, tries to retrieve his spirit, fails, and identifies with Billie Holiday, also a drug victim, in "for our lady." Having uttered her love in "poem for etheridge," she turns to "a chant for young / brothas / & sistuhs," using her own tragedy of the man "who went out one day & died." The section ends with "blk / wooooomen / chant," a demand that Black men appreciate their women who have been

> waiten. waiten. WAITEN. WAITENNNNNN
>   A long AMURICAN wait.
> hurrrrreeehurrrrreeehurrrrreeeeeeeeeee

In this section typography registers intensity, shifts in emphasis, rhythmical beats and breaks.

The last group, "TCB/en Poems," carries the acronym for "Taking Care of Business," or meeting one's commitments efficiently (see Clarence Major's *Dictionary of Afro-American Slang*, 1970). The business here is "blk/nation/hood / builden," in which Malcolm X, Elijah Muhammad, and Amiri Baraka receive praise as "chiefs." "TCB" humorously criticizes the substitution of rhetoric for action. Repeating "wite/motha/fucka" with alternate endings of "whitey," "ofay," "devil," "pig," and so on, it concludes, "now. that it's all sed. / let's get to work."

Two of the strongest poems in the section, "we a baddDDD people (for gwendolyn brooks / a fo real bad one)" and "a/coltrane/ poem," reveal a vital jazz influence. Using an improvisational flux of rhythms, they sometimes attempt to imitate sounds of the instruments, confronting the reader with possibly baffling passages of words and sounds to be sung, to be chanted. Nevertheless, beyond the poet's deep concern with music and craft, it is their political meaning and usage that stir the roots of her art and determine her view of the contemporary scene.

Three years after *We a BaddDDD People*, having remarried and moved to Massachusetts to teach at Amherst, Sanchez entered a new creative phase, and her lyricism flourished. *Love Poems* (1973) abounds in haiku. There are poems of love and loss; of father/daughter (two sonnets), parent/child, and man/woman relationships, mostly difficult, at times ecstatic. As the author notes on the dust jacket, "These poems are the sun stretching / like red yellow butterflies across / the sea, / these poems are you and me running / toward each other hands reaching / out to hold the morning."

Sanchez's finest poetry, perhaps her strongest artistic achievement until *homegirls & handgrenades*, is represented by *A Blues Book for Blue Black Magical Women* (1974). In 1972 she had joined Elijah Muhammad's Nation of Islam; she left it in 1975. Of this "mountain-top poem," George E. Kent writes that it "possesses an extraordinary culmination of spiritual and poetic powers. It is in part an exhortation to move the rhythms of black life to a high peak through deep and deeper self-possession; in part, an address to all, with specific emphasis upon women; in part, a spiritual autobiography."[5] Dedicated to the poet's father and to Elijah Muhammad, "who had labored forty-two years to deliver us up from this western Babylon," the book begins with an introduction addressed to Black women. Sanchez urges them to "embrace / Blackness as a religion/husband" and to turn away from acquired, false Western values. Her voice is that of the poet as teacher, a guide at one with her audience yet standing a little apart in order to gain and share perspective.

The second and longest of the poem's five parts, "Past" details the poet's physical and spiritual growth, beginning with an invocation to the "earth mother," whose voice responds. Birth, adolescence, the move from South to North, painful childhood experiences with a stepmother, confusion of identity with white culture, and then the rejecting, "vomiting up the past" until

> i gave birth to myself,
> twice, in one hour.
> i became like Māāt,
> unalterable in my
> love of Black self and
> righteousness.
> and i heard the
> trumpets of a new age
> and i fell down
> upon the earth
> and became myself.

Part Three, "Present," lyrically affirms her faith in the Nation of Islam. In Part Four, "Rebirth," the poet returns to an ancestral home imaginatively inspired by Sanchez's travels in the Caribbean and China; a plane trip becomes a metaphor for her spiritual odyssey, "roaming the cold climate of my mind where / winter and summer hold the same temperature of need." Purified, the poet has "become like a temple," made her form from the form of Allah, and is "trying to be worthy."

Part Five, "Future," begins with a kind of Blakean vision of the "day of accounting,"

> When the sun spins and rises in the West
> when the stars lose their boundaries
> when ancient animals walk together
> when the oceans recede

It continues with a series of five visions and concludes with a hypnotic chant of constant creation: "in the beginning / there was no end." The repeated chant leads to the exhortation to "begin again the / circle of Blackness," which introduces the closing lines:

> me and you
> me and you
> you and me
> me and you
> you and me
> me, me, meeeeEEE
> you, you, YOUUU
> & have no beginning
> or endddDDDDD!

I've Been a Woman (1978) presents selections from the previous four books plus two sections of new poems: "Haikus/Tankas & Other Love Syllables," and "Generations," the latter importantly celebrating a heroic heritage. "A Poem for Sterling Brown," one of two tributes to him, reveres him as a "griot of fire / . . . griot of the wind," with language and imagery that suggest Africa and its music. In the sonnet "Father and Daughter," the poet at last comes to terms with the relationship. And the final eulogy, the stirring "Kwa mama zetu waliotuzaa" (for our mothers who gave us birth), proclaims that Shirley Graham Du Bois, widow of the renowned "W. E. B.," "has died in china / and her death demands a capsizing of tides." By coincidence, the poet's stepmother died in the same year, 1977.

Sanchez's closeness to her own children sparks her interest, like that of Gwendolyn Brooks, in writing children's literature. *It's a New Day (poems for young brothas and sistuhs)*, published in 1971, is filled with inspirational poems that are "teachen new songs to our children . . . cuz we be a new people in a new land / and it will be ours." *The Adventures of Fathead, Smallhead, and Squarehead* (1973), an illustrated story about three friends on a pilgrimage to Mecca, teaches that "Slow is not always dumb / and fast is not always smart," and that "Just as a lion is never dangerous without a head / so a people never progress without a leader." *A Sound Investment* (1980) comprises short stories for young readers, moral tales followed by discussion questions. Sanchez is also drawn toward writing plays, chiefly one-acters in a variety of forms, which deal with the world as it is for Black people and seek to change it. In both poetry and drama, she maintains that she is trying to reach "all kinds of audiences."

Sanchez's next collection, *homegirls & handgrenades* (1984), earned the 1985 American Book Award in poetry. "I enjoyed doing that book," she told me, "because I was able to celebrate some homegirls and homeboys, like 'Bubba' and 'Norma,' who needed to be celebrated but never came through the Harlems of the world."[6] The volume takes the spiritual force from *A Blues Book* and applies it to social action. "Handgrenades," she explains, "are the words I use to explode myths about people, about ourselves, about how we live and what we think, because this is really the last chance we have in this country."[7] The image also evokes guerilla warfare and the various worldwide struggles for liberation. As in the work of Jayne Cortez (see Chapter 5), there is a strong influx of African and Latino influences, both in language and in the selection of heroes. There is also a continuation of the blues mode, love poems, and haiku.

A significant development is the abundance of poetic stories and prose poems that create their own fluid forms. In "Bluebirdbluebirdthrumywindow," a rhetorical question-and-answer form shifts quickly to harsh realism. This account of a chance encounter in a Pennsylvania Station restroom epitomizes the life of a homeless woman, a "beached black whale" who retains the will to keep going on; who, appreciating the gift of five dollars, advises, "Don't never go to sleep on the world, girl. . . . Keep yo' eyes open all the time." The story brings to mind Sanchez's observation in our interview and at the twentieth anniversary celebration of Third World Press: "The will is a muscle. You've got to exercise the will." "Just Don't Never Give Up on Love," recounts a conversation with an old woman on a park bench. "After Saturday Nite Comes Sunday" searingly describes the impact of drugs on a young family. "Norma" and "Bubba" tell of bright friends from the poet's childhood, two who stayed behind in Harlem among the rubble of their thwarted dreams. All the pieces are poetic, autobiographical. Focusing on youth, survival, and hope, they reveal the compassionate immediacy with which Sanchez relates to the lost ones of society; they express her felt responsibility to articulate their despair.

The richness of that voice culminates in the public poems of the last section. "Reflections After the June 12th March for Disarmament," introduced with "I have come to you tonite out of the depths / of slavery / from white hands peeling black skins over / america," is a speech poem, its parallel syntax invoking both secular and religious oratory. Sanchez makes historical connections, distinguishes between "humanitarians" and "inhumanitarians," and scores "the proliferation / of nuclear minds, of nuclear generals / of nuclear presidents, of nuclear scientists, / who spread human and nuclear waste / over the world."

Two open letters show the poet reaching for still another form of poetic discourse. While Brooks's "verse journalism" is clearly both verse *and* journalism, Sanchez's "A Letter to Ezekiel Mphahlele"—the South African writer-in-exile, returning home after twenty years—is a prose poem. "Bravery is no easy taste to swallow," it comments. "A Letter to Dr. Martin Luther King," on the other hand, breaks new poetic ground with a letter-prophecy to celebrate what would have been the civil rights leader's fifty-fourth birthday. The transition from a friendly, poetic prose that recapitulates the years following his death moves by stages to a chant ("ke wa rona," he is ours) listing great figures from Black history and anticipating the future: "Great God, Martin, what a morning it will be!"

"MIA's (missing in action and other atlantas)" is a major work in which visionary hopefulness transforms anger and pain into a Third World working-class call to action. Interspersed with Spanish and Zulu, it explodes its real and surreal images to light a landscape of suffering from Atlanta to Johannesburg, South Africa. The poem is structured around a trio of tragic circumstances: the series of child murders in Atlanta; the murder of Stephen Biko in jail in Port Elizabeth; and the revolution in El Salvador. The three sections approach their subjects with subtle differences: the first utilizes Black English as spoken by the victims; the second employs Zulu and ironically narrates in the voices of the jailers and the government; the third, its surrealism reminiscent of Pablo Neruda, sounds a refrain in Spanish, "quiero ser libre" (I want to be free), which extends "yebo madola" (come on men and women) in the preceding African section. Thus the theme obliterates geographical borders and takes a global perspective on Black solidarity and liberation. The concluding section moves to the imperative:

> plant yourself in the eyes of the
> children who have died carving out their
> own childhood.
> plant yourself in the dreams of the people
> scattered by morning bullets

Sanchez's quicksilver transitions and skillful tesselating make for excitement and dramatic expansion, for connections that draw the reader/listener through a widening terrain of action and sensibility.

The newest book by Sanchez, *Under a Soprano Sky* (1987), is dedicated to her father and to her late brother, Wilson Driver, Jr. The new poetry carries forward the poet's lyricism, her political commitment, her confessional/moral declensions, and what may be called her transcendental imagery: sensory images infused with spiritual awareness. Three elegies set the tone. "A poem for my brother (reflections on his death from AIDS: June 8, 1981)" is a brave poem that identifies the poet's life journey with her brother's journey into death. Its nature imagery and transcendence of death take it into the grand precincts of pastoral elegy.

> you in the crow's rain
> rusting amid ribs
> my mouth spills your birth
> i have named you prince of boards
> stretching with the tides.
>
> you in the toad's tongue
> peeling on nerves
> look. look. the earth is running palms.

The crow as death image also invokes Jim Crow discrimination, and "ribs" and "rust" have material connotations—the frame of a ship, a bridge, a skeleton, discarded food, a garbage heap, rust/dust (recalling "dust to dust"). But the context of sacred imagery overtakes the secular: Adam's rib, the unity of male and female; even more critically, the nails of crucifixion and the final piercing of Jesus at the rib.

The second of the three, "elegy (for MOVE and Philadelphia)," a strong, ambitious work in eight parts, treats of the "philadelphia based back to nature group" (as MOVE is described in a footnote) whose headquarters were bombed by the police, with the mayor's approval, on May 13, 1985, killing men, women, and children and destroying a block of houses in the ensuing fire. The tragedy gained national notoriety. The poet relates the events with heavy irony, through which she weaves biblical lamentation: "who anointeth this city with napalm? / who giveth this city in holy infanticide?" She concludes, however, with traces of hope: since "there are people / navigating the breath of hurricanes," there may be "honor and peace. / one day." In the related third elegy, "Philadelphia: Spring, 1985," a Philadelphia fireman reflects on the carnage after seeing a decapitated body in the MOVE ruins, when "the city, lit by a single fire, / followed the air into disorder."

A further extension of Sanchez's range appears in her attention to the visual arts. "At the Gallery of La Casa De Las Americas, Habana, dec. 1984" responds to two artworks, Arnold Belkin's *Attica* and Roberto Malta's *Chile: Sin Título*. The first poem provides a companion to the painting; the poet had visited Attica after the 1976 massacre of prisoners following an uprising. The second seems to use the painting to precipitate a vernacular indictment of the cultural wasteland back home.

In "Section Two," an interesting trilogy, "3 X 3," presents three monologues, each carefully made into eleven lines of matching parallel and incantatory syntax: "shigeko: a hiroshima maiden speaks," "Carl: a Black man Speaks," and "the poet: speaks after silence." The triptych becomes a lament for past, present, and future. Birth is not "trailing clouds of glory" from God and heaven, as Wordsworth believed; heaven for Shigeko is a "bleached sky that dropped silver"; the Black man comes from a white hell; the poet's future is "going unstyled into a cave," "a bluerain that drowns green crystals," suggesting a fallout of grief and premature death and the final knowledge, "I am going to die." Structural and linear equation support the triadic view: all are victims, doomed by the same forces.

In the third section, which celebrates Blackness, the major contribution is a moving tribute to Sanchez's paternal grandmother, Elizabeth ("Lizzie"), who died when the poet was six. "Dear Mama" is a letter poem, falling within the epistolary genre introduced in *homegirls & handgrenades* but more closely autobiographical. It details the gentleness and understanding bequeathed to Sanchez by "a long line of Lizzies who made me understand love. Sharing. Holding a child up to the stars. Holding your tribe in a grip of love. A long line of Black people holding each other up against silence." The poet remembers the woman's laughter, her music, and her respect for her granddaughter's identity:

> I still hear your humming Mama. The color of your song
> calls me home. The color of your words saying "Let her be.
> She got a right to be different. She gonna stumble on
> herself one of these days. Just let the child be."
>
> And I be Mama.

The fourth section is a series of carefully crafted love poems, often haiku or tankas, with one outstanding example of the blues, and the fifth mainly concerns children and displays a strong African motif. It opens with Bantu sayings: "We are the fire that burns the country" and "no one plans alone." The closely rhymed "Song No. 2" adapts the blues, recalling Houston A. Baker's words on the back cover, "She has formed a blue/black sound and transmitted it to the 'people' to make us free." "Endings," the epilogue, comprises a flourish of poetic prose, philosophical prose poems, and closes with the compelling, didactic lyricism of "Graduation Notes," directed at the young, particularly her sons Mungu and Morani.

The title poem, which opens the book, is an exquisite lyric that also bears on youth. It describes growing up into womanhood in earth-embracing strophes Dylan Thomas might have envied.

> once i lived on pillars in a green house
> boarded by lilacs that rocked voices into weeds.
> i bled an owl's blood

shredding the grass until i
rocked in a choir of worms.

Where Cortez (Chapter 5) explodes the body into a political
landscape, Sanchez sings it into transcendental unities. She appre-
hends its communion with nature and with itself. And when she
concludes, "under a soprano sky, a woman sings, / lovely as chan-
deliers," she is unmistakably a woman shaping her essence into an
art that reflects its prismic light.

Sanchez believes in a feminine sensibility. "Women are quite
different from men in what they feel and think and how they view
the world. I use feminine imagery which is drawn from ancient
cultures. . . . a lot of my poetry expresses what it means to let
people feel sweetness and power running together, hate and love
running together, beauty and ugliness also running together. . . .
My work, really, has always been motivated by love" (PPR, 357,
365). This view is consistent with her political activism. At the
Third World Press Twentieth Anniversary Conference in December
1987, she declared, "Because we love the country, we challenge the
country," and called Blacks to "expel the myths regarding Black
people."[8]

Two awards were bestowed on Sanchez at the anniversary
celebration. One, a surprise she shared with co-recipient Mari
Evans, was the first George Kent Award, established by Gwendolyn
Brooks. In accepting a Builder's Award from Haki Madhubuti and
Third World Press, she gave a rousing speech and, reaching a state
of spiritual intensity, seemed to relive the cries of children suffering
in South Africa and in the MOVE disaster of Philadelphia. She once
described how she "shook" when the chant came out in the
writing of the Martin Luther King poem in homegirls: "Forces had
come to me while I wrote it and I did exactly what they wanted me
to do" (PPR, 358).

Regarding her interest in African religions, Sanchez has ob-
served, "I was bringing into the arena of poetry the sense of another
sensibility, another way of looking at the world, another life force."
She does not flinch from "what might be considered a metaphysical
concept, this collective unconscious," because "I'm . . . using my
relationship to it to change real things" (PPR, 368). That purpose
does not waver: to alter society and to organize it, from the home,
the church, the school, the community. As it is for Madhubuti, the

word *serious* is frequently on her lips. "We are serious people," she says, and offers her life of commitment.

INTERVIEW WITH SONIA SANCHEZ

DH   What was the first art form that interested you? When did you start writing, and was poetry your first genre of expression?

SS   I think the first art form was poetry. I first started to write poetry when I was a little girl in Alabama. As a child I stuttered, and I was what Black people call "tongue-tied," too. It was a hell of a combination. [*Laughs*] So I would go, "Det-det-det-uhm"; I would go "Ah-ah-ah-ah-ah-ah-ah—I." I was a very introspective kind of child as a consequence of that, and I started to write these little things on paper, and someone finally told me, "That's a poem," and I said "Oh!" And I just kept writing.

When we moved to New York, I continued to write, didn't show it to anyone, actually. One day my stepmother called me into the kitchen. You know how children wash dishes sometimes. I mean the dishes aren't clean, and she had, the way mothers do, she had decided to fill up that sink with hot water again, and she proceeded to put the dishes—all the dishes—back into the sink. She said they were greasy; what a terrible job I had done. And so when I heard her call, I ran, because the kind of call she actually sent into that bedroom was like, "You'd better get here in one minute, Sonia." So, I was writing a poem, and I left the poem on the bed, something I never did. No one knew that I wrote poetry in that house or had continued to write poetry. And I ran in there and I said, "Just a minute." She says, "Right now, young lady." So I was—sort of like I had to do it at that point. Well, while I was washing dishes, out comes my sister with the poem in her hand, and I reached for it with my soapy hands, and she pulled away, and the whole family was in the kitchen, and she started to read this poem that I had written. I don't have a copy of it; I wish I did, about George Washington crossing the Delaware [*laughter*]—you can imagine, right? Because we were home on holiday that day; it was George Washington's birthday, when it was celebrated on the twenty-second. And she read this poem, "Da-da, da-da, da-da, da-da, da-da, da-da, da-da." Well, I was utterly mortified. I was utterly hurt, and I felt so betrayed. So I grabbed—I finally grabbed it and took it into the bedroom and hid it someplace, and I came back, and they were all laughing at this poem I had written, and I was very much upset. So, from that point on, no one actually knew that I was still writing, because they never found anything.

I would write at the darndest times. I would, in the middle of the night, get up and go to the bathroom when I was supposed to be, and everyone else was, sleeping, and sit on the toilet and read. I used to keep books underneath those bathtubs, old-fashioned bathtubs—they had yet a lot of space underneath—I guess the old-fashioned ones that people pay a lot of money for these days. And I would slip my books—we lived in an old building in Harlem—and I slipped my books underneath there. So I would come into the bathroom about three o'clock in the morning, because I couldn't read in the bedroom. My sister would complain with the light on. So I'd come into the bathroom and read from about three until six in the morning, or write, and keep my little book. I had no idea what happened to that book—the book I used to have. To this day I just can't trace it anyplace. I know once, when I was in college and I took a writing class, it was just a very traumatic experience for me. The person really didn't want to get involved with what I was writing about. I remember coming home and tearing up stuff. And so I could have very well torn that [book] up and pitched it out.

DH   You said that you stuttered. Now you are a beautifully articulate person. How did you get over it? Was it the poetry that helped you?

SS   When I was in high school—you know in high school when you have to give all these damn speeches?—

DH   Yes.

SS   We were in a speech class, and the most terrible time for me was to get up and give a speech, or to open my mouth and say anything. I just very seldom talked to anyone, period. As I was studying this speech, oh, almost day in and day—every night. And I would read this speech for my sister—she says, "Oh, it's fine, it's fine." But what she meant by that was that she understood what I said, and so she had no difficulty with the way I presented it. But I was determined that I was going to give this speech without one stutter, because everybody, I was sure, was just laying for me to get up and make this speech and then to try and speak very fast at the same time and just wreck this whole thing. So when I got up to give my speech—and I was about the last person to give a speech, too—I took my nails and literally dug my nails into my hand like this. [*Gestures*] And when I finished, I saw blood. And every time I heard a stutter begin, I would just go—[*gestures again*].

DH   That's amazing. You taught yourself, really, to stop. You conditioned yourself.

SS   That's exactly what it was all about. Every time I felt pain, I would just—[*gestures*]. It wouldn't come out. When I finished, I said to my sister—we were in the same class—I said, "How was I? How was I?" She said, "It was okay." I said, "No, but how *was* I?" What I was really asking her was, had I stuttered. And she really hadn't paid any attention to it at all, because she was accustomed to the way I spoke. But the difficult part about a stutterer is that he or she always hears the stutters, you see, in the back of the head. So for years, even though I didn't stutter, I always heard the stuttering. So it didn't make me all of a sudden, since I had "conquered" that—in quotes, okay—think that I was then going to jump up and just be a fantastic speaker. I was still quiet in school.

DH   [*Laughs*] Yes. It's like a fat person losing weight and still seeing that fat person in the mirror.

SS   Yes. I still heard—in fact, even the first time I had a reading in New York, I was going to chicken out and not read, because I figured I would get up there and just, you know, go out, stutter, whatever. And finally I said, "I'm not going to read." And they said, "Of course, you're going to read! Other people are reading, so you just go on out." So I went out and read a couple of poems, and I came back and I said, "How was it?" And they said, "Fine, Sonia," and I said, "I mean, really, how was I?" I went to another person, and he said, "Okay, Sonia." They thought I was getting a big head! What I was really afraid to ask was had I stuttered, because I still heard the stutters.

And it took me years, I mean throughout college days I always would be talking and still would hear the stutters. I mean for *years*, years, years. It's almost ironical that I decided to go into something which required talk, speech, whatever. And I don't know why I chose that. The interesting thing, when I was in school, when I was in college, I would say I wanted to be a lawyer. I wanted to go to law school, and again, the choice of speaking. It's almost really sadistic, I thought. [*Laughs*]

DH   Sort of an act of will.

SS   Probably. Well, you know, my name is *Wil*sonia. My father's name is Wilson—

DH   Yes.

SS   —W-i-l-s-o-n. So they expected a boy and, as the custom sometimes is in the South, sometimes they have relatives naming you, and I guess he was so disgusted with having another girl that he called someone in the family and said, "Well, I have another girl. I have no name. We were going to call this boy coming 'Wilson,' and now I have another girl." So she said, "Don't worry, I'll help you out." So she called back, my father tells the story, a couple of hours later. She said, "Well, name her 'Wilsonia,' after you. Benita. Wilsonia Benita." [*Laughing*] So I had a tag called "Wilsonia Benita." And I always think that people do name you, on some levels, in some ways.

And you're right. I have always made use of the will as if it's a muscle, which needed to be exercised and trained and disciplined. And as a consequence, the only way I have ever been able to do anything is via disciplining myself, sometimes very harshly, I think. But otherwise I couldn't have done twelve books if I hadn't. I mean, working the way I've had to work, in my time, without that discipline.

DH   Who and what were some important influences on your work? Haki Madhubuti, with whom your work has been compared, feels there have been only Black influences on his poetry. How would you view your own art in this respect?

SS   I would say, when I first started to write, I read everything, and I still do, to this day. I read all poets, and when I teach in the classroom, I make my students read all poets. Period. Because they don't get much Black poetry, I would quite often read a lot of Black poets to them. Or because they don't get a lot of Latin poets or African poets, whatever, I will read a lot of that, also. I begin a class, always, with a poem that's not in the textbook that we have, and in that way, I'm always able to share other kinds of poets with them, which I think is important.

When I first started to write, I was reading—there's a librarian in my neighborhood, not actually my neighborhood but in the library, and she used to see me. I used to *live* in the library; I was in the library all the time. And finally she said, "Well, you read a lot." And I said, "Yes." And she says, "Do you like everything?" And I

said, "Yes." Well, the next time I came she had Langston Hughes
for me, and she had Gwen [Brooks], also, and someone else . . .
Pushkin, also. I never forget this Black woman who worked in that
library, the first Black woman I found in the library. She said, "This
man, you should read, because he was a Black man who lived in
Russia." And my head just kind of swirled with that information,
and I remember reading some of his poetry, not understanding it all
but being very much involved with the imagery, and just the sheer
words, the power of the words, et cetera.

But I would just go in at will and pick up a poet's work—it
didn't matter, really, who it was—and would read. In that manner, I
stumbled across a man by the name of [Federico García] Lorca, and
it was really wild, just roaming through that library. And to this day
I love Lorca, you know, for the passion that's involved with his
work. And I remember reading his plays and also some of the
things he had done at that time. . . .

It was also my smutty period. One of the reasons why I was
going to the library so often was because I was reading novels
[*laughter*] and I was reading all the good parts of the novels. I had to
go through the whole book to get to the good parts, sometimes.
And so I always maintain that, like you leave people alone, even
when they're going through a smutty period, because if they're
reading, it really doesn't matter what they read, as long as they
continue to read. . . . So I would come into the library and sit there
and read a whole book in about two or three hours, just because I
didn't want to take it home, because someone might have realized
what I was reading. But I would come home from the library with
five and six books and just stay in the bedroom and just really read.
It was a real escape for me and also a great joy to read.

In class last night over at Haverford [College] where I do the
Black autobiography course, we were talking about Zora Neale
Hurston—that was a book we were on, *Dust Tracks on a Road*—
and a lot of the students were trying to be very critical of her. And I
said, I understand the criticism, I mean, the criticisms on her in
terms of some of the things that she said, and the kind of motion
and movement she made, which I thought were unnecessary, con-
sidering what she was and who she was. And then I also read them
excerpts of letters that she had to write to her patron, and the
question I posed was, what was it like to have been a Black woman
artist in your grandmother's time? It's already harsh enough being

a Black *woman* in your grandmother's time, but to have been a Black woman *artist* in your grandmother's time is a very, very touchy, damaging, almost disturbing question to ask. Because if you can answer that, then I think that you have a right to give out this criticism on her. Period. And also, I said, the question has not been raised in this class: what was it really like in terms of the men writers around her, too? Because you can imagine, the chauvinism that exists today, imagine how heavy that chauvinism must have been in her time.

So I read everybody and I still do, and my students still do as a consequence. They've got to see how people phrase things, how they write what they write about, what they don't write about, because art, no matter what, reflects the culture it comes from. Some people say, and I always tell my students, all artists, all poets are political. Some just maintain the status quo; some talk about change. Period. So on that level we read some people, and we can see what they are doing. They are out there to maintain the status quo. And there are some who are out there to change.

Also I read Countee Cullen. We had to memorize. When we were South, I remembered Paul Laurence Dunbar, because a lot of that was recited in southern schools. I really didn't like Dunbar too much in terms of the dialect. But when I read dialect years later, written by Sterling Brown, I liked it. Something instinctive about Paul Laurence Dunbar told me that it was just too coy or too—it was just something there—it just didn't seem right in my head. But when I read the "dialect poems," in quotes, of Brown, or when I read the poems where he made use of dialect or Black English or whatever you want to call it, or "the speech of Black people," in quotes, who are not educated as such, I was not disturbed, because he painted them with dignity. They were not minstrels. But one always felt that Dunbar was dealing with minstrels. I mean they were like minstrel songs were running out of their hands and thighs and eyes. With Brown, I didn't feel that at all.

DH   You've written some fine tributes to Brown in *I've Been a Woman*. Beautiful tributes. Your reading, as well as your poetry, is both dramatic and musical. How did you develop your compelling style of presentation?

SS   . . . It occurred to me at some point, and I tend to think that was in San Francisco, because in San Francisco we really, many of us really got out, began to get our teeth into that whole reading bit. And you must remember, when we were reading poetry at that time, there was not that interest in poetry. Period. People had their ears tuned to radios and whatever, et cetera, and you know, something with a beat. So you had to engage people in a dialogue to draw them into what you were going to do. So I began to, when I got an audience that was like really rough or loud, or perhaps saying, "Well, what is this?" before someone comes on the scene, or "Where is this poet coming from?" before the dance or whatever, I began to talk about what the poem was about, or something about the poem which would lead right into the poem. And then you had people, they'd listen to what you said, and then, when you had their ear, you'd take them into a poem.

DH   This was in the early sixties.

SS   This was in the early sixties. This was also when the poetry began to change and move towards Black themes much more. We're talking about '65, '66. And what that meant simply was that, for some reason, I began to understand the need to integrate the talk with the poem—

DH   The rapping with the reading—

SS   Yes. Right. And as a consequence, you didn't know where one began and where the other one left off, et cetera. It was such an integration of the two—which I think is quite often important.

DH   *We A BaddDDD People*, especially, reflects the influence of jazz improvisation. Do you want the reader to improvise interpretation of some of the musical passages, or do you prefer an attempt to achieve a uniform rendition?

SS   I think that sometimes when people hear me read from *We A BaddDDD People*, they say to me, "I didn't read it that way," and I say, "That's okay." I think poetry works on many levels. One level is to come hear the poet read her/his work. Another level is to take the poem home and then read it to yourself, quietly, silently. And then at other times for you to read it aloud. And it doesn't really matter what that's all about. I always hear the music when I write. Now the difficulty before was that I did nothing with it. I might have made a notation, or I might have stretched out words, or I might have done things in a very choppy manner that would give a sense of musicality or nonmusicality. But I always heard some distant music someplace. . . .

One of the first poems that I did where I actually said "to be sung" was in *We A BaddDDD People*. It was "a coltrane poem," but I never read it aloud. I would read it at home. When I was writing the poem—I wrote that poem, actually (I always remember where I write a poem) I wrote that poem in Pittsburgh, and I wrote that poem when I was teaching at the University of Pittsburgh, and I never read it. It was just there in *We A BaddDDD People*, okay? When I got home to New York, someone had asked me to read it, and I said, "I will," but I didn't at a reading. I just finished a reading in New York and never did. I said, "Oh, yeah, I'll do it next time." Because I really didn't have the grasp. And I remember—I can see myself quite clearly at my father's house—practicing reading *We A BaddDDD People* for a gig and being dissatisfied, trying to re-collect the music I had heard at that particular time, and I couldn't get it.

Well, to make a long story short, I was going to a gig at Brown University, and we had bad weather, and we were late coming into that place. And by the time I got there it was like nine-thirty, ten o'clock, and the reading was supposed to be at eight, and people actually had stayed; they had gone to get something to eat and come back, and so I said, I'll have to give a good reading—these people have waited all this time. So I gave a long reading, about an hour and a half; I was really tired when I had finished. And one little hand went up in the audience and said [*laughs*], "Would you read the Coltrane poem?" Right? And I looked down, as if to say, "I'm tired; we've been circling this damn place for hours, and thinking we were going to run out of gas and have to go back to New York"; I mean it was really that kind of terrible kind of set. And then I said, "Well, since you've been such a good audience, I will."

So I read that poem. And I did the whole thing, from like banging on my thighs to singing and tapping my foot at the same time, and it was really interesting, the response. People actually started to stamp their feet and cheer. And, I don't know, wherever it was I was working—sometimes they send the things back to the universities when you're working, like "Professor So-and-So was here, and I thought you might want to hear"—and it seems that someone, an editor or a newspaperman, was in the audience, and when I finished reading that poem, which talks a lot about Rocke-fellers—

DH   Yes—

SS   —and very graphic things—

DH   Right—

SS   —that need to be done, he said that I was there instigating students, you know, to stretch people's necks, and [*laughing*] whatever whatever whatever. Because what they had done was they responded, not only response but aloud, standing up, going "Yeah!"—that kind of thing, and people actually were doing that, and I had never read that poem before.

When I started off I was so nervous, but the section that says, "are u sleepen / brotha john / brotha john," which is the Coltrane section in there, and then when I actually got to the part where I literally had to do the sounds that he had done, I kept thinking—I was like looking down in advance at it, saying, "How the hell are you going to do this?" and I didn't really remember it. But the crowd was with me. It's amazing what a crowd will do, also. They were just that friendly and just such a good crowd that by the time I got to it, people were making sounds in the audience at the same time. It was just like, kind, of a very interesting set.

And so it just flowed, until by the time I got to "are u sleepen / brotha john," to the tune of "My Favorite Things," I literally had tears in my eyes, because I remember seeing Coltrane for the last time, here in New York when he was playing with Alice [Coltrane], and the whole group had left the stage and left the two of them on stage when she was playing the piano and he was playing, and they were playing back "My Favorite Things," and it became very apparent that each one was the other one's "favorite thing."

DH   And did you sing part of that?

SS   Yes, I did. I sang it, I sang. I did the actual "Woo-oo-oo-da" on down to the singing part, and I think I haven't read that poem no more than maybe ten times in my life, because it is an exhausting set, to do it. Period. But I think the times might demand that a poem like that come back, because it says a lot about capitalism and whatever. . . .

DH   Yes, I think it's an amazing poem, too. I know that you use slash marks in that, and in *We A BaddDDD People* you use slash marks a lot. Were they sometimes just arbitrary, or did you think of them in terms of breath or—

SS   I thought of them sometimes in terms of emphasis, sometimes in stoppage—

DH   Different reasons, different functions—

SS   Um-hum.

DH   Yes. Okay. Were there musical and dramatic influences in your childhood environment?

SS   Oh, yes, yes. My father, you see, is an ex-musician, and today, after I had finished talking, and he had come to hear me talk, a woman had come up, and I introduced my father to her, Queen Mother Moore, and he was talking about how people like musicians were always around us in the South, and even in the North.

I was raised on Art Tatum; the music that we heard—I would walk in someone's house and hear Art Tatum playing, and people would say, "Art Tatum—well, how did you know Art Tatum?" My father would let us hear Art Tatum and, you know, Count Basie, and he took us down to Fifty-second Street to meet people like Billie Holiday and introduce us to them.

DH   Oh—you met Billie Holiday—

SS   Yes, Sid Catlett, people who used to work those clubs on Fifty-second Street, you know, you would shake the hands, and whatever. He took us to the Paramount to meet Billy Eckstine, Count Basie, Art Tatum, Sid Catlett, the big drummer, people like that. But then at the same time, I remember in Alabama when they had parties at night, they would play songs by Billie and people like that, and I remember Bessie [Smith]. But they wouldn't play them during the day, interestingly enough, but during the day the radio would go on to a Doris Day singing "Que Será Será." [*Laughs*]

DH   Did your father play an instrument?

SS   Drums. Drums. He played drums. And so those are the people that we were involved with, and then, of course, living in New York, being involved with growing up on "Symphony Sid" [a radio program] on many levels, which had a lot to do with a whole lot of jazz things, et cetera. And then later on, always beginning to turn on the jazz stations here in New York; there's always been that kind of influence. I am not here to say that I was always a person who fully understood all the ramifications. I always know what I like. I don't always know the reasons why, if you know what I mean. The reasons why you like certain things, but you do know you like them—you know what I'm saying?

That's why I'm saying I would go and listen to Coltrane and other people. But I'm not a mixer. It takes a lot for me to get up and go out someplace. . . . After I come in from work I tend to stay home, unless I'm taking the children out to dinner and/or to the theater or to a movie. But I'm not a person who likes to hang out in nightclubs or bars or whatever, and quite often that's where you would go and hear music. It's an effort to do that. Like sometimes my students will come and say, "There's a band appearing here in a place up on Shelton. Come on, I want to go hear it, and I'll take you." So I'll go, you know, with a couple of students from my class, and I'll thoroughly enjoy myself for an hour, hour and a half, but I'm always very happy [*laughs*] to get back in the house.

So a lot of things I hear and enjoy—it does come via records that people get to me. One of the records I was stricken by, however, years ago, was Max Roach's and Abbey Lincoln's *Freedom Suite*. I will never forget hearing that for the first time, which, for the first time, made me hear some people talk about freedom on a record in such a—I guess it was almost a belligerent manner. And then there's a part that Abbey does on that record that is like a series of moans and groans. Have you ever heard *Freedom Suite*? It's a fantastic suite. I sat down and wrote from that piece because of what was happening there. It just kind of pushed you and propelled you. And then that swing and that movement of Max on a piece where he just kept—it was almost as if he was drowning you. Before you could catch your breath, he'd go "tschhh" and hit you again. It had that kind of impact and that kind of force. It was almost like he was hitting you in the skull, saying "Look, look, look!" and you were doing like, "Hey, hold it, hold it, hold it!" That was a piece that he had done on that level, too. And then I think, if I remember correctly, you couldn't hear it on the radio. It was that aggressive piece, belligerent piece, and they literally—I don't know if they banned it consciously. They probably banned it, but they wouldn't say they had; they just didn't play it. You know how D.J.'s are. . . .

DH In 1971 you stated in a *Black World* interview with Sebastian Clarke, "I think the prime thing with art, or being a writer, be it a playwright, a poet, or even a musician, etc., is to really show people what is happening in this country. And then show them how they can change it."[9] Does this substantially represent your position now?

SS I think so. And by that I meant that at the same time you show what is wrong, you show what can be or what could be. At the same time you show the horror, you show some beauty. You know, you always need that; you always need the movement of one and the other. You need the beauty, whatever that beauty is, if it's self, children, or ideas, whatever, to keep people moving. Otherwise, people will not move; if all they see is horror, they say, "The hell with it. I'm not going to involve myself anymore with any of this." So I think, yes, that's about true. I think it's important that artists not just involve themselves with themselves, and almost like an egotistical thing, I think we have, we do involve ourselves with ourselves. You can't help but do it on some levels. But at the same time, I think we must always be aware of what is happening in the world, and I think we've got to make statements about what is happening in the world.

DH   Gwendolyn Brooks has said, "To be Black is political." Do you feel the Black artist holds a uniquely political position, or do you recommend this combined vision to all writers?

SS   What combined vision do you mean?

DH   To be political and aesthetic at the same time.

SS   I think she's right.

DH   But do you think that—being human is to be political? Do you recommend being political for all writers, Black or white?

SS   Yes, yes. I think you have to. I think that we are talking about a world that will contain a lot of people here, and they're not just going to all be Black people on this planet. And so what we're talking about, when one talks about a white writer or a Latin writer or whatever, we are talking about people having to make those comments and saying those things about what is happening to them wherever they are. Period. So I think we are talking quite seriously about people taking positions when they write and not, and again, maintaining the status quo.

DH   You've spoken, in the *Black Collegian* ["The Role of the Black Woman"] of the 1970s as "ushering in an Age of Reason." How do you view the 1980s?

SS   I view the eighties as a very dangerous time for Black people, or anyone who intends to survive. I think it is a time of the humanitarians versus the inhumanitarians. I think that is very important for us to understand. I think it is time for us to recognize that we are now in the midst of a struggle to save Black people, political white people, people who have actually seen what America is about and recognize the fact that it must be changed, Third World people, people all over the planet Earth, who also must understand what this is about, that we're in a world struggle at this particular point to wrest control from the inhumanitarians who are in power and who could very well succeed in blowing up this whole damn world. You see, you can't keep on polluting the minds and bodies of one segment of your community or of your country, and then not expect for it also to seep among other segments of your community or country.

I mean, for instance, it was okay to do any damn thing you wanted to do with Black people: don't educate them; let them have a high mortality rate; let them live in the worst slums; it doesn't really matter what you do—kill them at will, whatever. And no one would say anything. A few people would raise some kind of loud, clarion cry. But all of a sudden we look up—now, in the late seventies and early eighties, and most certainly if we understand what happened in the Vietnam War—this country looked up, via Nixon and other people, Nixon and Company, and said, "Those crybabies!"—this is a Nixon—or, "Those people who think that they can say something about this country, we'll show you that we can treat you like a nigger." And so—I call it "the spread of niggerdom"—happened in America. And the top, the capping of that happened to have been Kent: that for the first time America actually killed her own—not just her own, but her best. You know, America has never killed her white college student, and Nixon pulled the trigger on the white college student, which told them, "Welcome to the club, anyone who disagrees with me. Period." And I think that many of us had to look up and see on many levels. That was a beast, you know, Nixon, doing this. He was literally just wiping out young people. You can argue or disagree about what they were doing, whether it was right or correct, whatever—that wasn't the point. He actually allowed the death of young whites, the best that they have in America, to prove a point, you know, to show exactly who they were in this country. But he was like a madman at that particular time. From that point on, we began to see the demise of this man on many levels, too.

DH   Do you see in the eighties, with their increased threats to both the economy and to world peace, a need for coalition or for working with non-Black organizations?

SS   I think that probably what we need to do is to make sure that people organize well wherever they are, and then people have coalitions for big, big, big, monstrous kinds of things that will have to come down in terms of power. Period. I think we'll see more of that happening.

DH   Black and white coalitions?

SS   Yes. Green, blue, whatever.

DH   Would you say your current thinking is closer to that of Madhubuti's Black Nationalist separatism or Baraka's Marxism?

SS   I don't know. I always steer away from tags, even when I teach people, because they have already ideas about what that means, and they either turn off or you can't reach them. I studied a lot still in the midst of all this madness and teaching. I think it so important that we study a great deal, and study in order to see where we're going to, and I'm not too sure that we need to say or we need to know exactly where we're going. But we do need to know some of the mechanics of it. We need to have under our belts information, alternatives, possibilities, and whatever. Those are the kinds of things that I'm trying to do today, like if we're talking economics, the alternatives to that, okay? If we're talking about a nation, what that really means in practical terms. If we're talking about America, what *that* means in practical terms. If we're talking outside of America, what *that* means in practical terms. That's what I mean. So I read a lot of people as a consequence and try to internalize what that's about and am still formulating a lot of that, what that really means for me. And I think that it means I won't ally myself with anyone at this point, but it will mean that I will continue to work and write and say what I think about certain things. It just means, in my head, no alliances with—I work with people. I'll do things for people and with people.

DH   In terms of issues? Organize in terms of particular issues?

SS   Always, always, always.

DH   In plays like *The Bronx Is Next* and elsewhere, and in public statements, you have recommended that people burn down their tenements. In the Bronx, as in other places, landlords have often been responsible for arson, to their own advantage. Do you still favor the position of "burn it down"?

SS   Well, I used to say, years ago, that as bad as Harlem is, they need to burn it down and rebuild it, because you just almost cannot do anything with some of the buildings there. The play *The Bronx Is Next*, you know, was about burning Harlem down and removing people from the urban cities. I still believe the urban cities have wiped out a number of generations here. I would not say that I would go and burn down Harlems of America, period. I think that you have to always organize people to make sure that they understand exactly what's going on. I don't think it's possible to do that today, let us say—probably not even then. That was symbolic of the need for Black people to perhaps leave the urban centers. I was speaking in symbol, symbolically about the need for Blacks to move out of that which is killing them and wiping them out. Blacks came North. Parents migrated to the North during those big migrations in the twenties for more freedom, et cetera.

DH   So you were speaking symbolically, rather than literally.

SS   I would say that was a symbolic play, in terms of people destroying that which was destroying them, and then making a decision to move out and on back to places which had nurtured them, or places perhaps where they would be the majority, other than, in quotes, a "minority" in the midst of the stone houses and apartment buildings, whatever.

DH   So you think that the freedom of the North is a myth for Black people?

SS   Always has been. Always has been.

DH   Then there's not—you don't see a substantial difference between the life of the Black in the North and life of the Black in the South.

SS   I just think that the differences are much more subtle here in the North. The interesting thing in the South, you can live next door to a Black, and a Black can come and take care of your children and cook for you, but you wouldn't sit down and eat together in a restaurant, which told us something about the social fiber of the South. In the "North," in quotes, you could not live next door to someone [laughs], but you could go downtown to eat, sit down to eat, because no one gave a damn. They understood their own separate societies, and they know that your child probably wouldn't go to school with the others, so it didn't really matter at all. Period. I guess what I'm saying is that it was like just a different emphasis.

DH   Differences more in style than substance.

SS   Yes. But I mean in this country it was still the same old same-o.

DH   At one time, your work expressed an important connection to the Nation of Islam, most apparent, perhaps, in A Blues Book for Blue Black Magical Women. What literary or religious works inspired that book's visionary form?

SS   That was a long book. It took me over a year to write that book. That book came out of a sense of wanting to get part of me down on paper, to give a sense of saying, "I'm here, and this is how I got here," without looking down on people at all, but just saying, "This is how I traveled here." I think [George] Kent is a very perceptive critic. I was actually amazed that he had picked up on some of the things that he had picked up on, because I discussed this with him. He has a class called "Black Autobiography," and I went out there to read that book for his class, and I'm always amazed at some of the things he picks up on. And he had said that it was what he calls "a mountain-top" poem, and I said to him, I smiled and said, "Yes, it's true. I was constantly climbing a mountain to get to that poem." And when I got there, two things could have happened. I could have said, "Goody-goody-goody, I'm here, and look at the rest of you, you aren't." The other part of that was to recognize that after what was there, you looked up and saw another one someplace, and you realized that that's what it's really all about.

I had visions during the time I was writing that poem, which was very interesting. And so people have asked me a great deal about what books, what was I reading during that time, and I always give some offhanded comment. But the point of that book is that during the time I was writing it, I used to wake up in sweats and with visions. I pictured a lot of this. The first part was a very obvious part in terms of being almost—it was a section I had written in Pittsburgh when some women had asked me to write something for them, to keep them holding together. So that's how I did "Queens of the Universe." And then I sent it to *Black Scholar* and they published it, from Pittsburgh, about '68, I guess, around that time. So that seemed like a logical, introductory theme to the book.

But when I went into the second part, Part Two, which is called "Past," I wanted to show people the movement of me in America, and what that meant in the South and in New York City, and during junior high, high school, college days, and the movement as a young Black woman, and then the movement as a woman, and then the ending of "Past" with the present, being a woman who was then involved with Africa and Africanisms as such, and reclaiming of the past. That's what that whole "Present" section is about. Then, after I went from "Present" I figured that that was the end of the book, because I had struggled through a lot of the writing of that book. It was just not very easy on many levels, you know, to do that whole book. I said, "That's it. Forty-two pages is enough for me." [*Laughter*]

Then I started—you know how you write a book, and you know that you're not finished, although you say you're finished. Well, I knew this book was not finished, and I'd start waking up in the middle of the night, and I had these visions of destruction in this country. I also—I went to China; I was in Guyana, then into China. Guyana reminded me—the Caribbean reminded me a great deal of the Continent [Africa]. Although I had never been to the Continent, I could see it. So the "Rebirth" section came next. I had seen all those Black people there, and the first time being in America and not really being around a lot of Black folk was something else again. You don't live in Black towns or see Black people running things in America. So that's what "Rebirth" is all about. That motion. You know, "when i stepped off the plane i knew i was home," that's what I'm saying. You knew what that was about. That whole section, which is very much part of nature and water and birth, walking out on the sea.

One line I like a great deal: ". . . i rowed out from boulevards / balancing my veins on sails"—it was moving from the cities, you know. Being there, amid the water, the water that was blue—the first time I saw water that was blue-green, as opposed to the Hudson River dirt. The ocean—I saw the ocean, seas, the way they should have looked before pollution hit them.

DH   Where was this—in Guyana?

SS   I was in, part of that time, in Bermuda, Jamaica, in Guyana, and on to China. . . .

DH   Did you spend much time there?

SS   I was on a cultural tour from this country.

DH   This was in the People's Republic?

SS   Right. In '73. I have pictures.

DH   Did you spend much time in China?

SS   Yes. We spent the whole month there. We went on a cultural tour that included people like Candice Bergen, Alice Childress, Earla Forrey (*Myth of Black Capitalism*), and some Broadway stars.

DH   And that was before you wrote the last section?

SS   Yes. That was before this was completely finished. I'm almost certain—I think I gave Dudley [Randall] this book—the book came out in '74, right?

DH   Yes.

SS   Right. I gave Dudley the book before we went to Amherst. So I finished writing the book when I came back. I had gone to the Caribbean and had written notes about the sea there, and all of that. It was not together. When I came back from China, the People's Republic, I finished up the book like in one—oh, about a week and a half, less than that.

DH   In Amherst or in—

SS   New York. . . . I had taken notes, because I always take notes. I had done the "Rebirth"; I did the "Rebirth" in about a couple of days. And then after the "Rebirth" I conjured up all the things in terms of Black cities and Black countries. And then the Part Two of that was the part that talked about perfection without being egotistical about it. Because at that point I recognized or realized this whole part, and I restored my perfection: I am pure, I'm a passenger. I was reading also at that point "praise poetry," a book of Swahili poetry. One of the poems was a praise poem which talked about not perfection as much as a very religious kind of thing. And I read it and read it. Before I fly, I always read anything— favorite poems or favorite people, or whatever, or music, et cetera. And then I realized that after I had talked about rebirth, then I had to show the physical rebirth. I had talked about being born with the water that I had sailed, and then walked in the water for nine months, and then really had given birth to myself again. Then I had to say, "I am, I am." You know, it hit me. I sat down at that point and put a Part Two, and then I had restored my perfection. It was that kind of motion and movement. And that's what I did, and it just flowed; it just like poured out. I always keep notebooks; I write in notebooks, so I have all those. Sometimes I go over that and laugh, sometimes, at that. And then, that poem, "Queens of the Universe," was done before. I put that in at the end.

DH   "in the beginning" was done before?

SS   Yes. I read that someplace downtown, before the rest of *Blues Book* was done, and I realized that it was tied up—the connection would be from "Queens of the Universe" and "in the beginning." The reason I know when it was done—because I did that before I came to teach or during the time I was teaching at Manhattan Community College, and Mungu and Morani were little little, just about two. And I was reading this poem, "in the beginning there was no end," and this poem was a specific poem I had done for—it was Baraka's play, *Black Mass*; I went to see Baraka's play, *Black Mass*— [*Telephone rings.*]

In *Black Mass*, Baraka discusses the Yakub myth.[10] But what had stricken me about it was the idea of inventing, and what I did in "in the beginning" at that time—I wrote this after I saw that play, that's what it was. It came from having seen something. Quite often I do that, I come in so full. And that's what that was about. The way they talked about being first man on the planet, you know, an original man on the planet, too. And then the idea of inventing or making people who would kill other people, because in the play *Black Mass* the scientist invents, makes what he calls a beast, and the beast turns around and kills all the people that are there. And I took that whole Yakub myth and put it into that poem. The reason why I remember that poem so well is because I knew I had done it before this book. It's a poem that I chant; it's not just read. It's a poem that is chanted altogether.

DH   It's a wonderful poem. I was wondering whether there was any thought of Eliot's "East Coker": "In my beginning is my end."

SS   No, I didn't—I hear what you're saying.

DH   Or even in the beginning of the Gospel of John, "In the beginning was the Word."

SS   Right. No, that came just on the level of—basically, I don't know where it came from. I walked into that house after I had seen that play, and literally it poured out almost just as it is. . . .

I don't know why I'm belaboring this, but the story I want to tell is that Mungu was two, and I had a reading at Manhattan Community College. I was not teaching there yet. I had come for a reading, and Mungu and Morani were sitting down in front with two students, and they had gone to sleep. They were sleeping. It was a long program, but I was the last person to speak, and Mungu woke up in the middle of the last poem I was reading—not from the book, because the book wasn't out yet, but from my notes. It was "in the beginning," and they had heard that poem before. That's why I knew that it had been written before. And Mungu pulled up from this young woman, and she was trying to get him back and he pulled away. And I saw out of the corner of my eye when I finished (I was finishing up a poem called "Queens of the Universe," which had never been in a book, either; I think it was in *Black World*, once, whatever). And I saw this little one come across the bottom and climb up these high steps. I mean, barely balancing himself, and walk across the stage in the midst of a reading, and I had gotten ready to start "in the beginning." Just at the point where I began to start "in the beginning," I said, "Just a minute," and I scooped him up with my right hand and put the paper which was very up— [demonstrates] because, you know, it was a manuscript at that point. . . . And I started, "in the beginning there was no end, in the beginning there was no end," and then I would sing [sings], "in the begi-i-ning, the-ere wa-as no-o e-end," and this little voice said, "in the begi-i-ning, the-ere wa-as no-o e-end." I have asked for that tape for*ever*! Someone was taping the whole damn thing. Then I said nothing, continued looking, stopped, and he sang, and the whole place just roared. . . .

We were living in the Bronx at that time. We got ready to come out again for a reading, because they were always going with me for a reading, and he said to me, "Am I going to read again? Am I going to read, too?" [*Laughter*] That's where that came from, that whole piece, as a piece, and at the end it's sung, the whole thing. It's just chanted. Period. And that came from that whole play that I had seen, and that whole myth.

DH   You have a lovely singing voice, too. Did you sing much?

SS   As a child, never! When I did, they used to say, "Shut up!"

DH   About the Nation [of Islam]—when did you leave? You have left the Nation.

SS   Right. I came into the Nation in, I guess, '72 and left the Nation in '75, the end of '75. I had gone out to Chicago in summer of '75, May of '75, when school was over in Amherst, and I had resigned as of, I guess, December of '75.

DH   Do you care to comment on this shift, at least its meaning for your work?

SS   Well, some people would like to always say that they have made a mistake. I don't think we make mistakes at all. I think that's not the point in terms of people. I think, looking back on the period that we all were involved in, when we all discovered Blackness in America, it was via two men: Malcolm and Elijah Muhammad. And I think that everyone had to go into that period, to move through that period, because they were the most viable people organizations going here at this particular time. It took a lot of strength to do that, because the moment you did that, America just right away just went slicing; I mean, it literally tried to destroy you.

Because it considered the Nation a very dangerous organization on many levels.

You know and I know that the schism that was developed between Elijah Muhammad and Malcolm was one that was set up because of the motion and movement of people, period, towards the Nation, just like for the first time people had seen something positively Black in this country. I guess it's similar to what people felt during Marcus Garvey's time. At some point you had to see something that resembled you, or something that was positive, besides the very negative stuff. I don't consider any of that time a wasted time, especially not when one looks, views *Blues Book*, and you see the work you've done. I put all that in perspective. I understand, I smile when I read *Blues Book* sometimes; I understand what that is. I understand the perspective of it. . . . I think it was a period that I had to go through, being political in this country, being Black and political in this country, with the kind of ideas that I had about change in this country. I think my movement on meant that there were other things I really had to do in terms of my politicalness and how I began to view other kinds of things, too.

DH   Your early books of poetry are written mainly in free verse, with the influence of blues and jazz. Then, in *Love Poems*, there are haiku and sonnet forms; haiku, the sonnet, and African rhythms in your new work in *I've Been a Woman*. What is your attitude toward the study and use of conventional forms?

SS   If you notice, in *I've Been a Woman* I have haiku, tankas, and again, the movement towards what I call "African" ideas and feelings, and also the movement towards a Black ethic and a feminine one, too. If you really read the poem that I did to Shirley Graham Du Bois and my mother, "Kwa mama zetu waliotuzaa" (for our mothers who gave us birth), that has a lot of feminine kinds of energy in there, woman kinds of things.

Repeat the question; that's the tiredness, now. I still have that headache, so you'll have to forgive me, from that blow. [The poet was referring to her fall in a supermarket. See end of interview.]

DH   All right. What is your attitude toward the study and use of conventional forms?

SS   I teach poetry, and people are always stricken—sometimes, when they first come into my class that—I teach form. I teach form on purpose. I do it in a way where we start off with something called "free association exercises." I do that from taste and smell, whatever, to release them from a lot of things that they might have, et cetera, and then I also move into the haiku. Someone said to me, "Sonia, you shouldn't be teaching college students haiku or the tanka form, because they'll never give you any great haiku or great tankas." I say, "That might be so, but I use the haiku and tanka form for discipline and for what I call 'word choice.' " I tell students they have three lines, and sometimes seventeen syllables or thirty-one syllables. They've got to choose the right word to make a certain motion come across. That's word choice there; that is work. Period. And so I make use of the haiku and tanka in terms of making them look up and recognize the fact that whether the poem is a haiku, a tanka, a sonnet, whatever, you are involved with choosing words, and quite often the best word that you can find in a poem. And once you get into that habit of choosing the best word, then you understand why, when you deal with free verse, the free verse also has discipline and also the need and necessity for choosing the correct words for that, and not just go and sprawl.

When students first come to me, they sprawl everything all over the page. What I do is I compress them. I start with something, the smallest forms you can possibly do, the haiku, tanka, cinquain, whatever. Then, after I compress them for about three or four forms of haiku, tanka, cinquain, and perhaps their own syllabic verse, I say, "Here, you can do a free verse," and all of a sudden they look up and they say, "Oh, I don't know. I had difficulty doing a free verse." And I do that on purpose, because I say, "I know; then you really recognize what a free verse is all about. It is *not* free. It is not sprawling all over that damn page. There's a reason for having one word on one line, not just because you feel like it, but there is also— you must begin to hear that reason, and understand that reason, also." And that's how and why I do form.

And then we do ballads and blues. You see, what I try to do in the English department is something a lot of the academic people don't really understand. They think that, sometimes, if you're Black you belong in Black studies, or if you're in Black studies, you really can't teach white students, whatever. But I teach my students, let's say at Tyler,[11] the majority of my students are white in that class. I teach the blues, and I read Bessie Smith's blues, and blu-blu-blum—they'll come in with some fantastic blues. And I say to the English department, "You don't know really what you're missing when you teach poetry and you don't include the blues in that also, that reality." Because those people can come into your classroom with some blues that are just like kind of fantastic. And they do this, and they deal with rhyme, and they learn a form. They sing it and have fun doing it. I mean, there are all kinds of reasons why I use form in the classroom.

DH   What drew you to the haiku—was it your travel to China, or was it before? Were you interested before that?

SS   No, I had done some haiku before my trip to China. . . . In *Love Poems*, if you will remember, there was a haiku that I wrote to the children, which I did in China. I missed them so much after I had been there for three weeks, I decided to call from Shanghai, and I figured this will cost me a hell of a lot of money, calling home. My aunt was with the children at the time. So I had the hardest time trying to make the operator understand in that hotel called the Peace Hotel in Shanghai that I wanted to call collect—that I didn't think I had enough money, you know. I was on a limited budget there. Well, she finally said, oh yes, she understood. And so about thirty minutes later, voom! the telephone rang, and "Here," she says, "your call," and I'm talking to my aunt in New York City. You know how bad the connections are coming from Brooklyn to New York? This was clearly clear. My aunt could not believe I was calling her from China. But when I finished talking to them, the children, who had instructed me exactly what they wanted, I said, "Three minutes. That, no more, I'm hanging up." I did a haiku that day. Well, I was explaining to them that it was seven o'clock in the morning, Wednesday, and it was seven P.M. Tuesday night there, and they couldn't—I said, "I'll explain it when I get home." I said, "It's in the morning here." I said, "It's Wednesday," and then they said, "No, it's not. It's night!" [*Laughter*] I said, "Yes, because the day hasn't reached you." When I went off the line, I did the haiku: "let me wear the day / well so when it reaches you / you will enjoy it." That was one I did there in China, to the children, to Mungu and Morani, because I wanted to explain what that was about, and then they understood it very well, as a consequence of that.

DH   Now the sonnet interested you in your earlier—

SS   Well, yes, I had done sonnets. [Louise] Bogan also gave us form—I studied with her—which like used to bore the hell out of me. I had to write a villanelle with Bogan, and I teach the villanelle also [*laughter*] and the first time my students—I gave them a villanelle, and they said, "Are you kidding?" But when they started dealing with the rhyme, an interesting thing happened. They learned that if you are going to repeat or if you are going to use rhyme, you really must, one, get a rhyming dictionary; two, you're not talking about "you" and "blue" for the rest of your life, the way some of us just hear easy rhymes; and three, you're talking about repetition. That means you've got to have strong lines. Any time you repeat something, you cannot have weak lines. It just teaches all that. Period. The sonnet was something that—I was doing a sonnet sequence to my father, three poems, three sonnets to my father, and I had done a couple of those poems at an earlier date, if I remember correctly. I think they were about '72 or '71, maybe.

DH What do you see ahead in your development? Free verse, or are you going to let the content dictate the form, so that you can use both free verse and rhyme?

SS I'm doing a book on my father at this point, which is a book about Black men surviving; southern Black men surviving.

DH Is this poetry or prose?

SS Poetry. But yet in all, some parts of it read like prose, and most of it is done, interestingly enough, almost with soliloquies and monologues. So it's interesting, the motion and movement. Because I couldn't understand what was wrong with the piece at first. I couldn't understand why it wasn't flowing, and I realized I wasn't hearing this man's voice at all. And so that's why I had to, in a sense, let this talk come out. You know, it's amazing how you can work on something so long, and all of a sudden you move away from it and you begin to talk it out in the head. At least, I do. I talk my poems out in my head. I kept saying, "Work at it some more, girl. You always tell your students, 'Work at it.' " I said, "It's not working, damn it! Something's wrong." And once I tell students, if it really does not work, you might as well look at a persona. You might have to look at something." That's what I had to do, stop and look and listen to my own words. And I realized that what was wrong was that I was telling it, and he had to tell it. It was a story.

DH Are you a reviser? Do you revise—

SS Oh, sure, sure. I write in notebooks, so I have all my poems as they moved towards a second, third, fourth, fifth revision, et cetera.

DH Do you wait for inspiration or do you write regularly?

SS I write regularly. If I waited for inspiration, I'd be finished. [*Laughter*]

DH   Right!

SS   So I'm a regular writer of poetry—of not just poetry, of many things. I keep a diary, for one, so usually I write in the diary impressions and thoughts and ideas. And it's something that I always go back on at night, sometimes, some days, and just really remembering what I was doing in 1974 someplace.

DH   Your poetry is generally lowercased—the "I," as in e. e. cummings, is lowercased in that wonderful poem that you mentioned—except in your most recent poems. Sometimes you spell phonetically. "Night," for example, is spelled n-i-t-e throughout, although in one poem you have both spellings. Sometimes you use speedwriting, like "cd" for "could," or the letter *u* for y-o-u. Now, what's your purpose in these different instances: the lowercasing and the contractions?

SS   Well, a lot of that, also, if you remember, came out of the movement of the Beat, and with disdain for a lot of the academic stuff that was existing at that particular time. That's why I read everyone and everybody, and I began to also do that kind of motion and movement with the "cd." The lower case I've always tried to deal with, because it just seemed to me that it's very easy to get involved with ego as a writer. And so I consciously—even when I write people in letters, I do that. It's not just in poetry. And I have to remember when I'm teaching, quite often—but students know, anyway, so they look up and understand. But when I'm correcting things, I have to always try to figure out if the person is really doing this, or if he or she doesn't understand. I have to put question marks.

DH   Standard spelling—

SS   But it has a lot to do with the ego on many levels, having to deal with and control it and move it in such a way that it is moving into the work, moving into a realm that is important, but also making the writer be less important.

DH   But the contractions—would you say that is for speed of communication?

SS   Sometimes it does happen with the "wd," "cd," you know. I also, sometimes, say "c-u-d."

DH   And it's also colloquial.

SS   Right. So it's always that. It depends on the voice, there, sometimes.

DH   *It's a New Day* and *The Adventures of Fathead, Small-*

head, and Squarehead show your interest in writing for children as well as adults. Is your main purpose in doing so didactic, or do you just enjoy writing for this audience?

SS   Most of it has been on the level of teaching, I would say. *It's a New Day* came about because I was in a junior high school and some of them said, "You know, they won't let your poetry come in here, because your poetry has cursing," meaning *Homecoming*, "and [*laughs*] we have had people—" And I said to them very dramatically, "Well, I will write a book for you with no curse words!" And I did. [*Laughter*] That's why when I sat down and wrote [*It's a*] *New Day*, there's not one curse word in *It's a New Day*, no place, nowhere. And then *Fathead—The Adventures of Fathead, Smallhead, and Squarehead*—came about because I heard some of the children playing together, four children in the house playing together. And one of the children was kind of a plump little one, and he was always slow, and so these children were just constantly getting on his case. And one of them stamped his foot and said, "You're so slow!"

DH   Yes.

SS   And so I said, if I come in there and go through this whole set about—that's not really what you say, because children forget that. So one night we had come in from school, a very rough day of picking them up from babysitters and bringing them home and feeding them and bathing them and putting them to bed, and I still had to go back and grade papers and read for the next day. I stretched out on the bed with them, and they said, "Tell us a story." So I reached for a book, and they said, "No, make up a story." Originally, the first part of that story was "The Adventures of Fathead." I started off with something silly. I said, "I'm going to tell you a story about three good friends." I don't know why I said "three," okay? And then I said, "One's name is Fathead," so they giggled. And they were tired; you know how children giggle—they must have been about four at the time, three or four, and they giggled about "Fathead." And I said, "and Smallhead," and they giggled, and the other was—

DH   "Squarehead"?

SS   Yes, but it wasn't "Squarehead," it was something like "Tinhead," something like that. And so they laughed, and I said, "They were going on a trip." And I told the story. I didn't have the moral at the end, at all. And the next night they said, "Tell me a story." So I picked up a book. They said, "No, the same story you told," and I started trying to tell it and couldn't remember all of it. And Mungu said, "It goes like this, Ma," and he told the damn story. And I got up—talk about breaking up!—and went and got a book and started to write down the story, because I had forgotten— I mean, I literally had told the story and gone to sleep! That night, in the bed with them—woke up with the lights on, maybe about one o'clock. They were sleeping, of course. We were all stretched out together, all bodies, whatever. I covered them up and just went on to bed, did no work that night at all, and didn't even think about the story the next day until they reminded me about it at night. And then I said, "Okay, what was it?" And I asked him to search, and I said, "Fathead?" because it was something that just came off some place. And he said, "No, it goes like this, and it went 'there . . . and there . . . and there.' " [*Laughter*] And I wrote it down, and then I worked it. I had just the frame of it, and put the juice and meat on it, whatever. And I said, "Whooof!" So it's a good thing they have a good memory, because I would have been in deep trouble. Didn't even remember that.

DH   What is the special appeal for you of writing plays?

SS   I don't know—I started to write plays—I think I still have to tell you, because I had written a first play for *Black Fire*.[12] Someone asked me, "If you write poetry, do you also write plays?" And I said, "Sure."

DH   [*Laughs*] And you'd never written one.

SS   Never written a play, except I had done plays in college. When I was pledging a sorority, I did a takeoff on *1984*. It was a funny play that I had done, you know, with commercials and everything. And also in teaching, I'd have students always do plays. It was always comedy, never serious plays. And so I said, "Sure, I do," and I literally sat down in my apartment again, one or two days, and wrote *The Bronx Is Next*, without saying "What should I write about?" and I wrote *The Bronx* and typed it up myself like this [*gestures*]—I'm a lousy typist—and sent that. Luckily enough, I had a carbon in there. Anyway, it got lost. Ed Bullins used it in *Tulane Drama Review*, the "Black Drama Review" [issue] of *Tulane Drama Review*. Then the next time I was in California and Ed called me and said, "Sonia, I'm doing a collection called *New Plays from Black Theatre*, and will you do a play?" I said, "Oh, sure, I'll do a play!" [*Laughing*] So, I guess what happens is that the head begins to work on it. I had the twins, and then Ed called me one day and said, "Where is that play?" All the plays were in except mine. So I said to Ed, "Oh, but you must understand, I just had these babies." He said, "Look, don't tell me your problems, I want the play!" [*Laughter*]

Well, D. H., I was so mad that that night—it was about their third month—I put the children down about ten-thirty, and for the first time they slept that night from ten-thirty until about six-thirty in the morning. The first time. They had never done that; they were up and down. Mungu was in my study, and Morani was in the bedroom, so I couldn't work in there. So I came down to the living room and sat in a rocking chair and on the couch and wrote that *Sister Son/ji* overnight. I wrote that play from ten-thirty to six-thirty, went upstairs when one of the babies woke up, and left a note on the door—I had students who lived over me, on the second floor; I asked them to stop by, and I handed them the one copy that I had and said, "Would you please type this up for me and make copies." And they brought it in that evening to me from school. I asked them to babysit. I drove my beatup car down to the main post office downtown, in San Francisco this is, the post office on Post Street there, and sent it air mail special. I heard from Ed about a week and a half later. "Dear Sonia: Yeah!" exclamation point. "Love, Ed." That was all. I was just pissed. . . .

I started a play when I was at home, in college, and never finished it. It was going to be a play about me living there at home. I still have that play, interestingly enough. The reason why I just remembered is because I just got to thinking about a play called *Dirty Hearts*, which I had done also. That is in a collection called *Breakout*, experimental plays. I did it right after *Son/ji*, at some point. A man who works at Brown University, but he used to teach at San Francisco State—he's a poet, he's a well-known poet [James Schevill]. . . . *Dirty Hearts* is about war and nonmovement of people, and "Dirty Hearts" is a card game where these people meet every—

DH   "Hearts"—h-e-a-r-t-s?

SS   Yes. "Dirty Hearts." Right. Some people just call it "Hearts." And the whole purpose is not to get hearts. And in this game there's a poet who is quiet and only writes about—makes up myths, because he can't deal with the world, whatever. And one is a businessman who is his roommate, who has left his wife, and is

about making money. One is Shiyeko, who is a victim of
Hiroshima, and one is a Black man. They play cards, Dirty Hearts,
every day. There's another person in there someplace, I think. And
they meet. And this particular time that we focus in on, the busi-
nessman gives the Queen of Spades to the Black man. The Queen of
Spades is the thirteen-point card; you don't want to get that, or
hearts, at all. And the Black man looks up, and each person has
something to say. They say it almost like a soliloquy, which is a very
poetic kind of piece. Shiyeko talks about being bombed in the war,
but she holds no bitterness for anyone.

I actually met a woman by the name of Shiyeko who had been
one of the Hiroshima Maidens, who had come over to this country.
So I have a whole thing with how she wears a big sun hat with the
veil, and she removes it only in that room there, and the scars,
whatever. And she talks about "It's not your fault." And then there
is the poet who is too timid to take on the world. Period. And lets
the businessman rule him. So he's like in charge of everything, this
businessman, you know. He gets the drinks, whatever. And then
there is the black man who comes in, hurried and harassed; he's a
businessman, he's coming in. Then everyone plays the game that
everyone else is playing. It's called *Dirty Hearts*, but it's also a
game, in terms of no one ever attacks anyone. And then when the
Queen of Spades is dropped on the Black guy, he gets angry, and he
just bursts out, just says, "what the hell." . . .

DH   Ed Bullins has called for "street theatre." Do you view
any of your plays this way?

SS   *The Bronx Is Next* was done for that purpose. We did it in
San Francisco. We did plays, poetry, whatever, in a van or whatever
to take theater to the people. It's a hard audience to play. . . . We
went into bars. We read poetry in bars. I remember one time we
went in and someone said, "Hey, ain't you the poet that came in
here to read?" That was good. It became an important cultural
event. They got to testifying in that bar, because they were listening
to poetry that was really dealing with what they were about.

DH   What kind of audiences do you want to reach in poetry
and drama?

SS   All kinds of audiences.

DH   What advice would you offer to beginning writers?

SS   Read and read and read and read everything you can get
your hands on. One of the things Louise Bogan told me was,

"Whatever you write, read aloud. Your ear will be the best friend you will ever have." And join a workshop at some point when you really feel you want to work more, and/or apprentice yourself to a poet or writer and study with him or her.

[Only near the end of our Wednesday evening interview, which had followed a heavy schedule of conference activities, did she mention her fall in a supermarket the previous Sunday. The accident had left her with an almost constant headache. Yet she had endured her discomfort without complaint, while putting her good humor, professionalism, and strict, personal discipline to social use.]

Sonia Sanchez: Works Cited and Suggested

Poetry

Homecoming. Detroit: Broadside Press, 1969.
We a BaddDDD People. Detroit: Broadside Press, 1970.
A Blues Book for Blue Black Magical Women. Detroit: Broadside Press, 1974.
Love Poems. New York: Third Press, 1973.
I've Been a Woman: New and Selected Poems. Sausalito, Calif.: Black Scholar Press, 1978.
homegirls & handgrenades. New York: Thunder's Mouth Press, 1984.
Under a Soprano Sky. Trenton, N.J.: Africa World Press, 1987.

Plays

The Bronx Is Next. Tulane Drama Review 12 (Summer 1968). Reprinted in *Cavalcade: Negro American Writing from 1760 to the Present,* ed. Arthur P. Davis and Saunders Redding, pp. 811-19. Boston: Houghton Mifflin, 1971.
Sister Son/ji, In *New Plays from the Black Theatre,* ed. Ed Bullins, pp. 98-107. New York: Bantam Books, 1969.
Uh, Uh, But How Do It Free Us? In *The New Lafayette Theatre Presents: Plays with Aesthetic Comments by 6 Black Playwrights,* pp. 161-215. New York: Doubleday/Anchor, 1974.
Dirty Hearts. In *Breakout: In Search of New Theatrical Environments,* ed. James Schevill, pp. 248-56. Chicago: Swallow Press, 1973.
Malcolm Man / Don't Live Here No More. Produced at ASCOM Community Center, Philadelphia, Penn., 1979.

I'm Black When I'm Singing, I'm Blue When I Ain't. Produced by Jomandi Productions, Atlanta, Ga., April 23, 1982.

Works for Children

It's a New Day (poems for young brothas and sistuhs). Detroit: Broadside Press, 1971.
The Adventures of Fathead, Smallhead, and Squarehead. New York: Third Press, 1973.
A Sound Investment. Chicago: Third World Press, 1980.

Editions

three hundred and sixty degrees of blackness comin at you: An Anthology of the Sonia Sanchez Writers' Workshop at Countee Cullen Library in Harlem. New York: 5X Publishing, 1971.
We Be Word Sorcerers: 25 Stories by Black Americans. New York: Bantam, 1973.

Miscellaneous

"The Role of the Black Woman in a Changing Society." *Black Collegian* 10 (April-May 1980): 128-30.
Two Speeches by Sonia Sanchez (includes "Crisis and Culture"). New York: Black Liberation Press, 1983.

Notes

1. The Sanchez interview took place on April 1, 1981, at the Statler Hilton in New York City, where the poet was staying while she attended the Fifth Annual Conference of the National Council for Black Studies.
2. The point is made in R. Roderick Palmer, "The Poetry of Three Revolutionists: Don L. Lee, Sonia Sanchez, and Nikki Giovanni," *CLA Journal* 25 (Sept. 1971): 25-36; rpt. in Donald B. Gibson, ed., *Modern Black Poets: A Collection of Critical Essays* (Englewood Cliffs, N.J.: Prentice-Hall, 1973).
3. The phrase appears in a review, largely negative, by Alvin Aubert, *Black Academy Review* (Winter 1970): 65; Liz Gant also found the "rite on wite america" theme tiresome (*Black World*, April 1971, p. 87).
4. Haki Madhubuti, *Dynamite Voices* (Detroit: Broadside Press, 1971), 50-51.

5. George E. Kent, "Notes on the Black Literary Scene," *Phylon* (June 1975), p. 197.

6. Telephone conversation, April 13, 1985. *Homegirls* and *homeboys* are American Black vernacular references to persons from one's home town.

7. Herbert Leibowitz, "Exploding Myths: An Interview with Sonia Sanchez," *Parnassus: Poetry in Review,* (Spring/Summer/Fall/Winter 1985): 357-68. (Cited as *PPR.*)

8. These remarks were made in a Dec. 12, 1987, workshop on "The Writer and His/Her Social Responsibility." The other participants were Gwendolyn Brooks, Mari Evans, Sterling Plumpp, and (impromptu) Ruby Dee.

9. Sebastian Clarke, "Woman of the Times: Sonia Sanchez and Her Work," *Black World* 20: (June 1971): 45.

10. In the myth, accepted by the Nation of Islam as interpreted by Elijah Muhammad, the magician Yakub creates the white man, who becomes a symbol of evil. Theodore H. Hudson calls *A Black Mass* "Jones' strongest dramatic statement of the original-virtue-of-black-people theme." In *From LeRoi Jones to Amiri Baraka: The Literary Works* (Durham, N.C.: Duke Univ. Press, 1973), 167.

11. Tyler School of Art, Temple University.

12. *Black Fire: An Anthology of Afro-American Writing,* LeRoi Jones and Larry Neal, eds. (New York: Morrow, 1968), a major statement for the new Black literature, introduced many of the writers to a general audience. In his foreword, Jones (Baraka) refers to Black artists as the "founding Fathers and Mothers, of our nation."

Mel Edwards

5. JAYNE CORTEZ
Supersurrealist Vision

The development of Jayne Cortez into a major talent has been as dazzling a rise as one might have hoped but not clearly anticipated from her first volume, *Pissstained Stairs and the Monkeyman's Wares,* in 1969. She came to poetry from acting and began writing in earnest in 1964. Her poems—banners and tributes—call to arms, to appreciation of political and artistic heroes and those of everyday Black life. Her fine ear for music, her dynamic imagery, and her disposition to orchestrate in a broad cultural span, both African and American, have led her social and political concerns into unique and risk-taking forms. The intense vision of reality in Cortez moves beyond the intellectual and unconscious aspects of Surrealism, itself a revolutionary movement, into a divine and infernal realism. Although I have referred to this as the poet's "superrealism," the term is applied differently in the visual arts. For this reason, I have adopted Cortez's own identification, "supersurrealism."

Jayne Cortez was born on May 10, 1936, in Fort Huachuca (Wa-CHOO-ca), Arizona, an army base where her father was stationed. One of three children, she has an older sister and a younger brother. Her father's family, traced by Cortez from Virginia and Carolina to Ohio and Arkansas, had lived in Arkansas for several generations. Her maternal grandfather, born in Tennessee, had served in the Philippines, where he met and married Julia Cortez, the poet's namesake, who bore him four children.

Cortez moved with her family to Los Angeles when she was seven. She attended the public schools and Compton Junior Col-

lege. Her earliest ambition, encouraged by her maternal grand-
father, was to be an actress. She was married early, in 1954, to a jazz
musician. Their son, Denardo, born in 1956, is an accomplished
drummer who has accompanied many of her live and recorded
performances. Cortez formed her own publishing company in
1972. Three years later, she was married to sculptor Melvin Ed-
wards, who has illustrated all her books. From 1977 to 1983 she
taught in the English department at Rutgers University.

     After her first marriage ended, the poet studied drama at the
Ebony Showcase in Los Angeles in 1960, and in 1964 she co-
founded the Watts Repertory Theatre Company, where she directed
plays, acted, and read her poetry, supporting herself meanwhile by
factory and office work. But the realities of discrimination drew her
into political action. In 1963 and 1964 she went to Mississippi to
participate in intensive voter registration drives with Fannie Lou
Hamer, the experiences that made a profound impression upon her
life and art.

     In 1967 Cortez fulfilled a dream by leaving for New York, and
soon she began to travel widely. She has since read her work and
lectured extensively in Africa (Ghana, Nigeria, Zimbabwe), in
Latin America (Mexico, Brazil, Martinique, Trinidad, Cuba), in
Europe (England, France, West Germany, the Netherlands), in
Canada, and throughout the United States. She has visited Nic-
aragua, the Ivory Coast, and Morocco. In Asilah, Morocco, she
made a series of monoprints that incorporated her poetry.

     Cortez's honors over the years include the Before Columbus
Foundation American Book Award for excellence in literature,
1980; Creative Artists Public Service Awards in 1973 and 1981;
National Endowment for the Arts fellowships in 1980 and 1986;
and a New York Foundation for the Arts award in 1987. In addi-
tion, a substantial portion of Cortez's recognition has come from
her compeers in the arts.[1] A present member of the executive board
of PEN and a member of ASCAP, she has also served on the
governing board of the Poetry Society of America (1985-88) and on
the board of directors of the Coordinating Council of Literary
Magazines (1986-88). She now serves on the advisory board of
Poets House in New York City where, on December 1, 1988, she
presented her tribute to Nicolas Guillén, the national poet of Cuba,
and read a moving encomium that she had written for the occasion.

     Travel has enriched Cortez's work with language, color, and

imagery. African languages in particular enliven the poetry. The poet's identification with Africa appears in the current name of her publishing company, Bola Press, adopted in 1973 for the publication of *Scarifications*. Her name in Yoruba, a Nigerian language, is Oyebola: *-bola* meaning "successful" and *Oye* deriving from Oya, the wife of Shango, an important deity, god of lightning. In Benin City Cortez was called "Emotan," the name of a woman helpful to the Oba (king) and meaning "poet," "wise." The vigorous images of "Ogun's Friend" (in *Mouth on Paper*) draw on the Yoruba god of iron and of war to interpret a sculptor who works in steel. The title *Firespitter* (1982) is taken from the name of a traditional African animal mask. When I asked Cortez whether she had considered notes or a glossary for that book's African references, she replied that she had put the idea aside; she wanted the reader to work at comprehension, just as he or she might struggle with allusions by white poets. Her later book *Coagulations*, however, does contain a glossary.

Pissstained Stairs and the Monkeyman's Wares is dedicated to members of the Watts Repertory Theatre Company. The title evokes ghetto life and, as the poet notes, its parasitical affliction of capitalism, symbolized by drugs. This passionate work abounds in eulogies—for Charlie Parker, Huddie "Leadbelly" Ledbetter, Dinah Washington, Ornette Coleman, Billie Holiday, John Coltrane, Theodore "Fats" Navarro, and (in "Sun") for "Aspiring Cosmobrating Men"—Black men. Love poems, revolutionary poems in which "R & B" (rhythm and blues) translates into "Revolution & Blood" (in "Ornette") and adaptations of the blues form within free verse show Cortez racing into the depths of feeling, the work occasionally faltering but charged with energy and power. Terminal rhyme, as in the blues attempts of "Dinah's Back in Town" and "Theodore," hampers her efforts, and she abandons it in subsequent works in favor of rhythm and repetition. "How Long Has Trane Been Gone," the poet's tribute to tenor saxophonist John Coltrane, effectively employs incremental repetition: The original question concludes, prodding, "how long / How long / Have black people been gone." "Forreal," a brave poem that skillfully relies on assonance, notes that

> Love lives
> & I wanna taste myself inside

Mmmmm that pure nigguh pain
I don't feel strange
I hate the welfare line

Anatomy as metaphor informs her dominant themes: identifica-
tion with the working class and underclass, with Black pride and
vitality, with heroic figures, and with Black music. Ahead lie the
African influences, what the poet refers to as "fusions."

Festivals and Funerals (1971), dedicated to her son, Denardo,
marks the development of Cortez's essential art: the fusion of
African language and imagery with American elements, unflinch-
ing use of the self/body as metaphor, surrealistic imagery, jazz-
influenced rhythmic repetition both simple and incremental, paral-
lel structures, lack of punctuation, improvisational features, and
worker-oriented perspectives. Body metaphor and repetition char-
acterize "Initiation," the dedicatory poem, in which the poet firmly
confronts African political upheaval:

During the season of cut organs we
shot forward like teeth spokes from runaways . . .
celebrated the slit nose reality of
our severed hands . . .
blood blood blood
and once again blood . . .
take us to the place for the new birth blood

"Today on This Day" encompasses with scorn an insensitive
culture: for example, the indifferent health department, "such an
audience of / mascara and white coats waving their bye bye's / to the
friday crowd of occupied stretchers" and "the basement smell of
their budget." Vernacular, unconventional language and imagery,
and synesthesic metonymy give form to both rage and its target.

The title poem, "Festivals & Funerals," repetitively mourns
Patrice Lumumba and Malcolm X:

I lost a good friend & i
loved him
I lost a good friend & i loved
him

C.O.D.

collect on death

collect on death
collect on death
. . . .

Who killed Lumumba
What killed Malcolm
Who killed Lumumba
What killed Malcolm

There are no tears
we have no friends
this is the word . . .

Inexorably, Cortez draws the threads of persecution, poverty, drugs, isolation, as they touch Blacks in the United States and Africa, toward introjection of the martyred flesh with its living testimony, toward solidarity and

the vanguard of precision
the virgin of communications
the erotic improvisation of uprooted
perfection the Blues

Festival and funeral, extremes of life and death, resolve their antinomy through celebration of creative essence and its cohesive symbol, "the Blues."

At the apex of the poet's Afro-American dynamic stands "African Night Suite," a noble poem of affirmation that begins:

Africa
take my hands from the newspaper shacks of
rotten existence and let my cataracts
flow into the red clay of your loyalty

In Cortez's dynamo of metaphoric exchange, her body's "cataracts" flow away from despair and stubborn poverty into the African terrain of pride, beauty, and sturdy character.

keep me in the mud of your belly
fed from the forest of your resistance
far from these mercenaries of illusion

I tell you i have to
live with my throat open to
the buzzards

my neck of our lines
my nose of gold studs
my lip ring flashing signals
to the moon against mount kenya . . .

Africa nurtures her; Cortez reciprocates. She hears the "afro suite of crickets in / the african blues tribe" as, with increasing intricacy, the cultural merging itself becomes the main focus. Transfigured, the poet declares:

> In cape coast
> in kumasi
> in Ibadan
> oyo oyo
> I am a ife woman
> biriwa fish woman of the sea
> night queen of night cities in nights
> I remember

Kumasi and the Biriwa area in Ghana; Ibadan, Oyo, and Ife in Nigeria, all typify the African references that distinguish Cortez's poetry from here on. The culture that blossoms through her imagery is a fierce flower, bound with the life of Blacks everywhere through shared pain, dedication, and a common foe:

> Listen
> from the lungs of a shark
> comes the gauntness of our agony
>
> the miracle of erections
>
> who were the peasants
> where are the bones
>
> my hat is off to the two toned
> double breasted birds of no hesitation
>
> who were the peasants
> where are the bones
>
> my hat is off to the two toned
> double breasted birds of no hesitation

The shark image, popular in Latin American portrayals of the United States (see Juan José Arévalo's *The Shark and the Sardines*), follows a stanza beginning with nature ("and the river knew / the ocean knew") and proceeding through transitional body images (miscarriage, knees, calluses, lips, ovaries, blood, navels, fists, fingers). After the shark stanza, these images continue their positive drive ("miracle of erections"). They end with a memorial acknowledgment of the peasants, their ancestral "bones," and with the spiritual survival of those "two toned birds" who inherit the two cultures.

Scarifications (1973) addresses life from the standpoint of a city dweller, using the Whitmanic identification with place and, again, the body as metaphor. Wild juxtapositions and crowded listing evoke the ambience:

> i am new york city of blood
> police and fried pies
> i rub my docks red with grenadine
> and jelly madness in a flow of tokay
> my huge skull of pigeons
> my seance of peeping toms
> my plaited ovaries excuse me
> this is my grime my thigh of
> steelspoons and toothpicks
>   i imitate no one

Neither does Cortez.

Politics and the Vietnam War compound the urban scene. "A New Cologne" grotesquely equates napalm with White Shoulders, Shalimar, and Tabu. "National Security" concerns Attica, and "the governor of shellshock," apparently Nelson Rockefeller, held responsible by many for the massacre of prisoners in quelling their riot. "Song for Kwame" (Kwame Nkrumah, prime minister of Ghana), "Back Home in Benin City," and "Orisha" (in which the Yoruba god and Louis "Satchmo" Armstrong converge) retain the African consciousness.

Although Cortez has the breath for long poems, she can be wryly concise in her social commentary. In "Making It," she defies adoption of a competitive system she feels will destroy her:

> I know they want me to make it
> to enter eye droppers and invade pills
>   turn around or get shot
> I know they wanna vaccinate me with

the fear of myself
so I'll pull down my face and nod
I know they want me to make it
    but i'm not in a hurry[2]

The poem thus connects the system to the drug culture that reverts
social anger to the self.

Mouth on Paper (1977) ascends into the full articulation of
Cortez's Afro-American fusion. An elegy "For the Poets (Chris-
topher Okigbo & Henry Dumas)," the former killed in Nsukka
during the Nigerian Civil War and the latter on a New York City
subway, unites the two cultures through insistent rhythm, jux-
taposed imagery, and the parallel martyrdom of the two poets.
Injustice is subdued in the crescendo of confrontations. These
culminate in a tornado of images summoned from the entire poem
and pounded into eulogy, shaping a monumental "delta" of praise,
which concludes:

i need spirits ah i need ankles ah i need hurricanes ah
i need gas pipes ah i need blood pacts ah i need ah
to make a delta praise for the poets ah

Cortez's urgent political sense is nowhere more apparent than
in "Give Me the Red on the Black of the Bullet," a poem for Claude
Reece, Jr., a fourteen-year-old Black youth who was killed by a New
York City policeman. Beginning with an impossible demand, terri-
ble in its simplicity—"Bring back the life / of Claude Reece Jr."—
the poet calls for the bullet from the boy's head to make "a Benin
bronze," and summons thunder, cyclone, earthquake—ultimate
powers of nature—in a call to justice. With the bullet she will
remake, like some deity, the life of the dead Reece. The final cry
gathers its thunder:

I want to make justice for
the blackness of Claude Reece Jr.
bring back the bullet with the blood of the blackness
of Claude Reece Jr.
I want to make justice
I want to make justice for the blackness of Claude Reece Jr.

The working-class perspective of "Ogun's Friend," inspired by
the steel sculpture of Mel Edwards, charges the poem with a special

intensity. The poet hammers language and imagery into short, syncopated strokes, gathers them into a list, moves to itemize tools, explodes into surreal images, while continuing to vary the theme: appreciation of a steelworker.

Cortez's "praise poetry," as she adopts the African term, includes instruments as well as people. The 165 lines of "Drums Everywhere Drums," her longest single piece, present an auditory feast in performance, especially with musical accompaniment. The poet's depth of control within freedom, exercised through physical, geographical, and historical imagery, sweeps the essence of African American cultural heritage into its percussive span. Drums pervade continents and existence itself, which in turn transforms into drums, the symbol of cultural power, communication, and solidarity. There are

> Drums made from rivers
> made from a multiplication of dance steps
> made from catfish heads in a tongues embrace
> made from a rosette of orange rosin cradle cap
> . . . .
>
> Fierce drums
> growling drums
> echo drums
> over mojo whoop whooping drums
> out of coo coo ka hooka drums
> ear drums khaki drums
> drums made of dynamite

drums in seemingly limitless number and variety, a people's consciousness, overwhelmingly inclusive.

Cortez's range includes an elegant simplicity (see "Commitment," for Paul Robeson). Appraisals of the "Blues Lady" of "Grinding Vibrato," (a fine example of blues adaptation), Josephine Baker ("So Many Feathers"), and Duke Ellington ("Rose Solitude") elicit the lyrical Cortez, who weaves a quieter magic.

> I am essence of Rose Solitude
> my cheeks are laced with cognac
> my hips sealed with five satin nails
> i carry dreams and romance of new fools and old flames

        between the musk of fat
        and the side pocket of my mink tongue

Yet even when reflective, the poet arrays the unsentimental, "hard,
dry images" once prescribed by Eza Pound's colleague T. E.
Hulme. She concludes: "i cover the hands of Duke who like
Satchmo / like Nat (King) Cole will never die / because love they say
/ never dies."

    "Alberta Alberta," an elegy for the murdered mother of Martin
Luther King, Jr., uses repetition as a keening chant, recalling the
chanted sermon that influenced Brooks's heroic "preachments."
"For the Brave Young Students in Soweto," like the collage of
strong faces (including the poet's) shown on the verso page, mounts
individual images side by side to survey a situation and design its
power. Solidarity among all colonized and oppressed people culmi-
nates in the heroes:

        Soweto i tell you Soweto
        when i see you standing up like this
        i think about all the forces in the world
        confronted by the terrifying rhythms of young students
        by their sacrifices
        and the revelation that it won't be long now
        before everything
        in this world changes

This vulnerability to change epitomizes Cortez's revolutionary
stance, in the explosion and re-vision of images that characterize
her work. Even when she seeks to write a blues, as in the humorous
"You Know," it is engaged, complex, presenting

            a serious blues
        you know
            a significant blues
        you know
            an unsubmissive blues

The last line titles *Unsubmissive Blues* (1980), a recording in which
she reads some of her strongest poems to a rich drum and instru-
mental accompaniment.

    Firespitter (1982) continues the drive toward pronounced
rhythms, jazz-infused; pyrotechnic imagery; African-pan-Amer-

ican fusions; and political statement. Like all her other books, this collection is enhanced by the powerful drawings of Mel Edwards, who interpreted the Firespitter for cover and text. Edwards, who had admired Cortez's work even before meeting her, observes, "It is a pleasure to work with her work." Poets often shun visual additions to their poems, but Cortez's art accommodates the senses, being visual, alive with form and color; aural, demanding to be heard. The auxiliary visual mode, here so finely attuned to the text, serves not as intrusion but as extension.

On November 13, 1981, a few months before publication of *Firespitter*, Cortez read from the book at Joseph Papp's New York Shakespeare Festival Public Theater, functioning as the poetic instrument in a jazz ensemble where each performer, in turn or as inspired, led the group into improvisation. The performance was distinguished by her voice, ranging frm shimmering silk to steel; her bearing, majestic in African robe; the stunning imagery of the poems; the democratic ambience and group sense that allowed each performer alternately to star; and the lively enthusiasm of the audience.

Firespitter typically garners musical and other public heroic figures of Black life: Charles Mingus ("Into This Time"); Count Basie ("Solo Finger Solo"); "No Simple Explanations (To the memory of Larry Neal)"; Fannie Lou Hamer ("Big Fine Woman from Ruleville"), of whom Cortez writes: "magnificent ancestor / warrior friend / most beautiful sister / I kiss the mud of this moment." The birthplace of Mrs. Hamer (1917-1977), the great civil rights fighter who challenged voting restrictions in Mississippi, suggests the rule of law and, further, the Golden Rule. "Mud" becomes an emblem of the struggle in which Cortez participated with Mrs. Hamer. Other figures include Léon Damas ("The Red Pepper Poet with the bull-roarer tongue"), poet and cofounder of the Négritude literary movement; and Afro-Cuban percussionist Chano Pozo ("I See Chano Pozo").

Also typically, there are Afro-American poems, from the triumphant "Firespitters (FESTAC 77)," honoring the 1977 Festival of Arts and Culture in Lagos, Nigeria, to "Nigerian/American Relations": "They want the oil / But they don't want the people," iterated twenty times. In a newer key, "If the Drum Is a Woman," popular with audiences, and "Rape," concerning the nationally prominent cases of Inez García and Joanne Little, turn to the

subject of physical abuse. Rather than as narrowly feminist state-
ments, the poet intends the pieces as "human rights poems."

There is celebration, too, of the humble worker. "For a Gypsy
Cab Man" eulogizes the African cab driver who enjoys taking
passengers to Harlem and other areas often shunned by
medallioned yellow taxicabs. The "friend and collector of green
cards," (the Immigration Bureau work permits for aliens) receives
the poet's

> . . . thanks for turning your automobile
>   into an ambulance
>   into a fire engine of red stallions
>   into a combat car of constant motion
>   and endless horn signals

Political pace quickens in this book, whose most unrelenting
attacks appear in three impressive longer poems. "Blood Suckers,"
about the Miami race riots, begins:

> In Miami
> the bood suckers came sucking in full speed
> twisting and sucking into
> a urethra of decapitated shrimp heads

and compiles a list of suckers and bloodsuckers that scores the
whole white governmental, corporate, and religious establishment,
together with dupes and collaborators both white and Black. It is a
deliberately unpleasant poem that hurls its enraged and loathsome
images without pause or mitigation. "Festival Fusions 81" marks a
dramatic change in tone from 1977 and "Firespitters." Four years
later the festival has turned symbol for the fraudulently hopeful
dreams of social change: "My festival is a parading pant leg of
vomit / my festival is a permanent archive of scar tissues," the poet
cries as she scans the "naked festival body . . . embedded with
scorpion dust . . . in the valley of shark pus."

Employing a simpler rhetoric of imagery, "There It Is" ap-
proaches the reader directly:

> My friend
> they don't care
> if you're an individualist
> a leftist   a rightist
> a shithead or a snake

Cortez renews the colloquial diction and familiar rhetoric ("the ruling class," "exploit," "killer cops," "enemies," "imperialism") by setting the stale words into fresh contexts ("The enemies polishing their penises between / oil wells at the pentagon"). This work approaches the speech poems of Baraka's *Hard Facts* and the "preachments" of Brooks. It reaches out to the audience; it calls to unity; it leads.

Coagulations: New and Selected Poems (1984) was the poet's first book with an outside company. A small but welcome glossary helps with the linguistic, geographical, and cultural references. Powerful drawings by Mel Edwards complement anew the raw energy of the poems. Selections from *Scarifications, Mouth on Paper,* and *Firespitter* gather many of Cortez's most powerful and popular works. "On All Fronts," the last section, comprises thirteen new poems that carry forward the poet's political concerns, audacious imagery, and percussive force. These three elements fuse at increasing degrees of intensity into "a work of resistance."[3]

The new poems clearly demonstrate that Cortez expresses the collective rage of the disenfranchised, the dispossessed, and the victims of discrimination. Militant and uncompromising, matching jazz and incantatory rhythms with parallel syntax and "unsubmissive" repetitions, she develops a heroic Black musical rhetoric of prophecy. Hurling the obscenities of contemporary life into a furnace of exploding images, Cortez exposes our paths to universal self-destruction, to a global Jonestown. "Stockpiling," inspired by the accumulation of nuclear weapons, arrays a series of hideous death images, "the final stockpile of flesh dancing in / the terrible whooping cough of the wind."

Cortez retains a ferocious humor. "Expenditures / Economic Love Song 1," merely repeats "MILITARY SPENDING HUGE PROFITS & / DEATH / / MILITARY SPENDING HUGE PROFITS & / DESTRUCTION" and reads as if it were nineteen banner headlines, but makes its point of lethal repetition. "Everything Is Wonderful" satirizes apathy, the assumption that all is well "Under the urination of astronauts / and the ejaculation of polluted sparrows"—*except* in various parts of the world, a lengthy list beginning with Grenada and El Salvador and ending with Beirut.

The pyrotechnical crescendo culminates in "Tell Me," a plea to rouse the conscience and consciousness of all human beings.

Tell me that the plutonium sludge
in your corroded torso is all a dream

Tell me that your penis bone is not erupting
with the stench of dead ants
that your navel is not the dump site
                              of contaminated pus
that the spillage from your hard ass
is not a fallout of radioactive waste
Tell me it's a lie
Tell me it's a joke

This is the prophetic Cortez at her mordant best, firing a warning
vision of judgment and impending holocaust at the body of the
listener/reader. In her total concern for the planet, Cortez may be
viewed as our ecological Jeremiah, or an Angela Davis by way of
Ralph Nader, "translated" and struck suddenly with Shake-
speare's "muse of fire" (via *Henry V*). Hers is no tranquil, Words-
worthian contemplation, although one could make a case for her
respect for life as "natural piety." Yet despite her dire perceptions of
present and future, she pleads for, even demands, the active essence
of hope.

Tell me it's a misunderstanding
Tell me it's not a human need
Tell me it's a crock of shit
Tell me it's propaganda
Tell me you really intend to go forward
Tell me
Tell me
Tell me

The reader or fortunate listener wants to spring up and reply, "Yes, I
will!" and, perhaps, to move into the aisle of action.
    When Cortez arrived at my apartment for her interview, I was
struck by her slender, almost slight, appearance, since, like
Sanchez, her performance projects a bigger-than-lifesized pres-
ence.[4] She is a very private person who talks little about her
personal life. "I consider that the details of my poetic processes are
personal; they're my private life," she told me. And though she was
warm and relaxed during our conversation, she did not at any time
forgo her alertness to a Black perspective on our discussion.

INTERVIEW WITH JAYNE CORTEZ

DH You spent the first seven years of your life in Arizona. What was it like for you there, as a child?

JC Let's see, Arizona—have you ever been there? It's very beautiful in its own way. There are fantastic sunrises and sunsets. The sky is a huge space of changing colors. There are mountains and canyons and a lot of cactuses, all different shapes of cactuses, and many flowers, and different kinds of insects, and snakes and lizards, and of course there's the desert—

DH Is it anything—

JC —beautiful rocks. Smooth rocks, broken rocks, rocks of silver flecks.

DH Is Africa anything like Arizona? Did you feel any kind of similarity?

JC Not really. Arizona is a state, Africa is a continent. Even the desert in Egypt is different from the desert in Arizona.

DH Not even in the climate?

JC Not in western Nigeria. I spent most of my time in Nigeria visiting the western and midwestern states. In the part of Arizona that I'm from, the southern part, it can be a hundred in the daytime in the summer, and in the evening the temperature can drop to fifty-five. And it's dry. But western Nigeria is not dry. It's moist. It's kind of like being in New York or in Houston, Texas—more like Texas. I did make a brief visit to Kano, and I guess that part, the northern part of Nigeria, is sort of like parts of Arizona in climate. The temperatures may be a hundred degrees in the day and drop to fifty at night, and of course the Sahara Desert is on the northern border of Nigeria. Nigeria is a very fascinating, dynamic, and beautiful country.

DH You mentioned the harmattan.

JC The harmattan starts in December and ends in February. What it is is a hot, dry wind that blows over parts of Africa behind clouds of red dust, which causes a thick haze and reduces visibility.

DH Your grandfather assured you that you would be an actress. Was he an important influence on you, and how did you become interested in acting?

JC I guess I was interested in acting because I used to like to act. Act up and act out! [*Laughter*] So, when you act up and you act out, they say, "Oh, you're quite an actress!" My grandfather said,

"You want to be an actress like Lena Horne, or somebody." But they didn't seriously sit down and talk to me and say, "Look, I know that at some point you are going to grow up and we would like you to be"—no. It was nothing like that.

DH   But I think it registers in your unconscious—

JC   I think they saw me acting and doing all those imitations, and they said, "Well, she's a natural!" But that's all. In the article[5] I said that because I was remembering my grandfather. Maybe he was serious, maybe I was serious, or maybe it wasn't a serious thing.

DH   Were there any other important early influences, apart from musicians and people like Lena Horne and Billie Holiday?

JC   I wouldn't say that Lena Horne or Billie Holiday were "influences." To be influenced means you're sort of under the spell of something or someone. I was under the spell of my mother and father! [Laughter] You know, they're early influences. I was under the spell of the environment, maybe, because I couldn't help it.

DH   Well, how would you say they influenced you?

JC   I was inspired by Billie Holiday; I liked the way she sang. I liked the way she sat down on notes and intensified. But I wasn't a singer. I was inspired by the acting of Lena Horne. She was Black and I thought she could act, and I liked her singing and acting. I thought she was really cute, and she attracted men in the movies, and you know, she seemed to have the world on a string with no problems, so naturally I wanted to be like her, the movie image her. So you're inspired for a minute, and you imitate the way they walk and talk. You go twisting through the neighborhood, moving your hips and lips a certain way and pushing your hair back—but at six or seven years old, who's going to take you seriously?

DH   How would you say your mother and father influenced you?

JC   Well, they were examples of how to live, how you take care of business, how you survive in a hostile atmosphere. They were my first examples of how to do everything that you do: how you take care of the house, how you take care of the family business, how you take care of children, how to have dignity and respect. Then later, you explore your feelings of whether you really accept all that.

DH   Yes. You say they had a strong sense of family.

JC   Yes, sure. A strong sense of family. Small family, but strong.

DH   The best kind. What were your interests in school, and was school in Arizona and in Los Angeles a positive experience?

JC   In Arizona, elementary school was one big room with all the classes in it. My sister was in her class, and her row was there; so-and-so's was here, and my row was over there. You would go from the first grade to the sixth grade in one room.

DH   It was a family experience.

JC   Yes. I remember liking my teacher. The principal of the school was also minister of the Baptist church. And later, he moved to California. I married my first husband in his house in Los Angeles. He performed the marriage ceremony.

DH   That's a wonderful story.

JC   My community in Fort Huachuca, Arizona, was a very close community. We knew everyone and everyone knew us. I went to school with mostly Black children and some Native American children. We were segregated from the white children, who went to white schools. This was my introduction to segregation. We moved to California. First San Diego, a very damp place that smelled of fishing canneries. A smell that was embedded in the skins of its workers. A smell that permeated certain sections of the city. It took some getting used to, because the only sea that we were used to was the desert. And the smell of the desert was quite different from the smell of San Diego.

My grandparents had moved from Arizona to San Diego. We lived with them for almost a year; then we moved to Los Angeles. We lived in West Los Angeles for five years. I attended the Thirty-sixth Street elementary school. Most of the sudents were African American, and a few of them were Japanese American children returning with their parents from the World War II detention centers. Later, we moved to the community of Watts, which was in South Los Angeles. I spent most of my teenage years in Watts.

DH   How did you feel about the move to Los Angeles and especially about living in Watts?

JC   I remember I hated to leave Arizona, because I had a cat and there were these insects, the ants and the bees. I used to get the bees in the summertime—catch them in the middle of a flower, hold the petals together so they couldn't get out, and they would buzz, buzz, buzz! Anyhow, I used to play games with all of the little insects. And of course there was my favorite tree, and friends. Well, I wanted to leave, but I didn't want to leave. As a kid you're attached to your friends and to your surroundings and all of that, but on the other hand, leaving is like an adventure. You're going to meet new people and have new experiences. The move was not disruptive to me.

DH   Did you like Watts? Did you like living there?

JC   Watts was okay, but I disliked the junior high school that I had to attend a few blocks outside of Watts. It was almost all white. We had integration and segregation and domination at the same time. And it was like, very miserable. Miserable simply because of the attitudes of both the white students and the white teachers. Almost every book we read was about their lives, their history, their values, their culture. Things would really get tense when we got to the slave era. It was replusive. They taught such lies about Africa. I tell you I had to fight every day. I mean when a white kid called me "nigger," I had to jump up and beat the hell out of him or her. And I did that constantly. My mother was always at the school.

DH   You learned early.

JC   Yes. I learned very early about what's ugly, and racism is very ugly.

DH   Turning to your work, now, I find it visual, kinesthetic, and musical, and yet you say you don't sing.

JC   I don't sing.

DH   Did you ever want to sing or play an instrment?

JC   No. I never thought about singing. But I did play several instruments. I played the piano like all young—

DH   All nice young girls. [*Laughter*]

JC   I took piano lessons. I played bass in junior orchestra. For a while I played cello. In high school I took a course in music harmony and theory. I was also interested in the visual arts. I attended Manual Arts High School, comparable to [the High School of] Music and Art here [in Manhattan]. I took drawing, painting, and design classes. As a child in Arizona I was exposed to the music of Duke Ellington, Count Basie, Jimmy Lunceford, and all the other big bands of that time. My parents had quite a collection of records; that's when I first heard Ella Fitzgerald and Billie Holiday. In 1947 I was exposed to the music called bebop. I fell in love with the music of Charlie Parker and Thelonious Monk.

DH   Your poem "Tapping" in *Scarifications* is dedicated to tap dancers. I wondered whether you ever learned to tap-dance.

JC   I took dancing lessons—

DH   You had the full middle-class treatment?

JC   Well, I don't think that was a middle-class treatment. A number of children in the Black community knew how to tap-dance, play an instrument, and peform acrobatic movements. Later I took modern dance and ballet. I couldn't tap-dance that well, but you could hear the sound of my taps!—because I liked the shoes.

DH   Well, I think that's all enriched your work very much.

JC   Probably.

DH   All the arts.

JC   About the poem "Tapping"—there used to be a place in New York City called the Jazz Museum, and on Sunday afternoon they presented tap dance concerts. I used to go. The dancers included Baby Lawrence, Chuck Green, L. D. Jackson, and Rhythm Red, and others. Baby Lawrence was known as the Charlie Parker of the tap dancers. He would dance the compositions of Charlie Parker and add his own complicated solo to the piece after the theme. The concert would continue like that, each dancer performing his own special steps. It was fantastic. I was so inspired by those events.

DH   You refer to your experiences in Mississippi as a catalyst that turned you away from acting—where white-prescribed roles for Blacks were restricted—to literature, where you could express yourself more freely. Was your work as cofounder of the Watts Repertory Theatre Company primarily in poetry, and was that the beginning?

JC   No, that was not the beginning. I wrote a couple of short stories when I was about fourteen. My best friend and I wrote these stories and sent them to a *True Confessions* magazine contest. We had dreams of winning the prizes and the money. We didn't win or place. We received rejection letters with our manuscripts.

DH   Oh, so then you were interested in writing pretty early.

JC   Sure.

DH   What about poetry—did you start that early also?

JC   The poetry? Let's see. I remember writing down words, lines, ideas, secrets. I know now that I was keeping a journal. I always read a lot of books, and I was interested in writing stories, but I didn't write that much poetry. However, in the community we were always rhyming.

DH   Did you play the Dozens?

JC   We alway played the Dozens, signified, told jokes, and performed for each other.

DH   That was in rhyme.

JC   Yes, that was in rhyme. We did it constantly. It was an everyday ritual. Oral poetry in an oral atmosphere. When I used to go to jam sessions and other musical events, I would sometimes write down my reactions to the music and the scene. Much later, I started to write poetry concerned with loneliness and need.

DH   So did I! That's the usual— [laughing]

JC   That's how you start. Right. You start with yourself. The "Why am I so sad?" kind of poetry. My experiences in Mississippi are important, because after Misssissippi I didn't write that kind of poetry anymore.

DH   Would you say your political awareness was charged after the Mississippi experience?

JC   Oh, sure it was. Of course, in Los Angeles I learned a lot about racism and politics, and we in the Black comunity always had problems with the police. They would harass and provoke people. They would stop Black men on the streets for nothing. They would say things like, "Well, you have a beard and so you look like you might want to do something." And you know, they used to be able to hold a person for forty-eight hours, for nothing. I think my political education started in the segregated school. Later, while working in a factory, I became more aware of the economic situation. I was working in a factory before I went to Mississippi. Through the work experience I learned about organizing and about protest. I was in the union. Before I went to Mississippi I already knew about discrimination, police brutality, and class and race problems. I took that with me. I mean—I wasn't just Jayne, you know, picking daisies and then she goes to Mississippi. I was Jayne facing the everyday routine in the factories with the bosses and the unions and with police brutality in the city of smog, suppression, and racism.

Mississippi was in the deep South—South Africa! In 1963 it was a place of fierce oppression, segregation, and lynchings. The people were struggling for survival. They were fighting for the right to vote. That's where I met Fannie Lou Hamer, a very dedicated woman in the Civil Rights Movement. After that southern experience, I became more aware of the need for political power. And like I said, the poems I wrote before going were concerned with being sad. In Mississippi I learned that you could get rid of a lot of sad feelings, and you didn't have to be isolated, lonely, and frustrated and sitting around without the necessities of life. Because you could do something about it.

DH   Rather than a personal sadness, you were really talking about sadness in the environment.

JC   Yes. Being unemployed and without food can make you very sad. But you weren't the problem. The problem existed before you knew there was a problem. The probem is the system, and you can organize, unify, and do something about the system. That's what I learned.

DH   You worked in a factory before going to Mississippi?

JC   Yes.

DH   What kind of factory was it?

JC   I worked in a shirt factory; then I worked in a belt factory; and I worked in other factories. I also worked as a waitress, a telephone operator, and an office worker, typing and operating business machines. I learned a lot from the women in the factories. We talked about many, many things. I got advice and tips on how to confront reality. How to be an independent woman. How to get your heels to clicking when you're being abused. How to cook. What to do about health problems. It was real sisterhood.

DH   What prompted your move to New York City?

JC   Well, I'll tell you. When I was a teenager, I always had this desire to go to New York City. I used to read in *Downbeat* all about the clubs and all about the concerts, and I felt like I was missing something. Since I liked music, I wanted to be in the place where the music was happening. At home I talked a lot about going to New York City. When I graduated from high school, my mother gave me a piece of luggage; she gave me a nice Samsonite bag. But I didn't use it until 1959, on my first trip to New York City.

DH   The poem that you wrote, "I Am New York City," in *Scarifications*, seems somewhat ambivalent about New York. Is that the way you feel now?

JC   I wrote that poem in 1973. In the poem I'm dealing with my relationship to New York City, using the objects and attitudes to conjure up images. By that time I loved New York—

DH   Warts and all?

JC   Yeah. New York was and is a big international city. The streets are popping with different dialects. The city is backward and advanced at the same time. I now have a hate/love relationship with New York City, with Manhattan. In 1972 and 1973 New York City was big, sloppy, and wonderful. Most of the poems in *Scarifications* are concerned with New York City images—connecting them and juxtaposing them against human interior and exterior body parts.

DH In the 1978 interview [in *Essence*] you said you spent seven hours a day writing and rewriting. Do you still do this?

JC No, I don't do that. Since I teach three days a week, I don't have enough time.[6] You know, it takes seven hours sometimes to start, to get started, to retrace your steps. I mean, you may be sitting there with one line—

DH What a mighty line! [*Laughter*]

JC Do you know that a minute becomes an hour, and an hour becomes three, and then it's seven hours and you hate to stop, even though you have accomplished—nothing. And you put it in the drawer with the other nothings, and the nothings pile up, and one day you turn the nothings into something.

DH Do you recommend writing regularly, rather than waiting for inspiration?

JC Yes, because you may never get inspiration; you may never get inspired. You can inspire yourself. I don't wait for inspiration. I write whenever I can.

DH Do you like teaching?

JC Um-hum, um-hum. I like teaching. I enjoy working with students, listening to their ideas, experiences, and interpretations. Teaching can be draining, but it's not a bad way to make a living.

DH Well, I guess with a caring person like you, it would take more time.

JC It takes more time because you have to prepare. I teach a Lit. course and a creative writing course at Livingston College. I usually have about twenty to twenty-five students in each class, which means that I have to read forty to fifty papers every time an assignment is due.

DH Your poetry is often political. Do you think poetry ought to be political, or do you feel that you just write what you can?

JC I think poetry can be political. If you're a political person and a poet, you will write political poetry. You make political decisions. At some point, your work will represent your political thought. You put the political thoughts, the emotional needs, and the poetic elements together.

DH Would you categorize your thought in any particular way? I'm talking about your political thought. Or do you think mostly in terms of issues and particular situations?

JC I think of issues, I think of situations, I think of the future. What our needs will be in the future. And how to eliminate needs. So it's good for the work and it's good for you to be political. I'm concerned with reality, illusions, contradictions, transformations.

DH Do you have any feelings about Black Nationalism? Your work doesn't seem to have that perspective. It seems more worker oriented and more general, class oriented—

JC But it's *Black* worker oriented. I'm a Black person in a Black family in the Black nation, so nationalism is a natural fact. I think that Black Nationalism has its place in the growth of the United States of America. I think the Black Nation—the oppressed African American nation—has a future.

DH I was thinking of it in a more specific way, pertaining to, perhaps the establishment of a Black state, a more segregated kind of existence, or maybe a totally segregated kind of existence, if that were possible, for Black people.

JC If it is possible to have a Black state within the United States—I would say wonderful! Most of our people are in the Black belt, and we speak the same language. Great! What's wrong with having a Black state in the United States? There are a lot of white states in the United States. What's wrong with having a Black state? Fine! I have a Black state of mind! I wouldn't be against that at all. It's called self-determination.

DH Sometimes you're called "a jazz poet." How did you get started working with musicians?

JC Well, as you know, I started writing poetry about my relationship to Black music, talking about the rhythms or what I liked about it, and of course, talking about the musicians who play the music. It's like praise poetry, the old African praise poetry. You write about another human being, about who the person is and what that person produces. When I started reading my poetry in public, I thought it would sound good with music. And I had a lot of musician friends at the time, and it seemed like an interesting idea.

DH   Is it a very difficult procedure, working the poetry into the music and music into the poetry?

JC   That part is not hard. The part that is hard is stretching the human voice. Everybody else in the group has another kind of a voice, a musical instrument that's much louder than yours [*laughing*]. That's the problem. How not to let the different pitch levels control your work. Most of the musicians who've played with me have all been musicians who play jazz. They are used to inventing off of different rhythm patterns and different sounds. So they relate to what I'm doing in the same way. They interject their own sound and attitudes. And I do the same thing. I listen to them and respond to their ideas and attitudes. I like working with music. It's a collective experiment. A collective composition.

DH   Do you plan to work in the future with musicians?

JC   Yes. I would love to. Working with the music has provided me with a lot of freedom. I don't feel restricted. My whole respiratory system is involved in an assemblage of free tones.

DH   I find it very exciting. I thought that your recent performance at Joseph Papp's theater was remarkably vital and beautiful.

JC   Yes, I liked it. I liked it because of the multiplying vibrations, variations, and extensions.

DH   Were you improvisational at any point during that?

JC   Yes. There are phrases or words that were not written but were added during the performance, especially in the Chano Pozo poem and the poem for the gypsy cab driver. The work sounded new and improvised because the approach to the new music was new. And of course the work is improvisational before it is written on paper.

DH   Yes, well that's what the lack of punctuation seems to do. It gives you that freedom, and it does seem improvisational.

JC   Yes. It goes back to the oral. It's like you don't say, "Come here. Stop. Go there. Stop." You say, "Come here let's do this babababababa," so it's just a continuation of rhythm and sound. When you stop, you stop; where you breathe, you breathe; and where you pause, you pause.

DH   From *Festivals and Funerals* on, there are strongly African elements in your work. Linguistic and cultural ones are obvious. Would you note any other factors that you might point to and say, "Well, that's African"?

JC   I would have to look at the work, because right now I can't remember—well, the use of African words. [Opens *Mouth on Paper*] Funny, I turned right to "Ogun's Friend," Ogun being the Yoruba god of war and iron, worshipped by metalworkers, hunters and warriors, truckdrivers, engineers—it's a praise poem dedicated to a sculptor who works with steel. Africa represents a link with the past. Africans and African Americans have many things in common. Our tastes, gestures, beliefs, ancestors. We share the same blood. We are connected in pigmentation and in our struggle against oppression. We are lovers of life.

DH   Would you say the African influences are primarily cultural, or do they also come from individuals?

JC   I've been influenced by traditional African art and inspired by African artists and musicians.

DH   And poets—

JC   Yes, and poets. I not only use traditional African elements in my work, but I also use details and situations of modern Africa. Soweto, Zimbabwe, Angola—the idea of a socialist system and attitudes in a neocolonialist situation.

DH   I'd like to talk about the process, your poetic process, in which your imagery seems to breed more imagery. How would you describe your making a poem?

JC   Well, you get up in the morning, you have tea or coffee, and you sit down at your desk and write. [*Laughs*]

DH   Well, I was referring specifically to this dynamic process of imagery. I mean you have a richer density of imagery in your work than I have seen in most other poets. It's quite unusual, and I was wondering what feeds that. I see surrealistic sources. It's as if the conscious and the unconscious were both rising and expressing themselves together.

JC   It's true. I use dreams, the subconscious, and the real objects, and I open up the body and use organs, and I sink them into words, and I ritualize them and fuse them into events. I guess the poetry is like a festival. Everything can be transformed. The street becomes something else, the subway is something else, everything at a festival is disguised as something else. Everything changes: the look of the person changes, their intentions change, the attitudes are different, experiences become fiercer. Voices become other voices. So that's what I do in my poetry. I keep making connections. I try to not wade in the shallow water of shallowness and I try to not get stuck in the mud of art council standards and the spectators' demand for messages. It's called multiplication, sub-division, and subtraction.

DH   I've called it "superrealism"; I've referred to your work as superrealism, and by that I mean a deep vision of reality, intensified by the emotional, imaginative, political, and surrealistic perception of it. Do you think that describes what you're doing?

JC   Sure. But the word "superrealism" means something else in the visual arts, so I would say "supersurrealism."

DH   You coin words, like "purrtongue," "stridulating," "cosmobrating," "contortionated." Is this mainly an intellectual process, or is it more intuitive? Do you try to get an onomatopoetic word for what you mean?

JC   The intellect and the intuition—that's all one thing. Can't be one without the other. I mean you select, and you think, you have an idea [*snaps fingers*], you reason and you don't reason. But it's all together; one reinforces the other. It's all one thing for me. And coining the words—like I told you, in the Black community we were always making up new words and phrases in our verbalization games. It's whose word was going to be the top word, and whose word was going to be the last word. If I say the person is con-tortionated, con-tor-tion-ated, I have made a decision of how to express myself intuitively and intellectually.

DH   What kind of audiences do you want to reach?

JC   All kinds of audiences. I've read in different countries; I've read all over the United States; I've read in libraries, in night clubs, and at political rallies. A lot of my readings have been in the Black community, and I'm certainly interested in reaching a lot of Black people. We share some of the same sentiments and responsibilities. They communicate to me and I communicate to them.

DH   I guess because I use initials, I'm interested in initials. It struck me that your initials are "J. C." I was wondering whether this ever interested you or anybody around you when you were growing up.

JC   No.

DH   In *Pissstained Stairs*, the poem "Race" refers to "A Race called Faggot," and seems to indict homosexulity. Is this so, and do you maintain this view?

JC   Well, first of all, "Race" was written for a friend of mine. I don't think it indicts homosexuals. I think it talks about the contradictions of a particular person. The poem is about contradictions and inconsistencies.

DH   Well, with the Gay Liberation Movement, which comes after the time of this poem, would you say that that has influenced your thinking at all? Do you have second thoughts about the views you had?

JC   Yes, I have second thoughts. I wrote the poem in 1968 at the request of a friend. He never rejected the tone of the piece.

DH   You were writing about a gay person.

JC   Yes.

DH   In *Festivals and Funerals* there's a brilliant poem called "African Night Suite," which ends with these lines: "my hat is off to the two toned / double breasted birds of no hesitation." Are the birds a specific or symbolic reference? What kind of birds are they?

JC   [*Laughing*] They're two-toned birds. You've heard of those two-toned birds of no hesitation?

DH   Since I've read you, yes! [*Laughter*]

JC   The two-toned birds definitely have to be the birds of America, and they're birds who are mixed, in race and in time. African Americans. Those are the two-toned birds of no hesitation, the people who are not going to hesitate.

DH   I'm so indoctrinated, every time I see the word "bird" I think of Charlie Parker!

JC   I wasn't thinking of Charlie Parker, but if we were all aggressive birds like Charlie Parker, we would definitely be birds of no hesitation.

DH   He didn't have much hesitation.

JC   No. I haven't read this piece in a long time.

DH   It's an awfully good poem. I recommend it. [*Laughter*]

JC   In fact, I haven't read from *Festivals and Funerals* or *Pissstained Stairs* in years.

DH   Do you prefer reading new things?

JC   I prefer reading new things, yes.

DH   I was curious about the poem "Rose Solitude." Was that inspired by a particular piece of music by Ellington?

JC   It was inspired by the creativity of Duke Ellington. I went to the funeral of Duke Ellington at Saint John's Cathedral.[7] I was very moved and impressed by the emotions of some of the people there. I happened to be sitting next to an older West Indian woman who said these lines to me, "Like Nat (King) Cole, like Satchmo," and I thought about that; I thought about the qualities of the people she had mentioned. I thought of their music, and I was sitting there, and I was thinking about Duke Ellington and watching all of the images in this church, the different moods, the different faces, the agitation of the wind outside, and I thought about the music. The poem is an accumulation of those thoughts, images, and other memories.

DH   Did you have the chance to meet Duke Ellington?

JC   I met him in 1966. We had a very nice conversation.

DH   You must have been thrilled.

JC   I was thrilled. He was so charming and so up-to-date. Like some of his music: melodious, swinging, and complete.

DH   To meet a myth that you write about—you mythologize. Your work does mythologize people. I think part of it comes from just loving the music, but I wonder whether part of it is also deliberate making, raising to heroic stature in the work, as people have raised themselves in life.

JC   Most of the names in my work are there as examples.

DH   Do you do a lot of revising?

JC   Not a whole lot.

DH   Do you ever go back to a book and say, "Gee, I would rewrite that line, and—"

JC   Yes, I've looked over *Pissstained Stairs* and *Festivals and Funerals,* and I've said, "God, how could I have done that?" But you know, it's there, and it represents that moment. It's too late.

DH   Not for a second edition.

JC   Yes, there are a number of things that I would change, but it would be hard to recapture the same sensations. They would be poems separating from themselves. They would be torn apart, because my solutions today are different. I don't have the same views as I had then.

DH   Yes, I don't think you should tamper too much.

JC   I like to do new things, build new structures, create new poems.

DH   You name several people who've influenced you, like Léon Damas and Aimé Césaire, Langston Hughes—

JC   I was inspired by them. I like the inner tension and rhythms of Damas's poetry. I like the way Sterling Brown articulates the blues, and I liked the oral qualities of Langston's poetry, and I like the levels of depth and complexity in the poetry of Césaire. I like the music and revolutionary stance in poems by Nicolás Guillén. I like Margaret Walker. I was very moved by her poem "For My People."

DH   Would you put Pablo Neruda in that group?

JC   Yes. I like Pablo Neruda's work. I liked his commitment, his consciousness. I liked the way he chose to explore events. Even when he was on a sentimental journey, it was interesting.

DH   You dedicated, I believe, your first book to the Watts Repertory Theatre Company. Would you say that they inspired you in any way?

JC   Well, yes. In fact, most of the pieces in *Pissstained Stairs* were written for them to perform.

DH   Now that's really interesting. How was this done?

JC   We wanted to present an evening dealing with Black music through poetry. So I wrote some poems for it, and three other poets in the workshop wrote poems. We presented an interesting program of poetry in praise of Black music.

DH   Do you advise other writers to publish their own works?

JC   Yes, if they can't get published by other publishers, they should publish their own works. I think that—well, one thing it'll do, it'll stop them from crying the blues. That's one thing. But I think in the sixties, it was about control. The musicians and writers wanted to have some control over their own works. This was one of the reasons why I decided to publish my own works.

DH   And you continue to do it as a matter of choice, now.

JC   I have continued to do it as a matter of choice—not that I won't ever publish with another publisher, because I will. My work has been published a great deal in anthologies and literary magazines by other publishers. I started my own publishing company in 1972, and I like it. Since I'm the owner of my own books, I have more freedom.

DH   Your mention of freedom reminds me of Amiri Baraka's current situation.[8] Do you think that his jail sentence may be an indication of the times, or do you think that's just a specific—

JC   It could have happened to me. Do you know how many arguments I've had on street corners with friends? Well, I know that whenever you decide to deal with the reality of the situation, the opposition gets all steamed up. They become very un-democratic. Now he has to serve time for trying to defend himself from being brutalized. Is this supposed to be a warning to artists? Is this supposed to put the fear of the reactionary gods in us? Are we supposed to put the lids on our mouths and shuffle along, enslaved as usual? I think this whole affair points up the contradictions of an unjust system. If anything, his courage and the courage of his family serve as a good example to many people.

DH   How do you view the 1980s and your role or the poet's role in the eighties?

JC   The poet's role is to make poetry. The eighties—the government is more reactionary. We are waiting in the wings of a false democracy. People are inflamed. We have a growing community of homeless people. The wealthy are getting wealthier and more toxic-wasteful. Friends are dying. Folks are in a state of stagnation, a state of passivity, a state of frenzy. Areas in Los Angeles resemble areas of Beirut in conflict and solitude. Near Douglas, Arizona, you can't see the sky through the dense pollution. The nuclear industry is still in the business of producing man-made radiation. Television is still dominated by white men and their views of the world. U.S. policies concerning Third World countries are designed to de-stabilize—to cripple and destroy independence. I'm opposed to those policies that promote death of people, death of land, death of a culture. I reject the notion that might is white, right, and supreme. I'm for peace and international understanding.

My role as a poet? I want to be creative, inventive, imaginative, free, secure, and make poetry. I'm interested in using the latest technology to reach a wider audience. I believe in diversity and in exchanging ideas. Travel means I have access to information from other sources. I think that poets have the responsibility to be aware of the meaning of human rights, to be familiar with history, to point out distortions, and to bring their thinking and their writing to higher levels of illumination.

Jayne Cortez: Works Cited and Suggested

Pissstained Stairs and the Monkey Man's Wares. Drawings by Mel Edwards. New York: Phrase Text, 1969.
Festivals and Funerals. Drawings by Mel Edwards. New York: Jayne Cortez, 1971.

Scarifications. Drawings by Mel Edwards. New York: Bola Press, 1973; 2nd ed. 1978.
Mouth on Paper. Drawings by Mel Edwards. New York: Bola Press, 1977.
Firespitter. Drawings by Mel Edwards. New York: Bola Press, 1982.
Coagulations: New and Selected Poems. Drawings by Mel Edwards. New York: Thunder's Mouth Press, 1984.
Merveilleux Coup de Foudre: Poetry of Jayne Cortez and Ted Joans. Paris, France: Handshake, 1982. Translations into French.
Word Within A Word (anthology issue), guest editor. *Black Scholar* 19 (nos. 4-5, 1988).
"Briefing." *Black Scholar* 19 (nos. 4-5, 1988): 108-11.

Recordings

Celebrations and Solitudes. Accompanied by Richard Davis. New York: Strata East Records, 1975.
Unsubmissive Blues. Accompanied by Bill Cole, Denardo Coleman, Joe Daley, Bern Nix. New York: Bola Press, 1980.
There It is. Accompanied by Abraham Adzinyah, Bill Cole, Denardo Coleman, Farel Johnson, Jr., Charles Moffett, Jr., Bern Nix, Jamaaladeen Tacuma. New York: Bola Press, 1982.
Maintain Control. Accompanied by Denardo Coleman, Al MacDowell, Charles Moffett, Jr. ("The Firespitters"), with guest artists Ornette Coleman and Abdul Wadud. New York: Bola Press, 1986.

Films

Poetry in Motion. Toronto: Sphinx Productions, 1982.
War on War. Paris: UNESCO, 1982.

Video

Jayne Cortez in Concert 1. Workhorse Productions, 1983.
Life and Influences of Jayne Cortez. Sao Paolo: Museu da Literatura, 1987.

Notes

1. Ishmael Reed, ed., *Yardbird Reader 5* (Berkeley, Cal.: Yardbird Publishing, 1976): 90-117, features a tribute to Cortez, with her comments, poems, photograph; a bibliography; also commentary and reviews by Steve Cannon, Stanley Crouch, Charles Davis, Deborah A. Gillam, Verta Mae Grosvenor, Eugene B. Redmond, Clyde Taylor, Charles C. Thomas, and

Quincy Troupe. See also Alexis DeVeaux, "Poet's World: Jayne Cortez Discusses Her Life and Work," *Essence* March 1978): 77-79, 106, 109; Nikki Giovanni, review, "Pisstain [sic] Stairs and the Monkey Man's Wares," *Negro Digest* 19 (Dec. 1969): 97; June Jordan review of *Celebrations and Solitudes, Black World* 24 (March 1975): 53, 63.

    2. "Making It," from *Scarifications*. Copyright © 1973, 1978 by Jayne Cortez.

    3. Barbara T. Christian thus characterizes *Coagulations* in her review "There It Is: The Poetry of Jayne Cortez," *Callaloo* 9 (Winter 1986): 235-38. See also Melba J. Boyd's review in *Black Scholar* (July 1985): 65-66.

    4. The interview with Jayne Cortez mainly represents a composite of two discussions: the first one tape recorded at my apartment, in New York City, Friday afternoon, January 22, 1982; the second, untaped, in a Greenwich Village restaurant on Saturday afternoon, May 22, 1982. Both constitute the interview that appears in my "Jayne Cortez: Supersurrealism," *Greenfield Review* 11 (Summer/Fall 1983): 18-47. For this chapter, however, subsequent clarifications and additions, including the two new closing paragraphs, were made by the poet in November 1988.

    5. De Veaux, "Poet's World."

    6. Cortez was teaching Black literature and creative writing at Livingston College, Rutgers, at the time.

    7. Funeral services for Edward Kennedy (Duke) Ellington (1899-74) were held at the Cathedral Church of Saint John the Divine on May 27, 1974.

    8. See Chapter 6, n. 7, below.

Don Farkas

6. AMIRI BARAKA
Revolutionary Traditions

Since the early 1960s, the figure to be reckoned with in Black political life and art has been Amiri Baraka. Controversial, responsive to changing social ambience, he has articulated the riotous "language of the unheard" (to invoke Martin Luther King's definition once again) within a vernacular and a new idiom of radical solutions. A founder of the Black Arts Movement of the sixties, he propounded a view that was, as the late Larry Neal put it, "radically opposed to any concept of the artist that alienates him from his community . . . the Black Arts Movement believes that your ethics and your aesthetics are one."[1] Baraka's impact has been such that as early as 1973, Donald B. Gibson placed him among "major influences on black poetry: (1) the Harlem Renaissance of the twenties; (2) the protest writing of the thirties as reflected in the work of Richard Wright; (3) the beat movement of the fifties; (4) the life and work of a single poet, Amiri Baraka."[2]

Amiri Baraka was born Everett Leroy Jones in Newark, New Jersey, on October 7, 1934, to Anna Lois and Coyette (Coyt) Leroy Jones. His mother, a social worker, had been a student at Fisk University; her father, Tom Russ, had owned businesses, helped found a Baptist church, and endured persecution in Alabama by envious white businessmen who three times burned down his establishments before he moved his family to Newark. Although he died when his grandson was eleven, Russ remained a significant figure for the poet. Baraka's father, a man of independent thought, taught his son the importance of self-defense.

Coyt Jones's grandmother had been noted for her storytelling,

especially about the era of slavery, and Baraka—recognized as a
prodigy by his parents—was encouraged in his ability to make
speeches before he was old enough for school.[3] His dynamic com-
petence as a public speaker and reader began in those early days.

After a year's unhappy encounter with Rutgers, Baraka at-
tended Howard University, where as LeRoi Jones, he studied with
Sterling A. Brown and Nathan Scott. Shortly before his twentieth
birthday, he left Howard to enter the air force, which he refers to as
the "error farce," serving two years, mainly in Puerto Rico and
Germany. In 1958 he and Hettie Cohen, a Jewish writer, were
married in a Buddhist temple on Manhattan's Upper West Side.
Two daughters, Kellie Elisabeth and Lisa Victoria Chapman, were
born to the couple. Baraka and his wife collaborated on publishing
Yugen, an important literary magazine (later, with Diane di Prima,
he edited *Floating Bear*). Since their divorce, Hettie Jones has
remained active on the New York literary scene.

In the sixties Baraka wrote poetry and jazz reviews, and began
writing plays with *The Eighth Ditch* (which is part of his 1965
novel, *The System of Dante's Hell*) and *Dutchman.* Turning to
Black Nationalism, deeply affected by the murder of Malcolm X in
February 1965, he left Greenwich Village for Harlem where, in the
previous year, he had already founded the Black Arts Repertory
Theatre/School (BART/S). In 1966 he was united with Amina Bar-
aka (née Sylvia Robinson) in a Yoruba wedding ceremony. For-
merly a painter, dancer, and actress, Amina is a strong poet in her
own right and coedited with him *Confirmation: An Anthology of
AfricanAmerican Women* (1983), in which several of her poems
appear (Brooks, Sanchez, and Cortez are also among the forty-nine
Black women writers represented). A woman of deep political
convictions, Amina shares her husband's world view and directs
the New Ark Afrikan Free School, which originated in Spirit
House, the community cultural center that he had organized in the
1960s. Her children with Baraka are Obalaji Malik Ali, Ras Jua Al
Aziz, Shani Isis Makeda, Amiri Seku Musa, and Ahi Mwenge.

Throughout the sixties Baraka steadily gained respect for his
work in jazz history, particularly *Blues People*; in poetry, with
books including *Preface to a Twenty Volume Suicide Note* and
Black Magic; in drama, with *Dutchman,* which won an "Obie" for
the best off-Broadway play of 1964, and *The Slave,* which won the
drama prize at the first World Festival of Negro Arts in Dakar,

Senegal (1966); and in fiction, with *The System of Dante's Hell* and *Tales*. Recognized as a political and cultural leader, he was welcomed tumultuously at the Second Fisk University Writers' Conference in 1967. In the Newark riots later that year, he encountered a different sort of tumult when he was nearly beaten to death by police (*Autobiography*, 258-64).

Home, a collection of his essays from 1960 through 1965, shows the development of Baraka's early thought. "After 1966," he says, "my work became self-consciously spiritual."[4] In this period, he wrote *Spirit Reach* (1972). Richly experimental, mimetic of instruments, its "Preachments" contribute to a moving poetic document of spiritual striving.

In 1974, as chairman of the Congress of Afrikan Peoples (CAP), which split off into the Revolutionary Communist League, the poet attended the Sixth Pan-African Congress at Dar es Salaam. The assembly marked a deepening schism among Black intellectuals: some clinging to Nationalism; others, like Baraka, embracing the new wave of socialism (see Chapter 3, n. 21). Ten years later, on the occasion of the writer's fiftieth birthday, Woodie King, Jr., asked, "What is it about Baraka that calls us to attention? I believe it is his daring" (*KT*, 107). In his candid *Autobiography*, Baraka, using a Mao-invoking metaphor, writes of his "long march to better understanding" (p. 325). For him, change is the constant present and presence, the quintessential fact of existence and growth. He dares to grow and chafes at being held back by his own former positions, whether they were error or insight. The anti-Semitism that marred some of his early poetry, for example, plagued him for years after he disavowed the sentiments. Even his "Confessions of a Former Anti-Semite" failed to remove the stigma. It persisted mainly because of his view of Zionism as nationalism and therefore incompatible with his later Marxist/Leninist/Maoist international stance. "People are always catching you where you were," he says. One recalls the hero of Brooks's "Boy Breaking Glass," who cries, "Nobody knew where I was and now I am no longer there." While many have known where Baraka was at a particular moment, they could not seize his protean reality, because he was always both of his time and ahead of it, struggling, in a Hegelian labor, to achieve a further level of synthesis.

As artist, Baraka wants "more than anything, to chart this change within myself. This constant mutability in the face of the changing world" (*Autobiography*, 18). And yet it is the reality of his changeless core that generates his vision. William J. Harris views him as a Manichaean and a vatic poet in the line of Whitman, Pound, Patchen, and Ginsberg.[5] In quest of philosophical truth, Baraka has turned to a variety of religious and political faiths. A serious artist, he has absorbed classical and modern literature and contributes uniquely to art that is experimentally alive to its social and political content. He uses music and multimedia to further the accessibility and impact of his works, in order to convey to the people his messages of strength, resistance, and political instruction. Like a great dancer (or skater), he risks all with bold leaps and turns, as evidenced by his play *The Motion of History* and *Money: A Jazz Opera,* neither of which quite comes off theatrically, and *The Sidney Poet Heroical,* which does. His work has moved from concern with self and schools of white poetry to placement of that Black self in a national and world community, at the same time developing an experimental Black art rooted in traditions of language, music, and religious and secular rhetoric.

Harris gives a solid interpretation of Baraka's methodology, which converts white aesthetics to Black aesthetic purposes: "Amiri Baraka's entire career is characterized by transformations of avant-garde poetics into ethnic poetics, of white liberal politics into black nationalist and Marxist politics, of jazz forms into literary forms. . . . I call Baraka's method of transformation the Jazz Aesthetic Process, a procedure that uses jazz variations as paradigms for the conversion of white poetic and social ideas into black ones" (KT, 85). Harris gives appropriate credit to Henry Louis Gates, Jr. (who, in turn, acknowledges Roger D. Abrahams) in perceiving that the process is one of suggesting structure by dissemblance, a form of "signifying," and that "repeating a form and then inverting it through a process of variation"[6] is the essence óf the jazz aesthetic (KT, 86). Baraka's own explanation of how he turned the Black Sambo minstrel image into the fear-inspiring Uncle Sambo revolutionary patches worn by Walker Vessel's Black army, in *The Slave,* exemplifies the process (KT, 89-90).

Because over the years Baraka has become a recognizable part of American popular multiculture, familiarity makes him appear less threatening than was once the case. As professor (since 1979) and director (since 1986) of Africana Studies at the State University of New York at Stony Brook, and recently as visiting professor at

Rutgers University, he may even tempt us to think of him as nearly an "establishment" figure (one can hear him chortle), though of a unique variety, to be sure. But he is ever Baraka: his mind, ranging freely, remains unfettered. His integrity as an artist and his ready polemics are partly witnessed by the history of some of his essays in *Daggers and Javelins,* pieces commissioned and paid for by such publications as the *New York Times, Black Enterprise* magazine, the *Village Voice,* and *Playboy* (Japan) and then not published— or, in journalistic parlance, "killed." Their survival and subsequent publication recall the mighty words of labor organizer Joe Hill in Alfred Hayes's ballad: "I never died, said he."

Dedicated to promulgating his views, Baraka has let nothing, not even enforced weekends on Rikers Island[7] or teaching commitments, ever prevent him from writing, publishing, and participating in functions and causes he deems worthy. Among other activities, he continues to participate generously in Black writer's conferences. At the Medgar Evers Second National Black Writers' Conference in March 1988 he discussed destructive stereotypes about Black writing (such as maintaining that it doesn't exist, that American writing is white, and that Blacks fixate on the subject of slavery) and called for the mass infusion of Black literature into school curricula. At the Langston Hughes Festival in New York the following November he presented a paper titled "Langston, McKay, and Du Bois: The Contradictions of Art and Politics During the Harlem Renaissance."

Baraka's stature in American letters was further evident on two occasions honoring Black writers. At James Baldwin's funeral "celebration" on December 8, 1987, at the Cathedral Church of Saint John the Divine in New York, where tributes were given by Baldwin's friends Maya Angelou and Toni Morrison and by the ambassador of France, Baraka—also a close friend—served as honorary pallbearer and delivered a memorable eulogy: "Jimmy was God's black Revolutionary mouth," he said, "if there is a God, and revolution his righteous natural expression and elegant song the deepest and most fundamental commonplace of being alive." The eulogy was printed by Baldwin's family as part of the memorial program.

On February 11, 1988, Baraka participated in the public television literary series *Voices and Visions,* in its tribute to Langston Hughes. Baraka regards Richard Wright, W. E. B. Du Bois, and

Hughes as the three most eminent authors of the Harlem Renaissance (*DJ*, 165). His appreciation of both Hughes and Baldwin has as much to do with music as with message.[8] His kinship with their knowledge, esteem, and application of Black music has been demonstrated by his own major writings on blues and jazz; he is vitally concerned with the relation of music to Black culture as a whole, the revolutionary impulse it expresses and the cultural tradition it embodies.[9] Currently, his weekly music and poetry series, "Kimako's Blues People," named after his late sister and codirected with his wife Amina, continues to project his vision of art merged with politics and to support the creative struggle of Black artists.

Baraka's deep concern with tradition is part of a pervasive concern among Black intellectuals with identifying and codifying an existing tradition. In addition to Black music, literature, and religious and secular oratory, slave narratives are also being perceived as "central to American culture."[10] The development of literary theory and the establishment of canons—begun with the prodigious work of W. E. B. Du Bois and the Harlem Renaissance writers; carried forward by Baraka, the late Larry Neal, and the legacies of Hoyt W. Fuller and George E. Kent—continue apace, along with emphases that range from poststructuralism to feminism.

Underlying or overt, the concern with tradition and traditions (also evident in the other poets discussed here) counterpoints both political and aesthetic radicalism, and it locates unequivocally in Baraka's major poem *In the Tradition* (1982), which he has both published and recorded (with music). Dedicating it to "Black Arthur Blythe," the alto saxophonist (whose 1979 record album lent the poem its title), Baraka calls it "a poem about African American history . . . a cultural history and political history." If a single work could sum him up "at a certain point," he says, it would probably be that poem. It incorporates his spirit, his energy, his musicality, all that he ever learned about and contributed to the visual and aural elements of modern poetry. As Joe Weixlmann points out (like Darwin Turner speaking of Madhubuti; see Chapter 3 above), "Baraka's recent work lives fully only in performance, yet rarely do Baraka's critics take that into account" (*KT*, 180). A stirring reader, he frequently shares the stage with Amina, herself a dynamic performer.

The recent poetry seems to be gaining power through its depth

and expansion. While it supports the range of his concerns—
"Soundings," a passionate outcry against war; "Wailers," a poem
for Larry Neal and Bob Marley that is essentially a tribute to Black
music (it has been reprinted in "The Music"); and "Why's/Wise,"
which, Baraka notes in introducing a published fragment, is a long
poem about "African American (American) History," recalling his
earlier description of "In the Tradition"—two new aspects bear
mention. First, the poet seems to be adapting his earlier connection
to Olson asnd the Projectivists within the framework of Black
culture. In his preface to "Why's/Wise," the poet mentions "the
tradition of the Griots," but also includes Melvin B. Tolson's
Libretto for the Republic of Liberia, William Carlos Williams's
Paterson, Charles Olson's *Maximus Poems* (one could also cite
Ezra Pound's *Cantos* here) as antecedents, "in that it tries to tell the
history/life like an ongoing-offcoming Tale" (*Southern Review,*
801). In the poem, which is still in progress, Baraka celebrates
heroes (and excoriates real and putative villains) from all aspects of
Black life. Utilizing the full vocabulary of his artistic development,
he is seen by one critic as "moving forward in the world armed with
both curiosity and wisdom."[11]

Baraka's new book, *The Music,* clearly locates in its very title
his focus for present and future. It is Black music that has provided
the lens, the cohesion, and the communication he has been pursu-
ing as he "investigates the sun." This anthology of recent work, of
Amina's poetry and his own poetry, essays, and "anti-nuclear jazz
musical," reveals a second and relatively new emphasis: Baraka as a
poet/musician of praise—a lover of "The Music" (by which Black
music is understood) and the family of Black musicians who create
and interpret it, and a lover of his own family, itself consanguine
within it. Witness his poetic and prose tributes to great artists of
jazz and blues, his instrumental articulations (he defines poetry as
"speech *musicked,*" p. 243), his remark that "Amina's poetry is
itself child of the music, as Jazz is Blues' " (introduction, 13), and
the poem to his sons, "Obalaji as drummer, Ras as Poet," in which
he affirms: "and when the music goes through me I swear I imagine
all kinds / of things. A world without pain, a world of beauty, for /
instance" (46). A Black Family man who remains lyrical with hope,
he is a formidable champion of the cultural contribution of African
American music and fierce defender against "The Great Music
Robbery," the plundering of its resources by whites (328-32; cf.

Gwendolyn Brooks, "Gottschalk and the Grande Tarantelle," Interview, Chapter 1).

Baraka's appraisal of Malcolm X may well serve as his own epitome: "A whole swirl of turnarounds hurricaned from him. The world was going through changes, and that world was in us too. We had to reevaluate all we knew. There were lives in us anyway filled with dynamite. We had a blackness to us, to be sure. It was always in us, we had but to claim it. And it claimed us" (*Autobiography*, 319).

To travel through the sprawling Black area of Newark is to be drawn into the nexus of Baraka's urgent rage: acres of slums, sullen in July—one imagines their bleakness in December. It is the Tuesday morning of our interview.[12] My cab drives on and on, through a city still partly burned out since the 1967 riots, until we come to a section of attractive private houses. And then: the red, rambling, Victorian-style brick house of Amiri Baraka. A tree, its trunk curving like a snarl, explodes into an umbrella of green to the left of the entrance walk.

Inside: Baraka, wearing a red T-shirt imprinted in black with a picture of the late Bob Marley. Inside: clean lines, beige walls; a fireplace with African art objects; an ample, beige sectional sofa. On the coffee table: Langston Hughes, *The Ways of White Folks*. Baraka speaks briefly with a telephone repairman after showing me to the living room.

Mike Bezdek, a pleasant southerner on assignment from the Associated Press to report on illustrious Newark citizens, is seated on the sofa when I enter. I had not expected a second interviewer. Baraka joins us. He is budgeting his time, trying to do two things in the space of one, aware of the days slipping past until October 16 when he will be sentenced, wondering aloud whether he might be "taken off" in prison. He explains that he has been speaking to the telephone repairman, who has just left. "This strange stuff that's going on with this phone," he remarks. "Every time I have to go to court, the phone is fouling up. You get a recording saying the phone is disconnected." He sits before us, flecks of gray in his hair and beard, poised yet intense as he mentions a "hit list" he will discuss in the interview, a list on which his name appears.

How does one live with fear and maintain sanity? Baraka's secret may be his productivity. During the interview he refers to a play, a jazz opera, a book of essays, a book of autobiographical essays, and an anthology to be co-edited with his wife—all works at various stages of completion and all subsequently produced or published.

The interview lasts approximately two hours. The poet speaks rapidly, but without haste, with seriousness and occasional humor, his manner forthright. The house is filled at times with sounds of activity from invisible children; no one invades the scene or interrupts the conversation. Baraka is to travel in the afternoon. Even though we are only one in a continuous series of commitments, he is relaxed. I am reminded of him at the New School, where I was first struck by his patience and quick intelligence as a teacher, his use of a socratic method, his description of "art for art's sake" as art created for the bourgeoisie. Once again I have the sense of constant reassessment or revaluation, of the very process of thought to which we are being admitted.

INTERVIEW WITH AMIRI BARAKA

DH   As a child, it seems you were regarded by your family as a prodigy. Did anyone at home or at school directly encourage you to write?

AB   In school I took a writing course as a senior in high school, before that in grammar school. When I was in elementary school I did a comic strip in seventh grade for a little seventh grade newspaper that we had, and I contributed cartoons for that. I didn't start really to get a sense of writing until high school.

DH   That comic strip you did, would you say that showed the influence of the radio and so forth—the comedians, mysteries, and dramas that dominated radio at the time? Would you say that the radio influenced your turn to drama?

AB   Well, I think the radio was probably the biggest influence on me—radio and movies. I was always really an avid radio listener. Every day, after the playground, I'd listen to all the adventure stories. I think they'd start coming on about five-fifteen, Hop Harrigan and Captain Midnight—

MB   The Shadow.

AB   Yes, that was on Sundays.

MB   That was one of your most widely publicized early poems—

AB   Right.

MB   —about the Shadow.

AB   Yes. All of those were. I guess what television is probably to little kids now, radio was to us then.

DH   Is the Green Lantern the Green Hornet?

AB   No. The Green Lantern was actually a comic strip character, and he had a ring, and he used to take this ring and he'd sort of, I guess, recharge it at the end of each one of his bouts with crime. Then he had this little poem that he would recite, "In darkest day, in darkest night / No evil shall escape my sight." [*Laughter*] Something like that. And I always identified with that.

DH   Your paternal great-grandmother was an accomplished storyteller. You have an exuberant relationship with words per se, as well as a remarkably fertile imagination. Would you say that your great-grandmother's talent influenced you in both respects, the lexical and the imaginative?

AB   I can't really be sure. I know that those stories were always fascinating. She would tell those stories out of the *Arabian Nights*—they were stories that I came to know later as the stories from the *Arabian Nights*—only in her own, unique, kind of way. But I think the whole language thing is the thing from the streets, really, from the playground, finding out that using words was as useful as being able to use your hands in some situations.

MB   Was this in Newark?

AB   Yes.

DH   Would you say that that joy in words is part of a Black cultural—

AB   Yes.

DH   —predilection?

AB   Yes, certainly the whole oral aspect of the culture, the fact of being kept out of formal replication just reinforces the oral quality. The fact that you couldn't just come off the farm and be a writer, you know, on the plantation and have access to the formal arts. It reinforces the kind of normally oral tradition of most people in the world. I think in saying that the African American people, because of being blocked in one area—it just reinforces that oral kind of tradition.

DH   Your identification with leadership seems to have begun early, with the independence and ego strength shown by both your parents, and your admiration for and closeness to your heroic maternal grandfather, Tom Russ, whom you refer to as "an American pioneer" in your dedication to *Dutchman* and *The Slave*. Would you couple his loss, when you were eleven, with the death of Malcolm X in 1965, as deeply significant events for you, influencing and even changing your life?

AB   Well, I don't know. See, the Malcolm thing was much more conscious, much more of a conscious commitment and seeing somebody you consciously had seen as important, killed. My grandfather was such a personal loss. I think the loss begins early when he got hurt. He got hit in the head with a street light they said fell off the pole and crippled him, which is still a wild kind of coincidence. But I think the loss begins there, because the kind of prestige he had in the community and the awe that I hold him in was at that point, you know, sharply kind of—just weakened, because he then became a paralyzed person who couldn't move, who had to sit in a wheelchair. That sort of eliminated a lot of the kind of heroic projections that I had around him. And then his death was kind of—anticlimax.

DH   Was he in a wheelchair long?

AB   Well, I guess the last few years of his life, about three years he lived after that, three or four years.

MB   What did he do?

AB   He was a storekeeper; he was a politician; he was in Black Republican politics. He lost his store in the Depression, and they gave him a political patronage job, which is very ironic. He was the night watchman in the election machine factory [*chuckling*], in the election machine warehouse where they kept the election machines. He was the night watchman in there, so we used to go over there in the evenings and sit around the election machines, protecting democracy, or something. [*Laughter*]

DH   More recently, do you consider Lu Hsun an important example for you of the writer as revolutionary?

AB   Oh, yes. Absolutely. Yes, absolutely. I think that it's a pity that his works are not known more widely in this country.[13] But he's a very, very skilled short story writer and an *acid* essayist—

DH   Like "A Madman's Diary"—

AB   Yes.

DH   —a great story.

AB   Yes. I have a book coming out in the fall, a book of essays, and I took the title from him. The title is *Daggers and Javelins*, and that's what he used to call his essays. He had some "dagger" essays, which were short and swift, and then he had some javelin essays, for long-distance [*laughs*] elimination.

DH   Who's publishing that?

AB   Greenwood. Academic Press. Essays, 1975-1979. [Later published by Morrow.]

MB   Speaking of academic life, you were well-known way back in the fifties. Do you have some trouble getting university positions? I seem to remember hearing that. Did that not further your anger, especially your home state where, for God knows what reason—

AB   Yes, yes. Well, in New Jersey, I applied to Rutgers, Newark, about three or four years in a row. Then I applied to Rutgers, New Brunswick; Rutgers in Livingston, a couple of times; then Princeton; Essex County College—I've applied to all of these schools around here with the exception, I guess, of Seton Hall and Upsala. But all the rest of the major schools I applied to. I know people inside these schools, and they tell me what's going on. They tell me, you know, in Newark Rutgers the English department says they will not have you. The head of the English department, a guy named Henry Christian, maintains that he will *die* first—

MB   Where is that?

AB   Newark Rutgers.

MB   And why?

AB   I think it's basically because my work in New Jersey has been—most people know it principally as political. And so it's different if you have a political professor who is essentially a professor and is political in that sense. But when you have somebody who people identify primarily as a political activist and only secondarily as a writer—a lot of these people around New Jersey and especially in Newark, they think of me primarily as a political activist. In terms of writing and stuff like that, they don't know a thing about that. [*Laughs*]

MB   Uh-huh.

AB   So it's like you want to hire a militant to be on the faculty. They don't want to do that. The fact that I can get jobs and go teach at Yale and George Washington, Columbia, you know, is lost on them. So that's essentially where it still is.

MB   Has that ever entered your writing? Have you ever written about that?

AB   What—the Rutgers thing?

MB   About New Jersey, specifically?

AB   I mentioned that in a couple of essays that I've done recently, in the last three years. I've mentioned that specifically in about three essays. One that Rutgers is supposed to be publishing in a collection called—you remember they had a conference on urban literature, something like that, a couple of years ago? They have a collection of those essays coming out in the fall, and one of those essays talks about Rutgers being a racist institution, and so forth and so on. And then I wrote about it in a couple of other essays, specifically about having applied and being turned down; having been sent a ditto sheet back, not even an answer—one of those purple ditto sheets from Rutgers. [*Laughs*] And all kinds of stuff like that. But I think it's par for the course. I don't see it as being weird, given the situation in New Jersey, specifically in Newark, the kind of intense political confrontation we went through, that I was involved with and identified with. You can see what their point is. I mean, it's so backward. Obviously, most people in the country look at it as extremely backward, you know, what goes on. I have yet to get even a grant from the State Council on the Arts in New Jersey, you understand? That kind of—refusal to identify me as anything but a political figure, a political militant that they don't want to deal with. Which is very interesting.

MB   Do we have any native sons who are more well known than you? I don't—

AB   I don't know—not in that particular field, I would think.

MB   I read about you for the first time in Alabama [*laughs*] and if they know about your poetry down there, my God—

AB   I don't think so. There are a great many well-known writers from New Jersey. Strangely enough, some of the best-known American poets are from New Jersey. Walt Whitman—

MB   Carlos—

AB   Yes, William Carlos Williams, Allen Ginsberg—

MB   He's from New Jersey?

AB   Yes. They're all from New Jersey. New Jersey has a particular, weird soil that turns out poets. Yes. But Ginsberg was born in Newark. He was raised, of course, in Paterson. William Carlos Williams lived most of his life in Paterson. Walt Whitman lived most of his life in Camden.[14] So there's something in New Jersey that promotes poetry.

DH I just want to go back to the childhood for a moment.

AB Yes.

DH There's a great deal of pain—inflicted and endured—in your work. As an adult, you observed discrimination in the army and suffered beatings by police during the Newark riots of 1967. Did you experience any comparable cruelty or discrimination from whites, Blacks, or anyone else when you were a child or an adolescent?

AB Well, see, interestingly enough, I'm writing this book now for Wyndham Press, which is a spinoff of Simon & Schuster, and it's memoirs. That's what they wanted, I don't know why.[15] I'm writing all about the youth part now, and I will put there one of the first incidences that I recognized—God knows what happened that I *don't* recognize—was when we went to the Bronx Zoo. Students—they took us to the Bronx Zoo, and I was sort of lagging along at the end, the group had sort of passed through and I was still in the elephant house. There was this white guy clearing the place up, so I go over to him; I said, "Gee, mister, how can you stand it?— you know, the elephant house stinks!" And he says, "Well, I don't worry about that. I live in Harlem," he says. And you know I was about nine, and I knew what he meant. I couldn't really get down and argue with him or anything like that, but it went right through me, and I knew what he meant. And I began then to be much more aware of—you know. And I think we lived close to the Italian community when I was in my middle—what is it, nine, ten, eleven, twelve?—and, you know, there were always incidents.

DH Well, *The System of Dante's Hell* and *Tales* are poeticized autobiographical—

AB Yes.

DH —works. Would you say that they're complementary? Would you consider *Tales* as, perhaps, an epilogue to *System*?

AB I'd say that there are certainly parallels, things focusing on the same things in a slightly different way. The things that I try to do in the Dante book I really wasn't even aware of, in a sense. I was just trying to stop writing like other people. And it's interesting that years later I read where Aimé Césaire did the same thing to get away from French Symbolist poetry. H says, "I'm going to stop writing poetry. I'm just going to write prose." And so then he turns up *Return to My Native Land*. But that's what I did when I started—I was tired of writing poetry like Robert Creeley and Charles Olson, you know, in principle. And so I said, "I'm going to do something that's going to very consciously break away." And so I just tried to just write spontaneously and without any kind of literary usage. Some critics say that's pretty obvious. [*Laughs*]

DH   They are unique. It really was a break.

AB   Yes. But I tried to get away from just literary—from "literature." Then I think what happened was that I was permitted to find my own voice, and once I thought I had it near the end of that book; then I sort of calmed down and began to write more recognizable narrative.

DH   In "Heroes Are Gang Leaders," the protagonist, sitting in a hospital bed, notes that "the concerns are still heroism." Does that show early interest in that whole theme?

AB   Yes. Oh, yes. You see, what has always intrigued me, and I've talked to my wife a lot about this, that they taught us to love heroes, and specifically in my youth, when the United States was not quite as bloody as it is now, I mean, in its pursuits all over the world, they were able to project the straight-ahead type heroes. Our heroes were people like Robin Hood, Errol Flynn as Robin Hood—you know, "take from the rich and give to the poor"—that was a clear, you know—[*Laughs*]

DH   [*Laughing*] That was a good idea.

AB   And so you really begin to be animated by those ideas in a real way; then later on you find out that it's all a lie. They don't really mean for you to believe that. But I internalized, certainly, a lot of—

DH   Is that ["Heroes"] an autobiographical story?

AB   That story? Generally so. I think writers always lie about something—

DH   That took place in a hospital.

AB   Yes—I think in taking autobiographical cores, writers always see parallel things that they blow up and other things that they leave out. [*Chuckles*] You know, it's never exactly, but it's generally so.

MB   Do you have friends still around Newark from when you were a child?

AB Oh, yes, yes. That's really the best part of being in this town. That's one of the reasons that I remain here. I do have friends that go all the way back to childhood, early childhood.

MB Do you have certain difficulties sometimes with your prominence with some of them? Do they have a hard time with that?

AB No. I think most of the people I know take it for what it is—you know, "It's a friend of mine." We get on pretty well. There's always some weird people. I know for instance I've gone to school with most people, probably with more people than [*laughing*] most people—then you find they went to school with you. You got a graduating class of three thousand! [*Clucking sound*] But aside from that, most people, I think, a lot of people feel good by what you do, because they know that it's part of them, that it's actually been made public, you know. They feel, "Hey, I know him, and now he says some things that other people are interested in, and part of me is in that."

MB It's important for your work, I would imagine, to keep in touch with people in the city, all kinds of people. I know Baldwin had some trouble—he's sometimes considered by certain Blacks to be a little bit of an elitist. Some say he's lost a little bit of touch.

AB Well, I guess maybe what they mean is he doesn't—you know, Jimmy goes back and forth to Europe; he stays in Europe a lot of the time. But interestingly enough, when we had that conference on urban literature, they were doing a movie, some English filmmakers were doing a movie on him, and because we were together, they asked me to show him around to see Newark, since I lived here. I took him to the Scudder Homes, which is about the worst project in Newark, and I think what most impressed Jimmy—first of all, when we came here, there was almost nobody on the street. Inside of five minutes there must have been three hundred people on the street, because they had camera equipment, and stuff like that. And I think what impressed him most was some of the young people, teenage types and young adults, saying, "How you doing, Mr. Baldwin? I read your last book." And so on and so on and so on and so on, showing how people never really, once they know you and identify you—that they do try to keep track of you, you see, and you might not think so. You might think that you disappeared from sight. But I think that's important to remember, that you never do disappear from sight. There are some people who always measure certain things in the world by what you're doing. I think it's a very important idea.

MB   Who is your preferred audience? Who would you like to meet on the street and have him say, "Hey, I just read your latest essay"?

AB   Well, I'd say the great majority of working people in this country. Certainly I'm closer to Black people, for the obvious reason of American segregation, you know, we've grown up in our own communities. And it's very very gratifying for some working person, some Black working—some person that you know goes to work every day, you know what I mean, in some factory or on some assembly line, but any kind of working person, let's say, whatever their nationality, that's the most gratifying to me. When somebody you know who's a real person, who's in the real world, dealing with the real world, has taken some time, has put some space in their life for what you're saying, that's really gratifying—much more than college professors or students, or people you know whose job it is, in the intellectual world. I mean, some guy who makes cars all his life, and says, "Hey, I read that book you wrote and I really liked it."

DH   Now this is your current target audience, but would you say that in the past you had a different audience you were writing for?

AB   Well, I'd say this: I think that my early days of writing—I think I wanted to reach everybody, but obviously, my concerns were not broad enough. I think when I was a Nationalist, obviously, I then wanted to focus strictly on Black people. But I think now, the difference between, say, myself as a young writer, when I really was just talking to anybody who would listen but my concerns were narrow—now I try to broaden my concerns to make that voice broad enough to touch different people's lives. Now obviously I'm speaking as a Black person, and any person has got to speak from their own experience and where they are, but I think it's a—you desire communication with most people at a level that they can deal with it, use it.

DH   Did you start writing poetry when you were in the army?

AB   I started writing poetry I guess in college. I started writing Elizabethan poetry, like [*laughs*] Sir John Suckling, Philip Sidney, people like that.

MB   Which college was that?

AB   Howard University.

MB   Did you go there first?

AB   No. I went to Newark Rutgers, when it was an all-white school. [*Laughs*]

MB   What about Columbia?

AB   That was later. That was much later. No, when I first came out of high school, I went to Newark Rutgers. I had scholarships to a lot of places, strangely enough. But I chose Newark Rutgers for some reason, I guess because it was in Newark, it was close, but I hated it once I got there. So I got out of there.

DH   Do you still consider yourself basically a poet?

AB   Yes. Sure. Fundamentally a poet and, you know, a political activist. But you see, I've always liked to write other things. I mean, I think—well, I always wrote essays, even when I first started writing poetry; a little while after that I started writing essay reviews, jazz reviews, first. I started writing plays about '63 and, you know, my work had gotten more and more dramatic. In the poetry there were people always talking. [*Laughs*] Suddenly in the poem I would have a conversation between two people, and it gradually worked itself into—*The System of Dante's Hell* had plays in it.

DH   "The Eighth Ditch"—

AB   Yes. I think that I developed the dramatic thing, and I liked that, because I think it's a much more ambitious thing to try and put people on the stage and make believe it's the real world or *some* real world, anyway.

DH   Your writing seems as visual as it is aural. How early were you interested in painting? And do you still paint?

AB   Well, I took drawing lessons when I was a kid. I guess my mother was one of those middle-class women who was trying to put you in these different places. But I think it helps, because it gives you some kind of attention to things as other than just random, boring kind of life. You then see, oh, there's such a thing as music. I took trumpet lessons. I took drum lessons. I took art lessons. She used to have me singing and dancing with my sister on the stage. And then when I got into the service, I painted, because I met a friend of mine down there, William White, who became a painter, who was a painter, a very good painter. He died of drugs, unfortunately. But then that stimulated me to want to paint. And then I got back to New York. I made a decision as to whether I want to paint or do I want to write. I decided it was easier to write. In painting you had to go through too many changes.

MB How many brothers and sisters do you have?

AB One.

MB One?

AB Girl—

MB One sister?

AB Yes.

MB Does she live around here?

AB She lives in New York, New York City.

MB And then, your folks—are they still living?

AB Yes. My mother and father. They're still living in Newark. They're both retired now.

DH There is often a fluid sense for me of exchange between your plays and your poetry and prose. Do you see them as distinct genres, or would you say your poetry is now being absorbed into your drama and prose?

AB Oh, I see them as distinct in terms of certain formal considerations, but I think my view has always been that poetry is the fundamental concern. If you're interested in words, then fundamentally you have to be a poet. I think that might be some poet chauvinism, but I think that fundamentally if you're really interested in words, then you will be a poet, because it seems to me that's the concern with words even before they become words, you know, sounds. And then I think that you have to utilize the poetic as much as you can in all the forms, because the poetic to me is just an intense sense of language, an intense concern with language; you know, rhythm, sound connote like "high speech," I call it. I think that you have to be concerned with that, whether you write a novel or a play or an essay. Lu Hsun said that he liked essays because in essays he could do anything. He could have a little poem; he could have a little novelistic bit of fiction, you know, but within the essay form. And so he could make that essay anything he wanted, but at the same time be talking in an expository kind of form about clearly identifiable reality.

MB If you had—it's impossible to do, but what would be a typical poem? What would be a poem that you would say, "That's what I'm all about"? More than some of the others mean? I know all—

AB Mine?

MB   Yes.

AB   I guess you always tend to want to uphold [*laughs*] your most recent works. I guess a poem I wrote recently called "In the Tradition," which is a long poem, a poem about African American history. It's a cultural history and political history. I think that would be, if I could say it was something that sums you up at a certain point, I would say probably that poem.

DH   Where does that appear?

AB   It was published in the *Greenfield Review,* and then it was—I read it with music last year at Soundscape. It's coming out on a record called *New Music, New Poetry,* with David Murray and Stephen McCall. In fact, I got the test pressing today, so it should be out momentarily.

DH   Is your departure from lyricism, basically—although you still are writing poems, but you seem to be turning towards satire and the historical pageant—would you say that it is simply a function of the genre? It's not that you're consciously rejecting lyricism as a mode?

AB   No. I've always had that, the lyrical thing, if you mean—to me, the highly personal song, which is what I've given up on, the lyric poems. On the one hand, I've always told my students you can't write lyric poems too long, only when you're a kid, because in those [*laughs*] you know, "I hurt, I feel, I love, I want"—after a while it gets to be—[*laughter*] kind of old, you know what I mean. [*Laughs*] So I try to—I think I do—maintain a connection with the lyrical urge, a sense of the self in the world, sensitive to it. But at the same time, that satirical thing that you perceive has always been present in my work, even from the first book that I put out, the poetry. There's edged in there, you know, the kind of satire and irony. And I think that's been a kind of characteristic of my view of things, even as a little boy, hearing these various dudes I know in this town talk about how I used to be when I was a kid. It was really the same thing. They were just subjected to the same kind of satire and irony, though, in speech, back and forth, back and forth, and that's why I always had to learn to run fast, because [*laughing*] you'd say certain things to people you didn't know would provoke them to such an extent. You had to get in the wind. But that has always been there, a kind of seeing, for instance, negative things in a very ironical and satirical way and really making them funny, with a bitter kind of humor. I think that's always been my way to a certain extent, and I mean I've suffered for that, God knows, in school and college, the service. If you make some comment to a sergeant or a lieutenant [*chuckles*], they wouldn't particularly like it. But I think that's always been there.

MB Do you think you're mellowing now? I don't mean—

AB No, I understand what you mean. I think in some ways, probably. But I don't think so. People still seem to think not. I mean in terms of reactions to various things that people—you know, they don't want to publish this, they don't want to publish that, so it seems like mellowing but it's still objectionable in a lot of quarters.

MB I mean do you think you're still perceived as a militant, angry, or—

AB I think in some quarters, obviously, because those people will not give you an inch. Obviously, a writer who's been around as long as I have is supposed to be able to make a living from magazine articles, those kinds of things, you know what I mean. A regularly published book a year—you're supposed to be able to make it. But I can't. And the only explanation of that is that the content still disturbs people. They still want to wrestle with you about your conception of reality. So it makes it difficult. I think the mellowing, if anything, has been, perhaps, a greater kind of understanding of certain things. For instance, I thought that revolution would be immediate, at one point. And I don't think that's so much mellowing but deepening your understanding to find that that's not reality, that it's not an event, that it's a process, and you have to be aware of that process, help speed that process up, but not get so frustrated that it doesn't come about, that you actually drive yourself crazy.

DH Do you think that any degree of revolutionary change can come through the polls or legislation?

AB Well, let's say this. To me, the use of electoral politics is only a tactic. I mean I think it does have to be utilized, because I think if you don't utilize it, you will find yourself in a position where you're backed up against the ovens, you know, and then the only thing you can do is fight for your life, I mean quite literally. Like people are talking about now they want to repeal the Voting Rights Act. They came on with an editorial on Channel 11, WPIX, "Repeal the Voting Rights Act." Now if you sit still and say, well, we can't fight against that, because finally, voting is not going to change monopoly capitalism—and it's not. I don't think, in the end, anything other than short of armed revolution will change this sytem of monopoly capitalism and end racism and women's oppression. But for you to sit quietly and let them wipe out the Voting Rights Act is just bizarre. For you not to fight for every kind of democratic right, inch by inch—you know what I mean, like they say, fight for every inch—is mad. It's like, I was very critical of a lot of people on the Left in the recent election, because their line was "Carter and Reagan are exactly the same." Well, look, they represent the same class, but there are different sectors of that class, and they are not identical, you see, as you now found out. Here's a man now talking about getting rid of Social Security—you can't say that's the *same* as Jimmy Carter. So I think that those kinds of sweeping, Leftist, ultrarevolutionary statements serve to do nothing but fog up the reality that you have to fight for every inch. Yes, you have to utilize voting. Absolutely you have to utilize it. People died in the South to get the right to vote, and then you're going to tell people, "Don't vote. It doesn't mean anything." That's bizarre. The question is, what *does* it mean? It has a limited and specific meaning, but it has to be utilized.

DH Do you see any progress at all, in Newark or elsewhere, since the sixties?

AB Well, yes, sure. There's been general progress. I think we're in a period now when they're trying to eliminate that, and you'll find that in this particular kind of society, that's what happens all the time. For instance, in the 1860s, a period of revolution, the Civil War—the Civil War was a democratic revolution: It eliminated slavery; it changed the Constitution to guarantee democratic rights, equality, you know, not only for Black people but poor whites, which is always a well-kept secret. But by the 1870s, 1880s, that had been almost eliminated. By that time, you had laws on the books now ensuring the inequality that had been fought in the 1860s. The same thing now: 1960s people struggled for affirmative action. Man comes along in the seventies and tch-tch—one signature, the Bakke decision [*whistles*].[16] Get rid of it. And the stuff that Reagan is doing now, to me, is the same that happened in the 1870s and 1880s, now in the 1970s, the 1980s, the same kind of attempt to eliminate what gain, what inch of gain was made.

MB Now there's talk—I don't know if it's some sociologist at Harvard or some place like that recently, in one of these vague generalizations about America, but he said that we are on the brink in some cities, I think Newark was one of them, with a permanent underclass of people, you know, who forever will be shackled to the situation. Do you think that that's—

AB Well, I think that as far as the present economy, that would have to be true, but since, if we understand reality, we know nothing stays the same. Things are not static. There is going to be motion; it's either going to be upward or downward. Then you know that those people are not going to stand for that, and the only thing you're doing then is preparing for some kind of broad, urban unrest. I mean, this Heritage Foundation has already advised Reagan to abandon the cities—don't give any aid to the cities, talking about the Northeast, in particular—abandon those cities, leave them, and the Midwest, the New Yorks, and the Detroits, and the Chicagos, and the Clevelands, and the Phillies, and Pittsburgh, abandon those cities, head for the Sun Belt. And then now, you see, even in this pseudopopular culture that they manufacture—there's a movie called *Escape from New York,* which actually now would turn New York into Alcatraz—

DH [*Laughing*] I find that insulting.

AB Well, if you see who's in there, locked up in there, you would really find that insulting: Blacks, Latinos, Asians, homosexuals, aggressive women, punk rockers. [*Laughs*] They're the ones who are locked up.

DH I wanted to ask you something about that. In terms of your current position, your article in the *Village Voice,* "Confessions of a Former Anti-Semite"—

AB —which is not my title.

DH Oh, it wasn't? What was your title?

AB My title was "A Personal View of Anti-Semitism." That's our friend [David] Schneiderman, who was the editor. That's his idea of something that would sell papers. Which apparently it did.

DH Okay. Well, in that article, you equate Zionism with white racism as "reactionary." Would you now add Black Nationalism to that list?

AB Well, I say this. To me, all nationalism, finally, taken to any extreme, has got to be oppressive to the people who are not in that nationality. You understand what I mean? If it's taken to the extreme, any nationalism has got to be exclusive and has got to say, "Us, yes; you, no." I mean, that's the nature of nationalism. But you have to make a distinction between, say, people who are oppressed as a nationality, who are fighting national liberation struggles. I think in terms of Zionism, the difference is this: that previous to the Second World War, Jews generally were not interested in Zionism, what Chaim Weizmann and, you know, the other dude put forward. Generally it was like some right-wing intellectuals, some right-wing nationalist intellectuals. Once the British got hold of that, the Balfour Declaration, in which then it's made a part of British foreign policy to settle Jews in a Palestinian homeland, you know, obviously to look over the oil interests—that changes into an instrument of imperialist policy. Now, a certain sector of the Jewish population becomes interested in Zionism as a result of the Holocaust, for obvious reasons, for obvious reasons. Once you knock off seven million people, then, if there's somebody saying, "Look, you got to get out of here, that's the reason, you got to get out of here," then that's going to become attractive.

But I do not believe that Zionism is the general ideology of Jews in the world. I think the great contributions that Jews have made in the world have been much more advanced than a narrow nationalism, and I think obviously what [Menachim] Begin and Company are doing now, it just isolates the State of Israel from the world. I think more and more people will come to see, and especially Jews, that the State of Israel and Jews are two separate entities. And I think that it's a great cover story for somebody who may jump on Israel, for you to say you're attacking Jews generally, and you have to shut up. But I don't think that's going to work. It's very interesting, for instance, to see a lot of Palestinian Jews, now, the kind of lines that have come out recently in some of these organizations. It's an incredible thing, but I think of course in New York, when you've got a stronghold of world Zionist organization, it's very hard for you to say things like that without people beating you to death as being anti-Jewish, which has been my fate. Even that article I wrote, which was an attempt to set the record straight, you know, was hacked up so unmercifully. It made you wonder just what they wanted to present. I mean, at the end it seemed like they wanted to present you as an anti-Semite, even though I volunteered to write the article.

DH You're talking about the editing of that article?

AB Oh, yes, yes, oh yes. You see, what I did—

DH The "Confession," with Jewish people I've spoken to, was not received as any kind of apology.

AB Oh, no. Well, the thing on Zionism, the minute you jump on Zionism, you're going to get it back, no matter what you say. You see, what was removed, to me, was critical, because I did a whole history of anti-Semitism. Essentially, it's an ideological justification for fundamentally economic and political oppression. Anti-Semitism rises, you know, in the struggle between the Greeks and Jews in the Middle East, and the Romans and the Jews, and basically then in the Middle Ages as an attempt to keep economic superiority. Economic attack is what it justifies: "These people are Christ-killers. Let's take their money." You know, it's like the Japanese you've put in a concentration camp: "These people are our enemies; let's get their truck farms. Let's get their truck farms; these people are our enemies." You know what I mean. There's always an ideological justification for some economic and political shenanigans. That's what it essentially is. No matter that you might have some people down the road who really believe it, like you might have some Klansmen walking around who really believe such and such a thing is true, when actually, what's happening is you've got some landowners who are not going to let Black people, for instance, have democracy down there because it means they're not going to control that land. They're not going to control the U.S. Senate or the colonies anymore. You always have people who walk around, who believe stuff on one level; but you also have the people who are putting that out, who are gaining from that. That's the real significance of that.

 DH I'd like to ask you about your thinking on homosexuality and also on the women's movement. Even as late as *The Sidney Poet Heroical,* which was published in '79, you refer to gay men as "faggots," referring in a derogatory way. Has your thinking changed with the movement for gay rights? Would you say—

 AB Well, I say this—

 DH —there's a certain parallel in, you know, the raising of your consciousness in thinking about those things?

 AB Well, in a certain way. You see, first of all, I say this. The use of the term "faggot," although obviously it's derived from homosexuality, from homosexuals, was not meant in the Black community simply as "homosexual." It meant, essentially, a weak person, you know, somebody who could not do what they were supposed to do. That's what it really meant.

 DH You're saying you absorbed this.

 AB Oh, sure. So that, a lot of times, calling people "faggots" did not mean specifically that it had to do with homosexuality. It had to do with the question of weakness, although obviously it is taken from that, and as such still is a kind of what would you call it—attack.

DH Yes, attack.

AB Yes, attack. I don't think I believe in any gratuitous attacks on homosexuals as such. I've tried to stop saying that, calling people "faggots," even though, still I would say when the majority of Black people say "faggot," they're not talking about homosexuals. You might say, "Reagan is a faggot"; I mean, you're not talking about him being a homosexual [*laughs*]; you're talking about him being a weak, jive person. But I think it does come from the denigration of homosexuality, and I think that, as I said, gratuitous attacks on homosexuals have to be opposed. We do have to oppose any kind of attempt to limit homosexuals' democratic rights, because when they're doing that, they're coming for *us*. You know, attack homosexuals' democratic rights—it's really coming for everybody's democratic rights, but at the same time, I believe this: that homosexuality is a minority issue, except in the way that I just mentioned, where it can be connected up to everybody's democratic rights. I think that living in L.A. or New York or San Francisco, one might tend to think that it's much more of a mass issue than it is. But the majority of people are not interested in homosexuality; they don't care anything about it. I think this: if you were to raise up as a mass question, "Do you want this homosexual to teach your children?" I think that, in the main, is going to be negative. I think most people are going to say, like, negative.

DH But how do *you* feel?

AB Well, I think this. The question is, if a homosexual is teaching my child in a way that I can see is beneficial to the child, it doesn't matter to me. You see what I'm saying? But obviously I don't want the child to be taught homosexuality, and I don't want the child to *be* a homosexual. I don't want that to be raised up as a positive thing, because I do believe that homosexuality is a social aberration. I do believe it's a social aberration, and I think it's a product of class society, essentially. I do not believe that homosexuality, by and large, is going to help human beings to make progress. But I do not believe that homosexuals need to be attacked.

DH So your thinking is somewhat modified, but not—

AB Oh, yes. It's modified in the sense that I think that just loose-mouthed calling people "faggots" is out of the question. I mean, even when some of my best friends—that sounds really corny, and it is—but see, even when some of my best friends were homosexuals, I still called people "faggots," and I didn't mean *them*. [*Laughs*] It meant something else. But I think that that question of dealing with homosexuals and understanding that you cannot attack these people's democratic rights—they cannot be subjected to any gratuitous attacks—does not, in any way, justify homosexuality, because I don't think I can justify it in that sense.

DH What about women's rights? Women don't seem to come off very well in your work, except, at best, in a passive—

AB Um-hum.

DH Has your consciousness been raised at all in connection with the Feminist Movement?

AB Probably, but I don't think the Feminist Movement per se; but I think the whole struggle for women's rights—the Feminist Movement is part of that; it's certainly in there. I would agree with you that until the last four or five years, works on women or about women have either been missing or, as you say, largely passive. In the last four or five years there has been some kind of significant change. I would attribute that to my wife, principally.

MB What is her name?

AB Amina, A-m-i-n-a. And to the whole question of—you see, when people like, for instance, Michele Wallace come off talking about it in that book that *Ms.* magazine wants to push to give a kind of a feminist interpretation of Black Liberation—that's completely off the wall, because what it does is it attacks Black women again.[17] Because if you think that because you weren't there, that the Black women in the Movement just went for that, just passively said, "Oh, yes, we must go and deal with these male chauvinists," well, you saddle your thinking, because our whole history of women's participation in the Black Liberation Movement of the sixties, from my own knowledge of it, was constantly marked by women fighting against the male chauvinism of people like myself, you know, and a great many other people. So that for somebody to come and make it seem that "Yes, you know, the problem with the Black Liberation Movement is male chauvinism, and none of these Black women knew it" is like the height of an attack, and the only person who could do that is somebody who didn't know, who wasn't there. But talk to the people who were in the Movement, who knew, and who know, and had to go through that, and had to be subjected to that, while people like Michele Wallace were off in some private school in Paris. It's ludicrous, because they actually had to be subjected to that and fight against that and have their lives crippled by that, and then somebody comes along and says, "Well, you know what the problem was."

MB   What do you remember about Newark in 1967, the riots—just immediately, what comes to mind?

AB   Well, the fires; seeing U.S. Army military weapons in a city that was supposed to be in America. I mean, you look up and see tanks, and soldiers fully armed; then you want to know where you are—this must not be America, because this is what they did in Vietnam or Korea. But then people, the police checking people's ID. . . . I was arrested the first night of the thing and was locked up through the period of the worst kind of burning and fighting. But the police came up into my house, which is the Spirit House on Stirling Street. My wife and child—young child was in there, oldest son—were in there, and they were on the third floor, I think, and then the National Guard and the cops came in on the first floor, destroying stuff, turning stuff over, breaking up things. They never went up to the third floor; they didn't think anybody was up there. And, you know, bullets through the windows, and stuff like that.

MB   What were the circumstances of your being arrested?

AB   Well, we were driving around looking at it, what was going on. A couple of friends and I were riding around the Central Ward—you know, I lived over there at the time—looking at what was happening. Picked up a couple of people, took them to the hospital; a guy got shot in the leg, picked him up, took him to the hospital, things like that, and then we stayed out too late afterward. People had cleared off the streets and we were coming down the street, and we were stopped by about twenty cops, I don't know. They pulled us out of the car and they started beating us. They split my head open, knocked my teeth out, I mean I couldn't see, I mean my face was so covered with blood I thought I was going to die, you know; there just was blood everywhere, I couldn't even see. But the people up in the window were screaming, there were Black people up there who kept screaming, kept screaming—that's what cooled it out. Otherwise, I was finished. When you feel the blood in your face, you can feel it warm in your face, and you can't even see for the blood; it's in your mouth, your eyes—

DH [*Softly*] And then you could have been killed.

AB Oh, yes. That was understood. That was understood, you know. Oh, that was it. I mean, that was really where they were going to take us off. But, after that, they charged us with possession of weapons, which was the first trial we lost, and then we got another trial because the judge was obviously out of his mind. He reads a poem and sentences. He reads one of my poems as a reason to sentence me. I knew that was out, even if he wouldn't do anything, I said this guy's a nut. As if the poem was the reason to—it was a poem about rebellion that had been written just before the [Black] rebellion. And so that was—I got a retrial and it was thrown out. It took about two years, three years.

MB Have you ever served time?

AB No. I've never served any; I've been in jail a lot but I never—except for a couple of days.

MB I mean, you've never been, like, sentenced, like this thing coming up.[18]

AB Well, even when I was sentenced to three years, no parole, for this gun thing—

MB This thing?

AB No. The thing in '67. I was sentenced to three years, but I didn't—I served about three or four days and got out on appeal. And I had done a couple of days before that. This time I did about four days and was discharged. But that's about the most time I've ever done.

MB What do you think of this ninety days coming up, if that goes down?

AB Well, that stuff is so wild that it's very hard to consistently take it seriously, but now we've been at it two and a half years; they've been on us for two and a half years.

MB This case?

AB Yes. From '79, June of '79.

MB You mean this incident with the argument? Is that it?

AB Yes. June '79. So, apparently they're serious they're going to lock me up. Why they will get so much satisfaction in locking me up for ninety days is something that needs to be looked into. I mean, they've had two years of court costs, five days of grand jury hearings for a resisting-arrest charge. You're wondering, "Why, why would you spend so much money when you're talking about the need to cut the budget?" Our boy William Butz just got sentenced to thirty days for a $96,000 tax evasion. [*Laughs*] What is it in this "resisting arrest"? But really, it's a form of intimidation—not only for me, but I think they want to intimidate, generally, people. They want the people to know, "Look. This is what we do." And then there's also the possibility that they're going to do something to you in the prison. You could never be sure of that. Especially with this hit list that's circulating. We just published this hit list of cultural workers and artists. Two people who work for the government leaked this out to a publisher—not a publisher, to a producer, and somebody in his office leaked it to me. And I've been trying to leak it to various people. We published it in our newspaper [*Unity*]; I've read it on the radio; I've sent it to different newspapers. Interestingly, one of the people who was on the hit list died last week—Harry Chapin, the folksinger.

DH   He was on that?

AB   Yes, he was on there. He got this mysterious accident—somebody hit him from behind. That is so spooky that I think that I'm going to reopen that whole thing. I've got a copy of it upstairs; I'll show it to you. But there are about twenty people on it, who they say have to be, you know, done something to—people like Pete Seeger, Bread and Puppet Theatre—

MB   Where did the list come from?

DH   Are you on that list?

AB   It was supposed to be leaked from a government—two people working in a government agency, who were cultural workers working in a government agency, and said these people would have two things going: blacklist, which is to make it difficult for these people to get their works out; and a hit list, that is, certain people within this list need to be done away with. And it talks about arranging accidents for some of them, and a couple of them who have already disappeared, a guy named Dan Silver, a guy who made films in El Salvador. Then there were a lot of people who do political theater, who are cultural activists, things like that. When that Harry Chapin thing happened, really, my eyes shot right open. Jesus Christ!

DH   Are you on either list?

AB   Yes. Oh, yes.

DH   You're on both lists?

AB   Yes, I'm on that list. They put them together. The ones that are supposed to be killed have asterisks by them. [*Laughs*]

Chapin was supposed to be—they said they were going to do something to remove him, something like that.

MB Do you know what agency it came from?

AB No. They didn't say. It was a letter, with a list attached to it. The letter said that "we are two people who work for a government agency, whose business it is to set up a blacklist on the following artists and also remove the ones that are listed on there." So we published it. Like I said, I broadcast it over the radio. I've sent it to a couple of big publications, but they haven't done anything with it. Recently, I just sent it back out, saying, "Well, look, since this Chapin thing, you can at least raise that up; you know, you might be able to sell a few papers." Because I believe that's the only thing that would really cool that out; to a certain extent, it's publicity.

MB Yes, sure.

AB Even if it turned out to be a hoax. Obviously, generally we know such things exist. I've got two thousand pages from the FBI that I had a lawyer get through the Freedom of Information Act, but now they're getting ready to close that loophole.

DH This list was published before Chapin's—

AB Yes. I'm sure. Published a couple of weeks before Chapin died.

DH That's scary.

AB Oh, yes. It was published in June.

DH That should really be investigated.

AB Yes. So we're going to try to get some more publicity on that.

DH In moving from Kawaida[19] to Marxist-Leninist-Maoism, did you have any strong influences on your transition before the Sixth Pan-African Congress in 1974?

AB Influences to change to Marxism?

DH Yes. And people, thinkers—

AB Yes. A lot of changes. First of all, I think my own experience in terms of dealing in this town with electoral politics; seeing a Black middle class benefit from those electoral politics and no changes for the majority. So I began to understand what "classes" and "class struggle" was about, you know, from my own experience. Meeting Black Marxists in different united fronts I belonged to, like the African Liberation Support Committee; beginning to see and talk to people who are on the Left; finding out that a lot of people that I admired who were African revolutionaries were really anti-imperialists and Marxists. They were not talking "hate whitey," as I was at the time, people like Amilcar Cabral in Guinea-Bissau; Nkrumah in Ghana; Samora Machel in Mozambique; the Pan-African Congress in South Africa—people like that. Beginning to see that, hey, there was a whole different view by Black activists around the world. And I think those are the things. I had read Mao, but I would always come to excise the part about communism, where he would talk about he was a communist, and stuff. [*Laughs*] You know, censor that part and try to read the rest of it, which was, of course, bizarre. And so then I decided that I was fooling myself, and I should go ahead and investigate and find out what was happening, and I did. I mean it was in a lot of ways a painful experience, in a lot of ways. Our organization nationally split in half. We had a large organization in some sixteen, seventeen cities, and then split in half.

DH   Which organization?

AB   That was the Congress of Afrikan Peoples. But I thought that it was necessary, and I still do think it is necessary and important.

DH   The deep concern of your leadership is with "unity and struggle." Whom are you seeking to unite?

AB   Well, the great majority of people in this country—in fact, the great majority of people in the world—who have the same general enemies. I think the great majority of people in this country are objective allies; they're fighting against the same class of people: I think the six- tenths of one percent of the people that actually own the land, that actually own CBS and NBC and ABC, that actually own Standard Oil and Exxon, I mean those of us who have been taught to think like them, I mean the six-tenths of one percent that actually own that, the rulers. I think a great many other people, let's say, 90 percent of the people—there's another 9 percent that will die with that six-tenths of one percent. But I think 90 percent of the people in this country can unite, and I think eventually they will. Everybody comes to it in different ways. You have some very deep problems in this country with that unity. Obviously, the whole history of slavery and chauvinism in this country makes that very difficult. But I don't think it's impossible.

DH   In looking toward unity, what about coalition on the Left? I mean the breach between Soviet-oriented communism, scorned as "Red Squad Functionaries" in your play *S-1*, and Mao-oriented communism, expressed by the "Revolutionary People's Union" in that? Do you see any possibility of a coalition?

AB Well, you see, no, because I think that if you look at the world with the view that I have, the view I guess best expressed by the "Theory of Three Worlds" of Mao Tse-tung, in my view, the United States and the Soviet Union are two imperialist super-powers, and while obviously a lot of people in the Communist Party U.S.A. are just—don't understand what's happening, are dupes, the people in the leadership there act as a kind of fifth column of the Soviet Union in the United States, and even make it difficult to struggle against U.S. imperialism; they make it more difficult to struggle against U.S. imperialism, even though it seems that they're struggling against it. And I say they make it more difficult because they are always putting out this line that reforms are the answer, that reforms are the end. They're even telling people that no, you can get socialism through the election machines—that's like some-body selling dope, you know. You're not going to get socialism; you're not going to elect the people's control of the wealth any-where in the world; I mean, Chile should have taught us that for all times. It was a legally elected socialist government in a modern, industrial country. What is it now? A fascist state. So I think the question is, if you've got people representing a superpower, imperi-alist country, whether it's the U.S. or the Soviet Union, then you can't make a coalition with it.

MB When you were young, did you ever talk politics with your parents? Your father, say, a Republican—you must have had a hard time with that.

AB No, no. My *grand*father was Republican. My father has always been a Democrat. My father says he voted for the man, not the party, whatever that meant. But he tended to be a Democrat. I think he was a Roosevelt man. Now, I don't know where he's at, but I would think that he's generally a Democrat-leaning person. But my grandfather was a Republican, obviously, even up until Wendell Willkie. We used to have Willkie buttons around the house. And, you know, my father was a Democrat, so there would be some tension in that. But I talked politics to them or raised up political issues, and we'd agree and disagree. I think for one thing, though, both my father and mother were radicalized *somewhat* by the '67 rebellion, and I think when my father, especially when he saw what they had done to me, it snapped him out, because he had been much more conservative before then. But I think that when he saw that they had tried to kill me, he knew that whatever I was doing, it wasn't that bad. I think it really snapped him out. And then he came to the court and saw the kind of obvious racism. It's one thing to see it abstractly, but when you see that it's your child they're doing these things to, that probably would light you up.

MB   Were you a fighter as a child, or were you more, as you mentioned earlier, a wordsmith? I mean you would say things—

AB   Really, when I had to fight it was because there was no other way out. [*Laughs*] But no, words became weapons for me a long time ago, and my physical prowess was in speed. If you couldn't talk your way out of it, then you had to decamp, change landscapes rapidly. But then when I got into the service was when I really started actually having to fight all the time. I'd never wanted to or even found it necessary to get into fisticuffs, but then I got into the air force and I really had to, first because of that kind of overt racism which I could not *stand*. It's one thing to see the Klan in the newspaper, but to have somebody call you a name, it always just set me on fire, and that's when I came in contact with that. Then I actually started to roll around on the ground with people, and I really had not done much of that before—especially when I didn't feel I could win, anyway. [*Laughter*] But in the service, though, I found that, always coming up with that.

MB   Did you grow up in the Central Ward?

AB   Yes.

MB   You mentioned Italian, so you must have been near the North Ward.

AB   West Ward, near the North Ward, yes, right by Central Avenue. I grew up, my early days, right in the Central Ward, Barclay Street, Boston Street, and then later on, Central Avenue, back over to the Central Ward, Belmont Avenue.

MB   What high school did you go to?

AB   Barringer; it's in the North Ward. At the time, there were very few Blacks in it.

MB   And how many children do you have?

AB   Five by the present marriage, two by a previous marriage.

MB   Five by the present; two by a previous.

AB   Um-hum.

DH   You're including the two children that are in Manhattan, before—

AB   No. She has two by a previous marriage.

DH   Oh—so there are seven?

AB   In the house?

DH   Yes.

AB   Well, there are six in the house. One of them is not here; one of them is actually on vacation somewhere, and the other lives elsewhere. There usually are six kids here.

DH   Three were in a play, weren't they—*S-1*—I saw three names—

AB   Yes. That's right.

DH   —"Baraka." Are they interested in the theater?

AB   I think so. Well, let me see, one of them, the oldest boy, plays the drums; he's a very good drummer. The next boy—I don't know if he's interested in drama; I think he wants to be a writer. The little girl is always reading poetry aloud, so I think she wants to be an actress.

DH   Um-hum.

AB   She's always proclaiming these poems, so she might want to act.

DH   Do you act?

AB   No, no. [*Laughs*] My mother was always putting me in different little things, skits, but I never did any serious adult acting.

DH   I was wondering about the response of Black writers, intellectuals, to your views. How receptive have they been to your view on these political aspects?

AB   Well, I think you'll find that there's a kind of class struggle raging among Black intellectuals like everywhere else, and I think that the people are divided around the lines they take. I think there are more and more people who are much less hostile, say, to Marxism than they were in '74, '75. In '74 and '75 people were calling us all kinds of bad words, you know, "traitors." I remember at the Sixth Pan-African Congress this woman actually went to the foreign minister, weeping, saying stuff that I had said and this other guy, Owusu Sadaukai, had said; that we were really betraying Black people. And I mean I thought that was kind of extraordinary. There is still, of course, a lot of sentiment in the Black community, but I think there's much less hostility to Marxist ideas.

DH   I just want to ask you a couple of more things on [Charles] Olson.

AB   Um-hum.

DH   Olson's theories of Projectivism and "composition by field" still seem alive and well in your work. Apart from your progress toward a Black aesthetic and the Marxist approach of your recent work, would you say that Olson remains your most useful poetic influence?

AB   Well, no. I think my most useful poetic influence is Langston Hughes. Charles Olson was important to me at one time, and I think the most importance that he had was that within the kind of aesthetic that I was actually involved in, he provided a kind of opening for the ideas that I saw, and then I said, Well, wow! A lot of the things that I think and want to do, he's actually expressing those things. You see? Because I was drawn to certain white poets, like Allen Ginsberg, even before Olson. I was drawn to them because they legitimized things that I wanted to do and that I felt. When I came up against the *New Yorker* magazine poets and the *Hudson Review* and *Partisan Review* poets, they made me weep, because I really didn't want to write like that; I really didn't think I could write that; I mean, it was dull, it was dead. The things that I wanted to write, I didn't think could even be called "poetry" by their standards, you know—so that was very depressing and discouraging. But then when I got to New York and discovered, wow! somebody like Allen, who was talking about, you know, the "nigger streets" and junkies and all kinds of things that I could see and I could identify with, then I said, yeah, that's closer to what I want to do. And then when I saw Olson's statement, he was saying, actually, that this old dead poetry that people have been writing is exactly that, exactly what you thought it was: old, dead poetry. Then it actually just encouraged me, because I had thought these things anyway. It's like somebody saying something that you've got bubbling around in your head, and then they come out with it, and it legitimizes what you're doing; it encourages you.

MB   What about [Jack] Kerouac—him, too, as part of—

AB   Well, in a way. But Ginsberg always was more important to me, I guess being a poet. Because Allen is an intellectual; Kerouac was not much of an intellectual; he was more of a—

MB   Street wise—

AB   —yes, kind of person. I think you could see that when his

later views became so backward, because he was never really rooted
in investigation of ideas. It was more like reacting to things, spon-
taneous, which, because it was so open and free in terms of its form,
was positive. Because there was no deep investigation into the
history of ideas, then the form could be undermined by the content.

DH   Ginsberg said, "First thought, best thought." Do you
agree with that?

AB   No. [*Laughs*] Obviously.

DH   Do you revise at all?

AB   Yes. So does he.

DH   In all genres—

AB   Yes.

DH   —in all genres, poetry and prose?

AB   Yes, sure. So does he—so what? [*Laughs*]

DH   I don't know whether he'll admit it, though.

AB   Oh, I don't see why not. I say this: what he means is that
you get to a point where at one point in the fifties people were then
showing you just—poems—"I worked on this poem *twenty
years!*" Really. There's so much more in people's normal percep-
tion that's worth being exposed to. But to tell somebody you're
working on something—getting a word changed for twenty years is
not really impressive anymore. It becomes like some prescription
for—a mummy farm.

DH   So then you're somewhere in between *le mot juste*—
Flaubert's *le mot juste*—and "if I write it, it's a poem."

AB   Oh yes, sure. I don't believe in "absolute spontaneity is
always the best." No. Absolutely not. That's why you have certain
levels of understanding. You know, there is perception where you
do perceive a thing, and sometimes that perception can hold. But
then you bring your rational mind to bear on it, and sometimes you
have to modify that, or sometimes you see a way that you can make
a thing stronger, and that helps. And then a lot of times you find
out, whoa! you're way off base; you might come back to something
a few years later and say, "Oh, Jesus—did I say that? Oh, get that
out of there." And that's obvious.

I don't like to . . . pretend that I never thought those things—
somebody says, "Well, look, you had these backward ideas on such
and such a date"—and then sneak around and cross them out. No.
I think the point is to say, "Yeah. Well, that's true. But, hopefully,
the later work has changed and shows some kind of growth and

development." But I don't think you can hide your tracks. And that's kind of—

MB   When is your birthday?

AB   October 7, 1934.

MB   So you're coming up for—

AB   Forty-seven. Forty-eight? [*Laughs*]

DH   A young man.

MB   Well, you'll be forty-seven—

AB   Yes.

MB   I don't want to say that too loudly in case your son was around and it was a secret he wasn't supposed to—

AB   Oh, no! [*Chuckling*] He asked me that the other day.

DH   There's an abundance of punning in your work, and you'll recall Olson's saying, "Pun is rime" in his "Projective Verse" essay?[20]

AB   Yes. Right.

DH   Did he to any extent spark that interest in punning?

AB   No. That's a street thing.

DH   That's just a street thing.

AB   Oh, yes. The pun—the rhyme and the pun are really part of the Black oral tradition. I think they're part of everybody's oral tradition—the whole first, what you'd call "delicious accident," and then a much more rational juxtaposition of sounds and things. But that always, I think, goes back to the oral tradition, the pun.

DH   The use of the word *Negro*, the pun "Knee-grow," and "New Ark"—these are your inventions?

AB   "Knee-grow" is: "New Ark" is the original name of the town. People resist that.

MB   That's what it's called in Delaware.

AB   Yes. If you look on the charter, it's two words, "New Ark," and obviously, it's a biblical reference, but when we started to use it, then people resisted it because it was identified with us, I mean, the backward people in this town. But that's the real name. And it's interesting that southern Blacks always say that to this day; you know, they keep saying, "New Ark."

MB   The town in Delaware is spelled the same way, and they all call it "New Ark."

AB   Yes, that's interesting. That's obviously the name. And I think the southern Blacks probably say that because they're probably going back to an older English, too, that's "New Ark."

MB   Actually Newark lately has become a sort of—when the
guy on the train announces it—"Nerk" [*laughing*], it becomes the
one syllable—

AB   It's not even there—

MB   "Nerk!"

AB   I know. That's another kind of speech.

MB   Speaking of speeches, can you—I'm sure your answer to
this is "yes"—you can go out there and talk jive, right? You can go
down to the corner and—you don't talk—

DH   Black English.

MB   Not only Black English. I mean you just—I don't really
mean Black English; I mean, just guys-on-the-corner sort of talk. I
don't know what the name is, but—

AB   Sure.

MB   I mean, you don't talk the way you're doing now.

AB   No, not altogether. But I think I've always had a reputa-
tion in this town—

MB   If I could borrow one of them at—

AB   No, I've always had a reputation in this town for talking
"funny." [*General laughter*] Obviously, I do speak more like these
people around here speak. I've always had a reputation of sounding
funny and so on. I know people—about the way I used to say
"motherfucker," they'd say, "I don't want you to call me that
because you say it too nasty. [*Laughter*] Because you pronounce—
you say '*mother*'—you know what mean? That is really *ugly* when
you say it like that." [*Laughter*] But no, I tend to sound more like
the people out there, I would imagine. But it be hard to get all your
training out of it. [*Laughs*]

DH   Would you say the Dozens were an influence in the
frequency of direct insult in your work? Like *Hard Facts*, would you
say the Dozens—

AB   Oh, sure.

DH   Did you do the Dozens as a child?

AB   Oh, sure.

DH   Did you play it as a rhyming game?

AB   Both, both rhyming and unrhymed, oh, yes. And I think
that was my real introduction to the strength and use of poetry.
Because by it you could actually keep people off you; with poetry
you could make them leave you alone. I mean if you couldn't fight,
if you could really use those words like that, they would get away

from you, because they didn't want to be called twenty-five different kinds of motherfuckers in twenty-five seconds, you know? So they would leave you alone. And then it did become very conscious to me. Yes, speech can be as effective, almost, as your fist. But that was my real introduction to the uses of poetry.

DH   So that was very young.

AB   Oh, yes. Oh, sure. But they used to have some people— still do, obviously—walking around, going for hours, rhyming, rhyming, rhyming, rhyming, you know, top speed.

DH   Yes.

AB   Just a whole flow of insults.

DH   In some of your recent work, do you use what Stephen Henderson refers to as "virtuoso free-rhyme"?

AB   Um-hum.

DH   Rhymes within a long sentence with lots of different rhymes strung—

AB   Yes. I have much more respect for rhyme, now. I've always used internal rhyme like that, because I felt that was, you know, slick, to do it like that; but I have much more respect for end rhyme, too. And it's like the old story about how, as you get older, you discover how wise your parents were [*laughing*]. I've grown to love Langston Hughes's poetry more now, because I want to use rhyme more. I begin to see then the strengths of that in ways I couldn't see when I was just dismissing rhyme completely. Obviously, rhyme can become a very dead weight in any kind of language. The kind of unrhymed verse that academic poets write is probably as deadly as rhyme. So—[*Laughs*]

DH   Yes. Well, in connection with that, apart from the critically important work you've done in writing *Blues People* and *Black Music*, you seem to be using music and musicians increasingly in your poetry and drama, the Advanced Workers, which is your musical group, specifically. Would you say there's a connection between the interest in music and the interest in rhyme? And what, specifically, is the function of the music?

AB   Well, the music, to me, is two things, but it's one thing first. The music, first of all, is poetry. I mean, to me, fundamentally, poetry is a combination. Poetry is a musical form, just like blues. I think blues is a verse form, but it's a musical form, too. You see what I mean? And to me, poetry has to be that, and at the same time, verse, but it has to be a musical form. I mean it doesn't exist as poetry unless it's musical, you know, "musicked speech," high speech. And I think that my own interest in poetry comes from the kind of love that I've always had for music, basically. I played trumpet when I was a kid, and I wrote this poem called "I Would Have Been a Trumpet Player If I Hadn't Gone to College." And essentially, that had something to do with it, because once I left this town and went away to school, I stopped playing the trumpet. I never lost my love for music. I began to listen to it, of course, to study it—I studied it informally with Sterling Brown. At Howard he had classes for a lot of us in the dormitory after classes, after *formal* classes. He took us to the dormitory in the evenings, and he'd teach us about the blues and early forms of jazz.

DH   You had some fine teachers there; you had Nathan Scott, too.

AB   Yes. Nathan Scott, right. He taught me Dante. That's where I got my interest in Dante. It wasn't even because I understood it, you know. He was so enthusiastic about it—

DH   Was it a course—

AB   —I said, "Jesus, this must be good!" [*Laughs*]

DH   It was a course in Dante?

AB   No. It was a survey course in Western literature. We got all the biggies, everybody we were supposed to get, in that one-year survey course. And when he came to Dante, he was so in love with it. And now I understand why—because he was religious. I didn't know that. He was a Reverend—something like that. He was a Doctor of Divinity, as well as a Ph.D.

DH   Yes, I think so.

AB   He was always connecting religion and existentialism. I guess that's what he was giving us then.

DH   In your adaptation of a Black aesthetic to Marxist, agit-prop aesthetics, you seem to be seeking new forms for the new content: for example, your historical pageants, *Slave Ship* and *The Motion of History*, and your satire, *The Sidney Poet Heroical*, in which you musically adapt a classical, Greek-style chorus. Apart from your self-criticism of *The Sidney Poet* as "petit bourgeois cultural nationalism," are you satisfied with these works? How do you feel about *S-1*? . . .

AB   *The Sidney Poet.* No, I'm satisfied with that as a work of a certain period; it said certain things. I think it still has some kind of general uses. It got Sidney Poitier mad at me, though, so I don't know—there was a negative feedback to it. But as far as *S-1* is concerned, and *The Motion of History,* I would like to see them done again. I directed both of them, you know; I had this thing of directing my works, at least one a year, every other year, when I could. I took the moneys that I had, whatever moneys I could borrow, and I would do some performances of the play, because I couldn't get any producers. Since this police harassment two years ago, I haven't been able to do that, and as a matter of fact, that interrupted the production of *The Lone Ranger* that was being done, which I was producing at that time, because I had to use all the money for the court thing, you see, so I didn't have any extra money to use for the production. I would like to see *S-1* done again; I would like to see *The Motion of History* done again. I think particularly *S-1* is relevant during these Reagan times, because what that was about was the attempt to bring fascism to the United States, and I think that's a very, very relevant play, now. I would like to get somebody who would produce it and direct it.

DH Was [Bertolt] Brecht an influence?

AB Brecht has been an influence, I'd say, in the last few years. In the last few years, certainly, this whole educational theater, in that sense, the "theater of instruction" is important to me, and a lot of the technical innovations. The jazz opera [*Money*] that I wrote a couple of years ago that we're going to do parts of the end of the year at La Mama, I think is closer to, say, Brecht than cold, traditional opera.

DH And the use of scene—one scene after another?

AB Yes. Well, certainly in the way I tried to direct *The Motion of History.* That was influenced by Brecht's wanting to use signs, you know, those kinds of things. I've always been, I think, interested in using audiovisuals along with the theater. In the play that we're doing in the fall, called *Boy and Tarzan Appear in a Clearing*—they're going to do that at the Henry Street in October. That uses a lot of video, television, and film at the same time. I'm interested in expanding the theater, using technological advances of society in general.

DH Which of your works would you say has given you the most satisfaction, so far?

AB Always the most recent one [*laughter*], when you see it produced—although I've done some bad productions myself. I think it's always gratifying to be able to see the most recent thing, the last thing that I've done, so I'm looking forward to the two things we're doing this fall and winter.

DH   You have a cinematographic technique in your later works.

AB   Yes.

DH   Who would you say has influenced you there—[Sergei] Eisenstein?

AB   Movies generally. Movies generally. I think Eisenstein intellectually, if I look at his theories on the dialectics of image. I think it would be impossible for anybody who makes film, whether they know it or not, to say they haven't been influenced by Eisenstein. The question of montage is impossible without Eisenstein, whether they know it or not. But then, I've been influenced by all the moviemakers that I've seen. I'm a moviegoer. I've always been a moviegoer. It always insults me when people try to say that movies somehow are some kind of inferior art form. I can never understand that. That always seems to me the most bizarre thing in the world to say.

DH   You said you would prefer a less sentimental ending for *The Toilet*.

AB   Yes.

DH   Although you don't turn your back on that time of your creative life.

AB   No. That ending was tacked on, that's what I meant, first of all. When I wrote it, I wrote it straight through and I tacked this ending on. The way it ended was first with the guy just left there, in the toilet, and then I tacked it on I guess as some kind of attempt to show some kind of, you know, reconciliation, or something like that. And I think that's where I was at that time.

DH   Is there any other work you feel that way about, that you would like to redo or revise?

AB   [*Emphatically*] Oh, yes. Shhhhh! [*Laughter*] Different things I see, the different reasons. Some, I might. But most, I won't, because, like I said, I don't want to cover up my tracks, you know what I mean? You should at least show where you've been, so people can understand how you got to where you are, and what have you.

DH   Okay. . . . What advice do you have for beginning writers, white, Black, or otherwise?

AB   Um-hum. Well, I say this, what I tell my writing students:

The only thing that helps you—I'm not going to say the only thing—I say the main thing that will help you learn to write is to write. That's the first step. That's the most important, is to write. The second thing is to read. Now those two things are very important, writing and reading. Of course the other thing, analysis, is observation, observation of everybody and everything: all classes of people and their relationship with each other; their ideas, how they contrast, how they be similar. And I say that the other thing is that for any serious writer in the United States, regardless of nationality, it's going to be difficult to get published. And so they better also learn how to run a mimeograph machine; photo-offset machine [*laughter*], learn how to bind and staple and how to put out their own works; and I would say, it's best you start putting out your own work. Don't wait to be discovered—

DH   Yes, right.

AB   —because for most people that's going to be a myth.

DH   Of desire.

AB   Yes, exactly. It's going to be a myth. You're going to have to do it yourself. Even if you're later discovered, it's best to start.

DH   Do you have any advice for contemporary American writers, Black or white or any other?

AB   Those things, and I think it's important that they be very, very aware of what is happening in society. Because I don't think your work can either be viewed, nor is it obtained, in isolation from society; and especially in this period now that we're moving rapidly to the right, it's very important. The rise of censorship, for instance—these kinds of wild things. I'm especially gratified to see this American Writers' Congress that they're going to have in the fall, that the *Nation* magazine is sponsoring, Victor Navasky. It's going to be, I think, a three- or four-day writers' congress at the Roosevelt Hotel in October; I'm supposed to be on one of the panels. I think that's a very important thing.

DH   Okay. What are your current or future projects?

AB   Well, like I said, this play *Boy and Tarzan* is going to be done in October. Then this jazz opera that we're going to do in workshop, that we're really going to try to raise money for; we're going to try to raise money to produce it. So those are two things in drama. I have a book of essays that's going to be published in the fall; I told you about *Daggers and Javelins*. And I'm working on that book of autobiographical essays. And then I've got some other projects that are on the back burner, unfortunately. Oh, another important project is my wife and I are doing an anthology of Black women writers—

DH   Oh!

AB   —that Morrow has just accepted. And so we'll be doing that. In the next couple of weeks we're going to start on that.[21]

DH   Are there any misconceptions—about yourself or your work—that you want cleared up?

AB   [*Laughing*] Oh, ho-ho!

DH   [*Laughing*] I mean, any *outstanding* misconceptions.

AB   I can't, I can't. No. Except that people are always catching you where you were.

DH   This is the last question. What role do you foresee for Black poets in the 1990s, and whom do you think they should address?

AB   That's a good question in this sense. I expect the same role from them that they have had—the same role that Margaret Walker had, the same role that Langston [Hughes] had, the same role that [Claude] McKay had. That is, intellectual leadership, you understand, commitment and struggle. But we must always learn from each other's lives. And in terms of the audience, the audience is all of the people, the majority of the people.

Amiri Baraka (LeRoi Jones): Works Cited and Suggested

Asterisk indicates work produced under the name Amiri Baraka

Poetry

Preface to a Twenty Volume Suicide Note. New York: Totem/Corinth, 1961.

The Dead Lecturer. New York: Grove Press, 1964.

Black Magic: Collected Poetry, 1961-1967. New York: Bobbs-Merrill, 1969.

It's Nation Time. Chicago: Third World Press, 1970.

In Our Terribleness (Some eleents and meaning in black style), with Fundi (Billy Abernathy). New York: Bobbs-Merrill, 1970.

Spirit Reach. Newark, N.J.: Jihad, 1972.

*Hard Facts (1973-75). Newark, N.J.: Revolutionary Communist League, 1975.
*Selected Poetry of Amiri Baraka/LeRoi Jones. New York: Morrow, 1979.
*Reggae or Not. New York: Contact II, 1981; rpt. in The Music.
*In the Tradition. Newark, N.J.: Rising Tide, 1982; rpt. in The Music. See also New Music, New Poetry. (Recording.) Accompanied by David Murray and Stephen McCall. India Navigation, 1981.
*"Sounding." BALF 16 (Fall 1982): 103-05.
*"Why's/Wise." Southern Review 21 (July 1985): 801-09.
*"Wailers." Callaloo 8 (Winter 1985): 256. In essay "The Wailer," 248-56. Larry Neal tribute issue.
*"Reflections," "Wailers." Black Scholar 19 (nos. 4-5, 1988): 8-9; rpt. in The Music.

Plays and Fiction

Dutchman (1964) and The Slave (1964). New York: Morrow, 1964.
The System of Dante's Hell. New York: Grove Press, 1965.
The Baptism (1966) and The Toilet (1963). New York: Grove Press, 1967.
Four Black Revolutionary Plays. New York: Bobbs-Merrill, 1969. Includes Experimental Death Unit #1, A Black Mass, Great Goodness of Life, Madheart, and statement "Why No J-E-L-L-O?"
Slave Ship: A Historical Pageant. Newark, N.J.: Jihad, 1969.
*J-E-L-L-O. Chicago: Third World Press, 1970.
*Three Books by Imamu Amiri Baraka (LeRoi Jones): The System of Dante's Hell, Tales, The Dead Lecturer. New York: Grove Press, 1975.
*The Motion of History and Other Plays. New York: Morrow, 1978. Includes Slave Ship and S-1.
*What Was the Relationship of the Lone Ranger to the Means of Production? New York: Anti-Imperialist Cultural Union, 1978.
*The Sidney Poet Heroical: In 29 Scenes. New York: I Reed Books, 1979.
*Selected Plays and Prose of Amiri Baraka/LeRoi Jones. New York: Morrow, 1979. See "The Revolutionary Tradition in Afro-American Literature," 242-51.
*Boy and Tarzan Appear in a Clearing! Music by Hugh Masakela. Produced at Henry Street Settlement's New Federal Theatre, New York City, Oct. 9, 1981.
*Money: A Jazz Opera (fragments), with George Gruntz. Produced at La Mama, New York City, in association with the Kool Jazz Festival, July 2-4, 1982.

Nonfiction

Blues People: Negro Music in White America. New York: Morrow, 1963.
Home: Social Essays. New York: Morrow, 1966.

Black Music. New York: Morrow, 1967.
*A Black Value System. Newark, N.J.: Jihad, 1970.
*Raise Race Rays Raze: Essays since 1965. New York: Random House, 1971.
*Kawaida Studies: The New Nationalism. Chicago: Third World Press, 1972.
*See Selected Plays and Prose (1979), above.
**"Afro-American Literature and Class Struggle." *BALF* 14 (Spring 1980): 5-14.
**"Confessions of a Former Anti-Semite." Village Voice, Dec. 17-23, 1980, pp. 1, 19-23.
*Daggers and Javelins: Essays, 1974-1979. New York: Morrow, 1984. (Cited as *DJ.*)
*The Autobiography of LeRoi Jones. New York: Freundlich Books, 1984.

Editions

The Moderns: An Anthology of New Writing in America. New York: Corinth Books, 1963.
Black Fire: An Anthology of Afro-American Writing, with Larry Neal. New York: Morrow, 1968.
*African Congress: A Documentary of the first Modern Pan-African Congress. New York: Morrow, 1972.
*Confirmation: An Anthology of AfricanAmerican Women, with Amina Baraka. New York: Quill/Morrow, 1983.
*The Music: Reflections on Jazz and Blues, with Amina Baraka. New York: Morrow, 1987.

Notes

1. Larry Neal, "The Black Arts Movement," *Tulane Drama Review* 12 (Summer 1968); excerpt in Arthur P. Davis and Saunders Redding, eds., *Cavalcade: Negro American Writing from 1760 to the Present* (Boston: Houghton Mifflin, 1971), 797-810.

2. Introduction, Donald B. Gibson, ed., *Modern Black Poets: A Collection of Critical Essays* (Englewood Cliffs, N.J.: Prentice-Hall, 1973), 15.

3. Theodore R. Hudson, *From LeRoi Jones to Amiri Baraka: The Literary Works* (Durham, N.C.: Duke Univ. Press), 5. For an account of Baraka's earlier life, I am indebted to his useful book and to Baraka's own extraordinary *Autobiography,* which discusses his life through 1974 and the "6PAC" (Sixth Pan-African Congress), held at Dar es Salaam, Tanzania. See also Werner Sollors, *Amiri Baraka/LeRoi Jones: The Quest for a Populist*

Modernism (New York: Columbia Univ. Press, 1978); Kimberly Benston, *Baraka: The Renegade and the Mask* (New Haven, Conn.: Yale Univ. Press, 1976); Benston, ed., *Imamu Amiri Baraka (LeRoi Jones): A Collection of Critical Essays* (Englewood Cliffs, N.J.: Prentice-Hall, 1978); and William J. Harris, *The Poetry and Poetics of Amiri Baraka: The Jazz Aesthetic* (Columbia: Univ. of Missouri Press, 1985). Harris's valuable work is epitomized in his essay (which inverts this title) appearing in *Amiri Baraka: The Kaleioscopic Torch, a Literary Tribute*, ed. James B. Gwynne (New York: Steppingstones Press 1985), along with pieces by Amina Baraka, Kimberly Benston, Allen Ginsberg, Jim Hatch, Maurice Kenny, Woodie King, Jr., D. H. Melhem, Joel Oppenheimer, Richard Oyama, Raymond Patterson, Sterling Plumpp, Arnold Rampersad, Eugene Redmond, Yusef A. Salaam, Clyde Taylor, Joe Weixlmann, and many others. Cited hereafter as *KT*.

4. Hudson, *From Jones to Baraka*, 36.

5. William J. Harris, review of *Selected Poetry of Amiri Baraka/LeRoi Jones*, *Greenfield Review* 8, nos. 3-4 (1980): 47.

6. Henry Louis Gates, Jr., "The Blackness of Blackness: A Critique of the Sign and the Signifying Monkey," cited from *Critical Inquiry* (1983); reprinted in Gates, ed., *Black Literature and Literary Theory* (New York: Methuen, 1984), 285-321.

7. In Greenwich Village in June 1979, police interrupted a dispute between Baraka and his wife, and conflict ensued between the couple and the police. Amina Baraka went to her husband's defense in the alleged assault upon him by four officers. Baraka was chargd with "resisting arrest," eventually convicted, and sentenced on October 16, 1981. Appeals by the public and community groups spurred the decision to permit him to serve his ninety days intermittently, with allowance made for his three days' initial detention. Between January 9 and November 6, 1982, he reported to Rikers Island from 9:00 a.m. on Saturdays to 5:00 p.m. on Sundays. See Amina Baraka's impassioned prose poem account, "June '79 livin is hard (a familiar story)," *KT*, 12-13.

8. The James Baldwin Jazz Tribute by great jazz musicians, produced by Marc Crawford at Art D'Lugoff's Village Gate on March 1, 1988, reaffirmed the significance of Baldwin's closeness to music.

9. See esp. *Blues People, Black Music*, and *The Music*. For an important study that seeks "to demonstrate that a blues matrix (as a vernacular trope for American cultural explanation in general) possesses enormous force for the study of literature, criticism, and culture," see Houston A. Baker, Jr., *Blues, Ideology*, and *Afro-American Literature: A Vernacular Theory* (Chicago: Univ. of Chicago Press, 1984), 14.

10. Bruce Franklin, in *Minnesota Review*, Fall 1975, as quoted by Baraka in "Langston Hughes and the Harlem Renaissance," *DJ*, 165. See also "*Black Boy* as Slave Narrative, *Black Boy* as Anti-Imperialist Narrative," *DJ*, 172- 81.

11. James A. Miller, " 'I Investigate the Sun': Amiri Baraka in the

1980s," *Callaloo* 9 (Winter 1986): 184-92, offers a balanced perspective on Baraka's transitions.

12. The interview with Amiri Baraka took place on Tuesday, July 21, 1981, in the morning and early afternoon. Although it appears substantially as it did in *BALF* 16 (Fall 1982): 87-103, the last question was posed on Nov. 24, 1988, at the Langston Hughes Festival at the City College of New York. Since the response represents Baraka's consistent view, moreover, and applies to the 1980s as much as it does to the 1990s, it provides an appropriate conclusion to the interview. Mike Bezdek's questioning is included with his gracious permission.

13. Important influences on Baraka's recent thinking include Lu Hsun, *Selected Stories,* 2nd ed. (1972), and Mao Tse-Tung's *Talks at the Yenan Forum on Literature and Art* (1967) and *Five Documents on Literature and Art* (1967), all published in Peking by Foreign Language Press.

14. Walt Whitman, born in 1819 in Huntington, Long Island, in fact lived more of his life in Brooklyn, New York. After his years in Washington, D.C., however, in 1873 he suffered a stroke and recuperated at his brother's house in Camden. Eventually Whitman bought his own house there, on Mickle Street, where he resided until his death in 1892.

15. This book became the *Autobiography* (Freundlich Books).

16. Allan Bakke was denied admission to medical school by the University of California at Davis because of a quota system. Bakke, white, contended that he was a victim of reverse discrimination and that his rights to equal protection under the law had been violated. In 1978 the U.S. Supreme Court ruled that special admissions programs were unconstitutional. Subsequently, Bakke was admitted.

17. Michele Wallace, *Black Macho and the Myth of the Superwoman* (New York: Dial, 1979).

18. See n. 7 above.

19. Kawaida is the Black Nationalist religious, ethical, social, cultural, economic, and political system developed by Maulana Ron Karenga in the 1960s and propounded by Baraka in his writings in the 1970s (see *Kawaida Studies: The New Nationalism,* 1972). The seven principles (Nguzo Saba) comprise Umoja (Unity), Kujichagulia (Self-Determination), Ujima (Collective Work and Responsibility), Ujamaa (Co-operative Economics), Nia (Purpose), Kuumba (Creativity), and Imani (Faith).

20. Olson's observation "Pun is Rime" occurs in his "Letter to Elaine Feinstein," which is appended to the essay "Projective Verse" in *Selected Writings of Charles Olson,* ed. Robert Creeley (New York: New Directions, 1966), 29.

21. This is the anthology published as *Confirmation* (1983).

THAT IS
CONSTRUCTION

> . . . And steadily
> an essential sanity, black and electric,
> builds to a reportage and redemption,
>   A hot estrangement.
>   A material collapse
> that is Construction.
>   —Gwendolyn Brooks, "In the Mecca"

The six poets who vivify these pages have "straddled the whirl-wind" of Black rage and ridden it into constructive courses. Their differing paths present a variety of options toward fulfilling the commitment they hold in common to Black pride, solidarity, social justice, and accomplishment. They epitomize the struggle which, despite more setbacks than victories since the 1950s and 1960s, continues undaunted. The ironic title of Alice Childress's novel *A Hero Ain't Nothin' But a Sandwich* (1973), for example, is countered by its recurrent theme, "It's a Nation Time," which recalls the name of Baraka's book of poems. These two poles—of despair and chaotic anger on the one hand, self-determination and unity on the other—have long impelled and ultimately empowered Black poetry.

Dudley Randall's poem "The Six" lauds Gwendolyn Brooks, Etheridge Knight, Audre Lorde, Sonia Sanchez, Haki Madhubuti, and Nikki Giovanni as Allah's creations of light "for the sons and daughters of men, to guide them and direct their steps."[1] What he expresses is the spiritual dimension of poetic leadership. The heroic essence of the poets in this study too is spiritual and exemplary, but it also manifests itself concretely: Brooks's untiring support of young people and her promotion of the writing of poetry, in prisons and outside them; Sanchez's personal courage, in overcoming the handicap of stuttering; Baraka's persistent expression, despite harassment; the independence and enterprise of Black publishing in Randall's Broadside Press, Brooks's The David Company, Madhubuti's *Black Books Bulletin* and Third World Press, Cortez's Bola Press, and Baraka's *Unity* and, as editor, the *Black Nation*.

The political thrust of the poets' work has been augmented increasingly by cultural action: giving readings, directing workshops; establishing reading and cultural series; founding educational and cultural institutions, literary competitions, and prize endowments; and supporting Black literary and cultural enterprise. The successful Black studies movement of the sixties has developed toward emphasis on writers' festivals and conferences, which have proliferated in the United States in recent years. Both have promoted pride and a sense of solidarity; they serve as intellectual exchanges where issues can be discussed, ideas developed and promoted, and alliances forged. The Langston Hughes Festival at the City College of the City University of New York, for example, which in 1978 inaugurated its annual awards by honoring James Baldwin and, the following year, Gwendolyn Brooks, expanded in 1988 to include an international interdisciplinary conference under the directorship of Raymond R. Patterson. It attracted many distinguished participants, among them scholars such as George Houston Bass, Hughes's literary executor, and Arnold Rampersad, Hughes's official biographer;[2] such poets as Amiri Baraka, Mari Evans, and Calvin C. Hernton; and honorees Alice Walker and Dennis Brutus. One active member of the festival committee over the years has been poet Jeanette Adams, a former student of Brooks at City College.

Theoretical questions of survival, moreover, in a contemporary climate of growing reaction and prejudice, take on greater immediacy. Madhubuti's concern with race draws on Marcus Garvey's Black Nationalist separatism. Baraka, who deprecates "skin politics," focuses on class and socioeconomic forces that look to Du Bois's communist ideology. Both race and class figure to varying degrees in the work of the other poets here. But the major intersection is with race, that crucible of Black survival in the United States. Nevertheless, the poets are not only universal within the context of the local (to recall John Dewey's dictum, "The local is the only universal; upon that all art builds"). They are also open to the so-called Third World and to oppressed people in various parts of the globe.

Despite the stresses of the social arena and also because of it, the literature produced by these writers has largely abandoned (wherever it had adopted them at all) the modes of irony and indirection. Those tools of the oppressed and depressed have proved more suitable to the modern antiheroic stance (or crouch). In general, the poets prefer free verse for its flexibility vis-à-vis content, yet their skill permits most of them to employ conventional forms on occasion, particularly Brooks, Randall, and Sanchez. And the free verse itself inscribes its own formal discourse. The lyrical, the incantatory, the sermonic, the rhetorical, the vernaculars of Black speech and music immerse themselves in contemporary life in order to render and retrieve its visible and submerged contexts.

The leadership offered by the poetry is enhanced by the example of these poets' lives. One would emulate Brooks's generosity, Randall's devotion to publishing Black writers (continued by Madhubuti), Madhubuti's visionary sense of self-definition and establishment of permanent institutions, Sanchez's open sensibility and devotion to her students, Cortez's fiery commitment to social justice, Baraka's ability to develop, express, and promote his dynamic thought. These models are distinct, yet they unite in service to Black needs. And further, if we can perceive that *Black* encompasses our common humanity, of which it is emblem, we will understand that the issue at stake is our common life, in which poets participate and share with everyone else. The heritage is there for us all. This Black heritage expresses the profound motives of our democratic intentions, carried from "the music of human flesh"[3] into poetry and action, into the poetry that defines craft in action for living.

These six poets will go on reading, lecturing, organizing, participating, proselytizing, and producing strong poetry whose vitality engages our deepest requirements for positive identifyings, for the spiritual force of possibility, of redemption, and of human solidarity as a fortress against chaos. And so, toward this continuity, a tribute.[4]

For Black Poets Who Think of Leadership

By song
through preacher
political
through field of hands and hearts
raising like wheat
the swords that are ploughshares
and the faces

that Malcolm and Martin saw
that Malcolm and Martin touched
with the colored strands
of their final vision

Black poets:
you enact the deep heroic line

Notes

1. Dudley Randall, "The Six," tenth anniversary poster (no. 6) with collage by Shirley Woodson (Detroit: Broadside Press, 1975); rpt. in *A Litany of Friends*.

2. See esp. vol. 2 of Rampersad's prodigious study The *Life of Langston Hughes* (New York: Oxford Univ. Press, 1988) for its many useful references to Brooks and Baraka (as LeRoi Jones).

3. Title of a collection by the Palestinian poet Mahmoud Darwish (Washington, D.C.: Three Continents Press, 1980).

4. The following poem, by D. H. Melhem, first appeared in an earlier version in James B. Gwynne, ed., *Malcolm X: A Tribute* (New York: Steppingstones Press, 1983), and was revised for this study.

INDEX

Note: Some poem and book titles are shortened in citation